That Our Daughters May Be As Cornerstones

A HISTORY OF IRVING COLLEGE

CHAD LEINAWEAVER

LOCAL HISTORY
PRESS
an imprint of Sunbury Press, Inc.
Mechanicsburg, PA USA

an imprint of Sunbury Press, Inc.
Mechanicsburg, PA USA

Copyright © 2023 by Chad Leinaweaver.
Cover Copyright © 2023 by Sunbury Press, Inc.

Sunbury Press supports copyright. Copyright fuels creativity, encourages diverse voices, promotes free speech, and creates a vibrant culture. Thank you for buying an authorized edition of this book and for complying with copyright laws by not reproducing, scanning, or distributing any part of it in any form without permission. You are supporting writers and allowing Sunbury Press to continue to publish books for every reader. For information contact Sunbury Press, Inc., Subsidiary Rights Dept., PO Box 548, Boiling Springs, PA 17007 USA or legal@sunburypress.com.

For information about special discounts for bulk purchases, please contact Sunbury Press Orders Dept. at (855) 338-8359 or orders@sunburypress.com.

To request one of our authors for speaking engagements or book signings, please contact Sunbury Press Publicity Dept. at publicity@sunburypress.com.

FIRST SUNBURY PRESS EDITION: May 2023

Set in Adobe Garamond | Interior design by Crystal Devine | Cover by Lawrenc Knorr | Edited by Taylor Berger-Knorr.

Publisher's Cataloging-in-Publication Data
Names: Leinaweaver, Chad author.
Title: That our daughters may be as cornerstones : a history of Irving College / Chad Leinaweaver.
Description: First trade paperback edition. | Mechanicsburg, PA : Sunbury Press, 2023.
Summary: Named after famed author Washington Irving, Irving College was founded during a nationwide trend in the 19th century to educate women. The school was typical of many small women's colleges training teachers, home economists and organists, and reached a golden age under the charismatic Dr. E. E. Campbell. But the college could not survive a lack of an endowment and the death of its famed president in the late 1920s.
Identifiers: ISBN : 978-1-62006-952-3 (paperback) | ISBN : 979-8-88819-042-5 (ePub).
Subjects: EDUCATION / History | HISTORY / Women | HISTORY / United States / State & Local / Middle Atlantic (DC, DE, MD, NJ, NY, PA).

Product of the United States of America
0 1 1 2 3 5 8 13 21 34 55

Continue the Enlightenment!

Cover photo: A student with trumpet at the gate on to Irving College, on East Main Street, Mechanicsburg, Pennsylvania, circa 1925, courtesy of the Simpson Library (courtesy of the Mechanicsburg Museum Association).

This book is dedicated to all of the Irving College Ladies, and also my three favorite ladies: Elise, Caroline and Michele.

CONTENTS

Preface   vii
Introduction: Women's Colleges   1

CHAPTERS
1. Irving's Administration, 1855–1957   13
2. Student Life, 1856–1929   85
3. Course Curriculum, 1856–1929   167
4. Faculty Life, 1856–1929   199

Conclusion: Irving's Legacy   216

APPENDICES
A. Irving College Administration   221
B. Irving College Student Statistics   224
C. Women's Colleges   239

Bibliography   244
About the Author   252

PREFACE

WITH an undying love for my hometown of Mechanicsburg, Pennsylvania, whose local history I researched while living there, writing on the history of Irving College has enabled me to study a topic near and dear to my heart. Though I had researched the only available information about the school years ago in a dedicated room of the Joseph T. Simpson Library, the subject and its available materials continued to grow through the efforts of Christine Metcalfe (the library's director when I first started this project), Sue Erdman (the current director) and the Library staff. Receiving a grant in 1993 to fund the cataloging and preservation of the collection of school annuals, student publications, and college catalogues that graduates and former students donated to the library since 1977, word spread about this Mechanicsburg college that closed in 1929. Portions of the grant money were allocated to publicize the collection which led to a greater awareness of the library's Irving College Collection among area residents and a greater number of donations of Irving memorabilia. Such news even spread to Iowa, where Jane Campbell Beard '29, daughter of the venerable Irving President E. E. Campbell, donated class records, trustee and faculty minutes, presidential correspondence, and land deeds. The grant also allowed the library to arrange oral history interviews of about twenty people associated with the college, from students to a former employee. Ensuring the longevity of the college records required the help of an archivist to develop a plan for preserving the collection using acid-free boxes, white gloves, and photocopied duplicates of documents. All the yearbooks and records were organized making their preservation and research much easier.

Preservation includes not only saving and caring for items within the collection, but also disaster planning for the worst-case scenarios; placing duplicates and photo negatives at other repositories ensures that something would still remain should a fire completely destroy the library's holdings. With the completion of the library's current building on Walnut Street, an HVAC system was instituted in a special Irving College room to protect the collection from humidity, light, and temperature differences which can often cause damage over time.

Though the library has now maintained an Irving Collection for decades, there has not been a full-scale work written on the college's history or the experiences of Irving's student body. With such a large collection waiting for research, it became apparent that my interest in local history and the absence of a secondary work of Irving College were to merge. The library's collection is a great resource for looking at a forgotten period of Mechanicsburg history or a family member's college grades, but the collection consists mainly of primary source material and cannot fully tell the Irving story without months of reading documents and pamphlets. The library needed a secondary source for patrons to check out, read for reference, and use as a guide to the library's holdings. Though a few past historians have covered Irving on a small scale (most notably Lenore Embick Flower, class of 1904 with her Irving College lecture given at the Hamilton Library), none had the resources available today, or appeared to have the ambition to turn their interest into a full-scale work. The following work meets those needs.

Although uncertain whether such a project could be undertaken and figuring upon a disinterested library staff, I was more than surprised with the encouragement and delighted responses I received from Christine Metcalfe and the staff of the Joseph T. Simpson Library upon our discussion of the project. Forgetting that libraries are non-profit/government organizations with a host of ideas but too few people to help, the fact that I walked in as the ambitious volunteer who would complete the massive project for *free*, certainly must have been a welcomed sight. Christine and her staff were more than helpful in accommodating me, not only introducing me to the collection, but digging in attics and back-office space to find newly acquired documents not yet displayed with the public collection. Certainly, no research project should initially be dubbed unworthy.

Talking with Christine Metcalfe and Cumberland County Historical Society Director Linda Witmer about the publication of this project led to opportunities for publishing the work in an easier form for the library. Since the college is quite significant to the area and developed a larger following because of their grant project, it would benefit the library to have a published work for easier use for the majority of patrons. Incorporating pictures from the library's collection into the book would create a user-friendly guide to the Irving collection and would act as an introduction to the collection, as pamphlets and books often do for museum exhibits. Though publication is not always available, researching organizations and publishers that would consider printing the book strengthen the future benefits for the library.

Though Mechanicsburg history has been a hobby of mine for years, the chance to expand my interest into a full-scale project that could act as an aid within a public setting is very exciting. Through the preservation of the Irving Collection, the Simpson Library[1] is not only teaching residents that there was indeed another college in the area besides Messiah College, but tells the story of women attending segregated colleges run by men who excluded them from attaining the best education possible. The library's holdings can teach better lessons through the help of a secondary source to spur further research, intrigue readers, and interest scholars, not only allowing for greater usage of the collection, but the wider knowledge that "those buildings by the hospital" weren't always just apartments.

---

1. Numerous artifacts have been transferred to the Mechanicsburg Museum Association.

INTRODUCTION

WOMEN'S COLLEGES

EUROPEAN settlers first landed in Massachusetts in 1620. Harvard College, founded across the Charles River from Boston, opened for young gentlemen in 1636. The colony of Virginia was well-established by 1670. Young gentlemen pursuing a higher education began to attend William and Mary in 1693. William Penn laid out plans for Philadelphia in 1682. The University of Pennsylvania opened its doors to young men in 1740. However, none of these colleges founded in the seventeenth and eighteenth centuries allowed women, and none of these men's schools admitted the "fairer sex" until more than two hundred years later. The first colleges exclusively for women began appearing from the 1830s–1850s, though it took another several decades to match the curriculums offered at men's colleges. Vassar had nearly achieved this in 1865, but even with this academic recognition, Vassar could not open itself to as many students as space allowed, since most women failed to meet the entrance requirements due to the lack of college-preparatory education available. Two hundred years separate the opening of Harvard for men and Georgia Female College in Macon, Georgia, showing the inadequacy of educational opportunities for both sexes, and how slowly the opportunities for women trudged along.

Female seminaries offered the first glimpse of women's higher education, as pioneer women sought to establish schools to bring extended educational opportunities to young women. Troy Seminary in Troy, New York, founded by Emma Hart Willard in 1821, provided liberal arts, fine arts, dancing, and music courses to women taught exclusively by women. Hartford Seminary, founded by Catharine Beecher in 1828, enrolled 100 students in its first year, providing courses from calisthenics to English.[1] Though many of these seminaries were really well-established secondary-school academies, sometimes involving the work of juniors and seniors at men's high schools, they were a step forward in bringing advanced education to women. Mary Lyon achieved the most success through her seminary Mount Holyoke, which she established in 1837. Though categorized as a seminary, Mount Holyoke offered a variety of college courses to women and spearheaded the movement.

Seminaries like Mount Holyoke enacted strict rules to ensure proper education and many colleges later adopted these regulations for use at their institutions. The students awoke at an early hour (5:00 A.M. in summer, 6:00 A.M. in winter), followed a system of bells that marked the periods of the day, took part in communal worship three times a day, abided to a clear, strict schedule, drew on female relationships with teachers as mentors, and reported their own misdeeds during probationary periods.[2] Rules became relaxed at many colleges after their incorporation from seminaries, but similar rules still applied at many colleges.

The seminary education attracted a variety of women from different classes, since Mount Holyoke catered to educating farmers' daughters and the middle class. However, the private women's colleges that would develop by the 1860s and 1870s received students of the upper middle class with professional fathers in medicine and law.[3] Even schools that developed in the South as "finishing schools" taught more about the proper etiquette of a Southern lady than chemistry or Latin, and catered to middle- and upper-class women, who tended to be the only people able to afford higher education.

Women's colleges hit their initial flourish right around the Civil War. A popular trend emerged in public education creating normal schools, high schools, and colleges as the Civil War opened factory jobs to some

---

1. Solomon, Barbara Miller. *In the Company of Educated Women: A History of Women and Higher Education in America*, New Haven, CT: Yale University Press, (1985), 19.

2. Horowitz, Helen Lefkowitz. *Alma Mater: Design and Experience in the Women's Colleges from Their Nineteenth Century Beginnings to the 1930s*, Boston, Massachusetts: Beacon Press (1984), 14–17.

3. Gordon, Lynn D. *Gender and Higher Education in the Progressive Era*, New Haven, CT: Yale University Press (1990), 28.

women causing a re-evaluation of the role of women; a fervent expansion and maturation of education grew in American colleges.[4] After Mount Holyoke and Georgia Female College, the latter which opened in 1836, other female colleges followed suit providing some college level courses. But, all of the schools still offered an education far below the level of men's colleges. With the opening of Elmira College in Elmira, New York (1855), and Vassar College in Poughkeepsie, New York ten years later, curriculum and admission requirements for women's colleges made further strides toward men's schools, though still not reaching equality. Though these schools worked toward equality in education, because of the limited educational opportunities offered to young women, many could not pass the Vassar or Elmira entrance exams. Because women received a diversified education across the nation, one woman from Connecticut could have been much further along than a Georgia woman of the same age. By 1875, with Smith and Wellesley Colleges offering equal admission standards and course requirements, women's schools bridged the gap, despite continued objections from conservatives who feared that education posed health threats to women.

Long an obstacle for women's education, the thought of a "delicate" woman learning male-oriented subjects and attending universities which had been solely a man's track for personal growth was largely frowned upon throughout society. American Victorian culture was characterized by distinct roles for both sexes: public life for men, domesticity for women.[5] Creating glorified responsibilities within the home and sentimentalized motherhood as integral facets of the Victorian Era, the period's ideals limited women's political voice and economic options, granting them few legal rights.[6] "Some people believed women *could* benefit from higher education but claimed they *should* not, either because God had decreed the subordination of women or because physiologically and socially it was undesirable for them to do so."[7] If women continued their learning through college, they would lose their spirituality and faith; if

---

4. Solomon, 43–45.
5. Gordon, 4.
6. Gordon, 13.
7. Burstyn, Joan N. *Victorian Education and the Ideal of Womanhood,* Totowa, NJ: Barnes and Noble Books (1980), 52.

women lost touch with God and became mothers, who would influence their children and, more importantly, how would Christianity survive?[8] If God wasn't against educated women, then Mother Nature certainly was, as various theories developed stating that higher education could damage a woman's health. Some people believed that educated women did not give birth to eminent sons and some went so far as to say that education made women sterile.[9] English philosopher Herbert Spencer (1820–1903) claimed in his "limited energy" theory that women, who put forth serious mental effort in studying, depleted the fixed amount of needed energy for their reproductive system.[10] Edward Clarke (1820–1877), a Harvard medical professor, wrote his famous *Sex and Education* in 1873 stating that women should not exert the energy needed to study at the college level of a man or else face the consequences of diseases to the nervous system: "An excess of mental exertion [for women], especially during that critical week of every month, would compromise their reproductive capacity and would thus deprive society of the biological function of intelligent, upper-class women."[11] Clarke claimed that educated women would produce horrid offspring with monstrous brains and small bodies, abnormally active cerebration of the brain with abnormally weak digestion and constipated bowels.[12] He argued that women should not study during their menstruation periods; women were to rest and thus follow a different pattern of education than men.[13] Clarke's book was popular among the general public and pushed many parents to rethink ideas about sending their daughters to college.

Clarke's book and various other theories forced women's colleges to enforce strict rules to ensure parents that their daughters would be monitored carefully and presented their studies at an acceptable rate. Many colleges instituted curfews, jam-packed schedules, and chaperones on walks and with visitors to ensure that no single student ruined the school's reputation as a safe setting for women to learn.

---

8. Burstyn, 108.
9. Burstyn, 95.
10. Eschbach, Elizabeth Seymour. *The Higher Education of Women in England and America, 1865–1920*, New York: Garland Publishing, Inc. (1993), 83.
11. Clarke, Edward H. *Sex in Education; Or, a Fair Chance for the Girls*, Boston: James R. Osgood and Co. (1873), 134–161 as it appeared in: Eschbach, 84.
12. Clarke, 41 as in: Eschbach, 84.
13. Burstyn, 92.

Besides the unknown physical problems that people associated with women gaining education, many were warned that no man would marry an educated woman, causing fear that college was a route to becoming an old maid. Many people felt that marriages of educated women would be unstable, as the educated woman would argue with and challenge the opinions of her husband.[14] Men supposedly wanted subservient and quiet wives, fearing that an argumentative wife could potentially beat them in an argument. The many opponents to women's education drove home the idea that if young women wanted marriage, they should not seek higher schooling. Though some women college graduates never married, many just postponed the ritual until after their additional schooling (as many men and women have done today because of college). In the first 35 years of Irving College, 126 out of the 176 graduates married (71.5%), while from 1891–1911, only 100 out of the 291 graduates married (34.4%). Though, many of these graduates were younger at the time President E. E. Campbell posted these figures and may have married later in life. Of the entire 855 graduates of Irving, 507 are known to have married, representing 59% and probably a truer amount of Irving girls who proved the critics of women's education wrong.[15] Some of these students certainly married later as well, being only in their early twenties upon graduation.

Wanting to avoid scaring potential students into thinking that they would become men after attending college, new women's colleges modeled themselves after other women's schools. Mount Holyoke became the prototype as Wellesley and other schools adopted many of Mount Holyoke's ideas and college structure. Despite the liberal idea of educating women, "[f]rom the beginning, women's college administrators identified institutional intellectual goals with men's colleges, though their social aims remained conservative."[16] Therefore, many schools continued the process of educating women using the seminary practices and incorporated little social change until the students pressed for it.

---

14. Burstyn, 42.
15. I use Irving "girls" sporadically throughout this paper since that is often how the women students at Irving referred to each other. Many of the former students who were alive in 1998 still referred to each other in that manner, and I use it only in an historical sense. According to the list of graduates in the college catalogues there are 879 names of individuals who graduated, but 24 names are repeated in the lists since some students achieved multiple degrees in multiple years (thus 855 total graduates).
16. Gordon, 26.

Students tackled the traditional Victorian ideals themselves in an effort to widen their college experience. Systems of self-government undermined Victorian rules, as colleges set up such systems to decrease the responsibilities on the college teachers, who otherwise monitored student behavior for 24 hours. Bryn Mawr launched the crusade for student self-government, by initiating it soon after its opening in 1885. Wilson College, in Chambersburg, instituted self-government for students in 1904, with a new president after numerous student petitions, essays and debates on the issue. By 1900, students began holding mock Presidential election campaigns, debates, basketball and soccer matches, and plays, which involved women dressing up and acting out men's roles. The appearance of women participating in these male-dominated roles in sports, debate, and politics, added to the social benefits of college, but also enabled intellectual growth and the rise of an equal voice in society.

Having to tackle opponents of women's colleges concerning health and still maintaining a strong curriculum that approached that of men's colleges was a challenge for many women's colleges. Curriculum strength posed a constant problem for women's schools, as many of the colleges laid behind the Vassars, Smiths, and Wellesleys of the time, which had the reputation and the course work making them the Harvard, Yale, and Princeton for women. The U.S. Commissioner of Education further separated women's colleges in 1887 by dividing schools into two divisions of education level: Division A consisting of the greater schools and Division B of the lesser schools. Though Vassar, Wellesley, Smith, Bryn Mawr, and three other schools achieved Division A status, 152 women's schools resided in Division B, showing the room for improvement still needed at most institutions. Even though by 1907, 15 schools reached Division A status, 110 still remained in the Division B category, showing the continued lack of emphasis placed on women's higher education even into the twentieth century.

Women in the South faced a tougher road in receiving an adequate college education. Georgia Female College, which claimed to be the first women's college in the U.S., actually instituted a curriculum less strenuous than some seminaries, typifying the inadequacy of Southern schools as compared to those in the Northeast. Southern students had limited access to colleges in state systems, and students did not study legitimate college-level work until the 1890s.[17] Formal education in the South had been hampered by the devastation withstood during the Revolutionary War, and faced further educational stagnation throughout the Civil War and Reconstruction.[18] Many Southern academies and seminaries often called themselves colleges, though in the 1907 U.S. Commissioner of Education report, 75% of the 110 Division B schools listed came from the South, but only three out of the 15 Division A schools. While the Northeast and Midwest established women's colleges with true college courses, Southern schools often resembled finishing schools, teaching students how to be proper and polite Southern ladies.[19] Many graduates of Southern women's schools often found the need to earn a second B.A. from a Northern school to receive the accolades usually attained from one.[20] Despite the finishing school problem, the desperate need for education in the South immediately following the Civil War called upon women to teach. Northern schools grew into teacher's schools, as a large majority of women attended college to begin their own professions as educators.

Though teaching added academic merit to women's colleges, they suffered greatly with the admission of women into men's colleges throughout the late nineteenth and early twentieth centuries. Oberlin Collegiate Institute, founded in 1833, and Antioch College, founded in 1853, first opened their doors to men and women, eventually paving the way for men's schools to admit women. However, Oberlin forbade its women students from delivering graduation orations or public speeches, while requiring them to perform domestic work for the college (while the men performed heavier and more physical chores). Following a similar pattern, Antioch College completely separated the genders except for in the classroom. Most of the established men's colleges, especially the Ivy League and other prestigious schools, postponed admitting women for as long as possible. Both Harvard and Columbia organized coordinate colleges within their institutions where women students could take classes

---

17. Gordon, 8.
18. Solomon, Barbara Miller. 21.
19. Eschbach, 141.
20. Gordon, 48.

from Ivy League professors, but in classrooms exclusively for women. Once state schools began admitting women, more opportunities were afforded, and many young women preferred to attend schools with men than those without. The University of Wisconsin integrated women in 1873 after about twenty years of debate, and most Midwestern colleges faced the same debate, when considering women students in the 1850s. The University of Iowa stood as the only original men's college that admitted women before the Civil War.

Since several of the most prestigious schools had not yet allowed women in classes, co-education became a source of embarrassment for those who did adopt it.[21] The University of Chicago, which originally opened with women in attendance, began segregating classes by 1901 in order to curtail the number of women students, which had reached 52% of its enrollment. With women representing 21% of all college students in 1870, and soaring to 47% by 1920, a fear quickly arose among coeducational colleges that women would overrun the schools.[22] Problems arose with the male college administrators and faculty when women students at these coeducational schools not only began to outnumber the male students, but received more of the honors and awards, prompting the administrators to limit women students' coursework or degrees in various fashions.[23]

Attending co-educational schools as the availability increased, the women students of the 1910s renewed their interest in boys, stemming from the fear of becoming like their unmarried college teachers:

> Contemporary charges of frivolity and lack of purpose made against women students of the Progressive Era stemmed from their elders' perceptions that these young women were entirely too concerned with what men thought of them. For their part, women students began to view their unmarried teachers as unfulfilled or even sexually deviant old maids.[24]

---

21. Eschbach, 108.
22. Gordon, 43, 63.
23. Solomon, 58.
24. Gordon, 39.

Introduction: Women's Colleges

With jazz music, cigarettes, alcohol, and automobiles on the horizon, the gap between student and teacher grew from the seminary-like mentorship to that of strictly a lecturer. Though disengaged reluctantly by many college administrators, old seminary-based regulations concerning chaperones, dating, and men on campus dissipated with the 1920s in order to attract more students and steer them away from co-educational schools.

Women encountered other limitations throughout the first half of the twentieth century. Colleges devised many course programs to divert women into certain spheres of education such as domestic chores, secretarial, and office work. Home Economics, Secretarial, Normal (school teaching), and even Social Work Departments arose at colleges, maintaining the status quo of women as housewives, directing women to entry-level clerical jobs, and creating a larger pool of schoolteachers. By 1910, home economics became the leading field for college-aged women to enter, redeveloping cooking, sewing, household economy, sanitation, and childcare as sciences of the home.[25] With many women flocking to colleges to enroll in home economics and secretarial courses, women's collegiate education stepped backwards, encouraging students to enter these domestic fields instead of math, science, and other academia historically dominated by men.

If college limitations frustrated women students, limitations on teachers were equally trying. Most colleges did not offer master's degrees or doctorate level work for women students, preventing women teachers at colleges from rising to the higher ranks and pay scales of the faculty. Women occupied the lower ranks of lecturer, assistant lecturer, or demonstrator instead of professorships,[26] and lived with the students in the residence halls, adding constant monitoring of students to their responsibilities. With duties to perform day and night, women teachers were expected to maintain their single status, despite the negative stereotype that pervaded with the single women teachers: "Cast in a light that rendered them as unfortunate spinsters leading dull, gloomy

---

25. Rossiter, Margaret. *Women Scientists in America: Struggle and Strategies to 1940*, Baltimore: Johns Hopkins University Press (1982), 65 as it appeared in: Eschbach, 166.
26. Eschbach, 195.

lives, women scholars, like single women in other professions, were often stereotyped, pitied, and derided."[27] Men faculty received more benefits and respect, enjoyed higher pay, attained higher degrees, resided in living arrangements off the college campus, but received embarrassment for teaching women students instead of men.

The variety of women's colleges and seminaries that opened in Pennsylvania between 1850 and 1875 represented the broad range of women's education, though many barely lasted their initial years. Metzger College and the Carlisle Female Seminary stood in Carlisle, Wilson College started in Chambersburg in 1868, Fayetteville Female Seminary originated in Franklin County, Irving in Mechanicsburg, while Shippensburg, Harrisburg, Newburg, Pittsburgh, Allentown, and Bethlehem all had schools for women in the nineteenth century. None of these schools obtained the success of Bryn Mawr College, founded in 1885 in the Philadelphia suburbs. Bryn Mawr not only offered Ph.D. programs for women, but united with the Seven Sister colleges (which represented the Ivy League of women's colleges), the only school from Pennsylvania to do so.[28] By 1928, Irving was one of only seven women's colleges left in the state, most of which struggled to compete with the co-educational schools which now attracted most of the women students. Each of these seven schools (Beaver College in Jenkintown, Bryn Mawr, Cedar Crest College in Allentown, Irving, Moravian College for Women in Allentown, Pennsylvania College for Women in Pittsburgh, and Wilson College in Chambersburg) offered an A.B. degree, while Cedar Crest, Irving and Wilson graduated B.S. degrees, Irving offered a B.A. in music, and Bryn Mawr offered advanced study with an A.M. and a Ph.D. With the multiplicity of colleges to choose from in a populated state like Pennsylvania, Irving struggled with others for respect, educational reputation, and students, all necessary to sustain growth and survive into the twentieth century.

---

27. Eschbach, 197 as taken from: Clifford, Geraldine Jonçich, ed. *Lone Voyagers: Academic Women in Co-educational Universities 1870–1937,* New York: The Feminist Press at the City University of New York (1989), 30–31. A spinster in this quote refers to a woman past the normal age for marrying, or one woman who will likely not get married.

28. The Seven Sister Colleges are largely still in existence: Wellesley College, Wellesley, Mass.; Mount Holyoke, South Hadley, Mass.; Smith College, Northampton, Mass.; Radcliffe College, Cambridge, Mass. (which merged with Harvard in 1999); Barnard College, New York City; Vassar College, Poughkeepsie, N.Y.; and Bryn Mawr.

Introduction: Women's Colleges

Irving College of Mechanicsburg followed the standard pattern of women's education, beginning in the era just before the Civil War with women's collegiate education in its infancy, growing through the turmoil of the conservatives against higher education for women, trying to mature by adopting the home economics and secretarial programs that women apparently wanted, and suffering from the draw of women into co-educational schools. Irving stands as a prototypical example of this history of women's culture in America, and its development will be examined through its administrative practices, student life, curriculum history, and its faculty. Chapter One covers Irving's presidential and administrative history, from its founding in 1856 to the disassembling of the board of trustees in 1940. Irving grows with several of its educational leaders who display the passionate and effervescent personalities to turn a college into a success story, while it suffers alongside other schools who cannot handle collegiate finances. Irving is not the story of a well-endowed school, not of a strong board with ideas, but of a proprietorship, one that simultaneously undermined and brought success to the school, but possibly closed the school on the eve of the Stock Market Crash of 1929.

Chapter Two focuses on student life as student organizations, activities, college life, regulations, and educational workload are presented as the main focal points to describe Irving from a student point of view. With the school largely open to different educational levels of students, many classes, activities, and clubs formed to fill social calendars over the course of time. However, more unofficial activities existed in student life than the annual publication, student groups and graduation indicated as students tried desperately to bring boys and smoking into the rigorous schedule imposed by Irving. Student attitudes of individual teachers, upcoming vacations, the strict regulations, and student groups reveal the atmosphere of learning and social life at the college.

Chapter Three chronicles the classes of these students, covering the curriculum at Irving following the two lives of the school from 1856–1882 and from 1888–1929. Irving followed the trends of other colleges by establishing men's courses in the era of the Civil War and by adding secretarial courses as needed at the turn of the century. Irving also developed a famed music conservatory. Teaching methods, required courses, regulations for taking classes, and models used for its educational development, help to reveal the educational organization of the university and the changes imposed by student enrollment, national trends, and able-bodied administrators.

Chapter Four presents the lives of the faculty and workers of the college from what little evidence still remains. Faculty lifestyles are covered as much as possible, while individual faculty who helped Irving to grow educationally are also presented. In addition to teachers and professors, the activities of some campus help such as dining room servers and caretakers appear from available primary sources to present the often-overlooked history of an institution. Subjects such as wages, responsibilities, and college life through the eyes of an employee offer comparisons to student and administrative views, despite limited resources.

Where does Irving College fit in this history of women and higher education? Was Irving a conservative school that opened courses up to women only as they became more socially acceptable? Was Irving a groundbreaking college providing facilities to women that other colleges could not or would not offer? Where does Irving fit into this picture? Placing any person or institution into the realm of American history varies with the historian; some historians would claim that Irving requires little mention, while educational and gender historians could realize the college as an excellent case study with its extensive records and interviewed alumnae. Irving did become the first school in Pennsylvania to offer advanced degrees in the arts and sciences to women, but to the 4,200 women who attended Irving for five years or even one class, it meant opportunity, education, personal freedom, a strict home away from home, and a chance to develop the underprivileged minds of women.

CHAPTER ONE

IRVING'S ADMINISTRATION, 1855-1957

SOLOMON PERRY GORGAS AND REVEREND A. G. MARLATT, 1855–1865

That our daughters may be as corner stones, polished after the similitude of a palace.
—Irving College Motto, from Psalms 144:12

The origin of Irving College begins with one man's aspirations. As with Milo Jewett's founding of Vassar College with Matthew Vassar's money in Poughkeepsie, New York, Solomon Gorgas (1815–1887), a landowner, lawyer, and bank executive, had similar ideas for Mechanicsburg, Pennsylvania. Solomon Perry Gorgas had lived in Mechanicsburg only five years after farming in York County, Pennsylvania when the idea of Irving presented itself. Born the youngest of seven children in Lower Allen Township, Cumberland County on August 31, 1815, Solomon quickly became an established citizen in Mechanicsburg. He served with the local fire department, the Episcopal Church, and co-founded the First National Bank of Mechanicsburg. A staunch Democrat who even served two terms in the State Legislature,[1] Solomon and his wife, Elizabeth Eberly (1822–1905) "[stood] high in the estimation of all who [knew] them," and Solomon was "one of the honest, upright, solid, business men."[2] Purchasing 56 acres of land in the eastern portion of the borough, Gorgas made his most liberal contribution to the community by donating the land between Trindle and Simpson Roads to be used as a women's college. "In selecting a site on which to erect a suitable building, the following advantages were considered especially desirable: that the location be central, easy of access, healthy, in the midst of a moral and religious people, and surrounded with such scenery, that the intellectual and moral nature of the students would be elevated and improved by holding communion with nature as well as with books."[3] What inspired Solomon to try such a feat is uncertain, though this liberal tendency, the growing rise of several women's colleges across the country at the time, and the fact that he had three daughters may well have been influences.[4] By 1855, Mount Holyoke was well established, and at least three women's colleges had sprouted up in Pennsylvania alone,[5] possibly creating the idea of a women's school in south-central Pennsylvania. There was certainly some talk of the idea in the Harrisburg area as the mid-nineteenth century saw the establishment of not only Irving College, but Metzger Institute and Emory Female College in Carlisle, Fayetteville Female Seminary and Wilson College in Franklin County, and Female Seminaries in Shippensburg and Newburg.[6] All this interest in instituting a women's school in the area certainly must have been on the mind

---

1. It is important to keep in mind that before the advent of the Civil War, America's political party system was much different. It was not until during the Civil War with the creation of the Republican party that the modern difference between the two parties began to surface. Even though Gorgas clung to a liberal ideal in beginning a woman's college, the idea was widespread by 1855. Just because he registered as a Democrat, he cannot necessarily be equated with Democrats of today. Being a businessman and banker Solomon quite possibly could have been a staunch Republican in the twentieth century.

2. *History of Cumberland and Adams Counties, Pennsylvania*, Chicago: Warner, Beers and Co., 1886, 413.

3. Marlatt, Rev. A. G. "Sketch of Irving Female College," *Irvington Annual*, Vol. I No. 1, 1858, 2.

4. Solomon Gorgas had five children that survived into middle-adulthood: Kate E. (Gorgas) Clark, Anna B. (Gorgas) Kohler, Mary E. (Gorgas) Hicks, his son, William F. and his son, J. Wesley. In all Gorgas had ten children, four which died within four months, and one that died at five years.

5. Eastern Pennsylvania had The Pennsylvania Female Seminary founded at Collegeville and Beaver College at Jenkintown, both in 1853. In the west Pittsburgh Female College was founded in 1854.

6. Oddly enough only one of these schools survived through the twentieth century, as Wilson College, founded 1869, still is in existence today.

of Gorgas, who planned on Irving accepting students in the fall of 1856. Reverend Archibald G. Marlatt, who would become Irving's first president, said at the 1858 commencement that Gorgas was "impressed with the necessity of an institution which would rank with the best Female Colleges of our land . . ."[7]

Washington Irving, named the "first great American author" because of his nationalistic, American short story subjects, was the inspiration for naming the school, though his connections with the school are uncertain. There is no definite proof for why Gorgas and his board of trustees decided to name the school after the author except for the fact that he was so famous and well respected. Apparently, the author was elected to serve on the board of trustees, though there is no record of him ever attending any board meeting or coming to Mechanicsburg. Even though the school honored Washington Irving, such acclaim came right and left to the esteemed author, and he may very well have passed Irving College off as a nice gesture, politely declining any involvement with the school.[8] One letter that Washington Irving wrote to an unknown gentlemen may be a letter he sent to Gorgas in March of 1856 declining any trustee involvement with the college:

> My dear Sir,
> I am sorry to learn that the scheme of your proposed institution has appeared in a pamphlet form in which my name was given as a trustee. I had no intention of committing myself, as such, in the conversation we had a few evenings since but reserved the matter for after consideration. That determined me to decline the responsibility when we should have further conversation on the subject, and now I beg you will have the kindness to omit my name in any further publicity you may give to the undertaking.

---

7. Marlatt, 1.

8. There is another school that was named after Washington Irving in the nineteenth century, located in Manchester, Carroll County, Maryland (though a military school instead of for women). In an annual school publication, a very short letter from Washington Irving is reprinted in which he thanks the school for the honor. It seems very clear from this correspondence that Irving had only a passive interest in the military school.

> I thus decline the honor you are disposed to confer on me, not from any doubt of the merit and advantages of your proposed institution but from a consciousness of my own deficiencies and short comings which makes me avoid committing myself for any post or office which I cannot faithfully and thoroughly discharge.
>
> Very truly and respectfully / My dear Sir / Your friend & Servt
>
> Washington Irving[9]

Though Irving gave no names in this letter, it seems quite clear that he is referring to Irving College, which was in the planning stages in spring 1856. Most likely, Gorgas had public relations literature printed up early in 1856 and Washington Irving obtained a copy either directly from Gorgas or an outside source, thereby renouncing his involvement. No primary records survive stating that Irving served as a trustee, only secondary accounts which probably found his name on the trustee listing from one of these early public relations brochures.

College folklore has Washington Irving, "in recognition of his appreciation," donating a complete autographed set of his works to the college, which establishes a closer tie between author and school.[10] Along with the collection of Irving works, the ivy that grew on campus buildings was even said to have sprouted from the original shoots of ivy from "Sunnyside," Washington Irving's home on the Hudson River.[11] It is quite possible that these Washington Irving legends are true, but needless to say, Irving could not have had a great effect upon the college nor its board of trustees since he died three years after the school's opening in 1859, making any large involvement with the school nearly impossible.

---

9. Irving, Washington. Letter to unknown person, March 4, 1856. As reprinted in Irving, Washington. *Letters Vol. IV, 1846–1859, from The Complete Works of Washington Irving,* edited by Ralph M. Alderman, Herbert L. Kleinfeld, and Jenifer S. Banks, Boston: Twayne Publishers, 1982, 579.

10. The following sources list Irving as donating the collection of books to the college, though they very well may have just recirculated the same information: "Irving College . . . ," *Greater America,* Vol. II, Nos. 10–11, July\August 1899, 1; Irving Female College. *Irvingiana '01,* 1901, 12; Brunhouse, Robert. *Miniatures of Mechanicsburg,* Mechanicsburg: Thomas Printing House, 1928, 85; Donehoo, George P. *A History of the Cumberland Valley in Pennsylvania,* Harrisburg: The Susquehanna History Association, 1930, 474; Bradley, Carol June. *Irving Female College,* essay given at the Hamilton Library, Carlisle, 1952, 1.

11. The ivy was supposedly donated from Washington Irving's Sunnyside residence, and from those original shoots, the ivy in place on Irving College's Columbian Hall (built 1893) grew up the sides of the college residence. Apparently if the shoots were donated for this building, it would have had to have been by the heirs of Washington Irving's estate, since the author was dead by the construction of the building.

It is entirely plausible that upon Irving's death, his estate provided the school with his works or even shoots from the estate, but again there is no primary evidence to corroborate this.

With a college campus in place, Gorgas constructed the remainder of the pieces in order to complete his collegiate atmosphere. Construction began on Irving Hall, the all-purpose building for classes, dining, and residence, in 1855; one centrally located building for residence and classes became the model for women's colleges arising in the mid-1800s. Vassar, who would construct in this vein, infused three floors of the president's residence, a dining hall, a chapel, two parlors, classrooms, housing for faculty and their families, student rooms, and an exercise corridor into one building.[12] Wellesley copied Vassar's design and incorporated College Hall with presidential living space, rooms for 350 students, a chapel, library, dining hall, drawing room, and other facilities. Like Vassar's and Wellesley's buildings, Irving Hall, though much smaller, became home to student and faculty rooms, the chapel, a college parlor, and the residence of Reverend Archibald G. Marlatt (1829–1865), of Mechanicsburg, who accepted the position of Irving's first president.

Marlatt, born in Warren, New Jersey in 1829, graduated from Dickinson College (in Carlisle) in 1850, received his A.M. at Wesleyan University, and assumed part of the Carlisle Methodist Episcopal circuit of churches as a junior preacher.[13] He was not without some educational experience, as he left the Methodist circuit in 1854 to become the head of a "male literary institution" in Washington, D.C., then leaving the nation's capital to fill the Irving position. The *Weekly Gazette* out of Mechanicsburg described Marlatt as an "accomplished scholar and an experienced instructor having been engaged in that capacity for many years," and it was not long into his tenure before he started receiving accolades for his fine work in constructing Irving.[14] One graduate of the

---

12. Horowitz, 34–35.
13. Marlatt was married to Sarah Agnes Marlatt (Aug. 8, 1831–Jun. 22, 1872), who is buried with him along with four other names (Annie, Lilly, Archie, and Arthur), all of whom may have been infant fatalities. According to Lenore Embick Flower's *Irving College*, Marlatt had two children at the time of his death, Mary H. and Sarah A. It seems quite possible that both Mary and Sarah grew into adulthood and married thus having a foreign plot with their husbands as their resting place instead of the Marlatt family plot at Chestnut Hill Cemetery in Mechanicsburg.
14. *The Weekly Gazette*, January 14, 1857, 3.

first commencement said Marlatt "possessed . . . an intellect keen and discerning, a judgment true and unbiased, and a zeal and ceaseless energy, which, combined with his marvelous *social* qualities, at once, made the college a reality and a success."[15]

State recognition for the institution was surely important for its future, and Solomon Gorgas sought a charter from the state to incorporate Irving with authority to grant degrees to young ladies. On March 28, 1857, the State Legislature of Pennsylvania granted Irving a charter without an endowment, and the ability to grant degrees essentially as the college saw fit. The charter allowed for the board of trustees to:

> have the power to erect such buildings as may be necessary for the purposes of said college, and to provide libraries, apparatus and all other needful means of imparting a full and thorough course of instruction in any or all the departments of science, literature and the liberal arts, and to do all and singular the matters and things which may be lawful for them to do for the well-being of said college . . . That the faculty shall have power to confer such literary degrees and academic honors as are usually granted by colleges, upon such pupils as shall have completed in a satisfactory manner the prescribed course of study.[16]

The words are vague, giving Irving administrators the liberty to interpret "literary degrees" and "satisfactory manner" in their own fashion to establish the courses and requirements for the school. The charter gave ten men (of which included Gorgas), who were most instrumental in implementing Irving, the honor of being trustees and the privilege of choosing the remaining of the maximum of 25 trustees for the school.[17] The charter clarified that the trustees:

---

15. Aldred, Julia Adkins, '58. "Rev. A. G. Marlatt, A. M.," *The Sketch Book*, Vol. I No. 2, March 1895, 58–59.

16. Pennsylvania State Legislature., Act No. 152, *Charter to Incorporate Irving Female College*, (1857), 132. Irving College was incorporated on March 28, 1857.

17. The ten men who made up the original trustees were Dr. Ira Day, who would be the board president until his death in 1868, Dr. P. H. Long, Solomon P. Gorgas, Ephraim Zug, John Riegel, John Brandt, Robert Bryson, John B. Coover, David Coover, and George S. Adkins.

"shall have the power to fill all vacancies in their own body . . . adopt and establish their own by-laws and regulations; they shall appoint a president and faculty of instruction, who shall be charged with the direction and management of the literary affairs of the college, prescribe the course of study, text-books to be used and the discipline for the government of the pupils."[18]

Although the charter required the hiring of a president and faculty, Rev. Marlatt and his staff of educators had been in place teaching students for eight months before the charter was issued.[19]

Despite the appointment of a board of trustees as instructed in the charter, the college building and property were not officially vested within their care. Since Gorgas had financed the building of Irving Hall and purchased all the acreage for campus, Gorgas still officially owned title to them. In the school's first few years, Gorgas essentially was the college, possibly allocating money to President Marlatt whenever expenses appeared.[20] Though in direct conflict with the charter, Gorgas continued to own the school and the land for the remainder of Marlatt's tenure, a practice which caused administrative problems for Irving in later years.

Irving did not begin with the grandiose beginnings of a Vassar, nor did it have the established reputation of a Mount Holyoke. Though Vassar had 353 students in its first year (1865), and Mount Holyoke had enrollments of 250 during the 1850s, Irving Hall could accommodate only 40 boarders, leaving the remainder of the student body to commute from the surrounding area.[21] But after the school hall's completion in 1856, students arrived at the new college that September, to congratulatory remarks in the local papers:

---

18. State Legislature of Pennsylvania. *Charter to Incorporate Irving Female College*, March 28, 1857.

19. The faculty for that first year are as follows: Pres. Marlatt—Mental and Moral Science; D. R. Coover—Natural Science and Ancient Language; Rev. Henry I. Comfort—Math; Miss Mary A. Homans—*Belles Lettres* and Philosophy; Alexander J. Schem—Modern Language; Mrs. S. J. Coover—Piano, Guitar and Singing; Henry R. Kouer—Instrumental Music; Miss J. Maria Seavey—Painting in Oil and Colored Crayons; C. C. Bennett—Landscape Color and Composition.

20. Flower, Lenore Embick, '04. *Irving College,* Irving Alumnae Club, 1966, 4–5. Even when Marlatt died in 1865, Solomon Gorgas put $7,000 in U.S. gold bonds and purchased 13 shares of bank stock to help support Mrs. Marlatt and her family.

21. Enrollment numbers courtesy of: Horowitz, Helen Leftkowitz. *Alma Mater: Design and Experience in the Women's Colleges from Their Nineteenth-Century Beginnings to the 1930s,* Boston: Beacon Press, 1984, 25, 40.

"This Institution is rapidly improving, and bids fair—at a very early period—to hold a high position among the best institutions of the kind in the Union.—May success attend all the efforts put forth by its gentlemanly President, and able and experienced faculty."[22]

"The Institution is truly in a flourishing condition, and possessing as it does a healthy location, and an able and experienced faculty, cannot fail to attain a high grade among our Institutions of learning."[23]

"The increasing patronage of this well, conducted institution is fairly indicated by the additions recently made to the board of instruction. We take pride in noting its increase of patronage, which is already nearly equal to the facilities for the accommodation of pupils. Irving College, although in its infancy, is fast gaining an envisible [sic] reputation as an institution of learning and will at an early day, under the direction of the present President and faculty, rank among the first Institutions in the Union."[24]

"The building itself is a fine specimen of superb architecture, well arranged, and properly sub-divided into compartments, both large and well ventilated, to secure health and comfort to the student. The campus containg [sic] several acres of ground all of which is planted with ornamental shade trees, interspersed with shrubbery, and beautiful flower plots, affords delightful walks for amusement and pleasure during the hours of recess."[25]

An article from 1863 said that Irving "has attained a popularity, which any institution might envy, and our citizens can feel proud that in 'Irving,' they possess so excellent a school for the education of their daughters.

---

22. *Weekly Gazette*, Vol. II, No. 18, March 19, 1857, 3.
23. *Weekly Gazette*, Vol. II, No. 21, April 9, 1857, 3.
24. *Weekly Gazette*, Vol. II, No. 49, October 22, 1857, 3.
25. *Weekly Gazette*, Vol. III, No. 8, January 14, 1858, 3.

Not only is this locality blessed in the possession of this institution, but the cause of education generally, in having so efficient an auxiliary."[26] The faculty of Irving "are eminently qualified . . . having had long experience in teaching and hitherto have received the approval of all patrons . . ." as four of the nine teachers had collegiate degrees.[27]

The growth and prosperity enjoyed in the first few years of the institution was short-lived. In 1865, Marlatt died at the age of 36. Marlatt, who had been "enfeebled by an insidious disease,"[28] did not let up from his collegiate duties, continuing his work until dying in the early morning on January 2. An anonymous student said of him after his death:

> "We loved him as a teacher, because there was blended in all his acts the sincerity of a friend and the kindness of a parent. We looked up to him for counsel and direction, and the path of duty he marked out was always found the safest and best. For all of us he had the consideration of a father . . . In his large and noble heart there was room for all, and towards all he showed an impartiality and a thoughtfulness that was as uniform as it was praiseworthy. . . . The radiance of his Christian example shall gild, we hope, our pathway all through life."[29]

"Marlatt, evidently a well-liked and much respected man in the town, always spoke on behalf of the institution, and in such a manner as to make the college seem a part of the town."[30] It was also said of Marlatt that "None knew him but to love him, None named him but in praise."[31] He was an adored man whose endearing personality enabled Irving to prosper.

---

26. *Cumberland Valley Journal*, Vol. VIII, No. 9, March 19, 1863, 3.
27. *Weekly Gazette*, Vol. III, No. 8, January 14, 1858, 3.
28. Aldred, 58–59.
29. *Cumberland Valley Journal*, Vol. IX, No. 50, February 23, 1865, 3.
30. Brunhouse, Robert. *Miniatures of Mechanicsburg*, Mechanicsburg, Pennsylvania (1928), reproduced by the Mechanicsburg Museum Association (1986), 87.
31. News clipping, "Death of Rev. A. G. Marlatt, A.M.," *Cumberland Valley Journal*, January 5, 1865.

REVEREND THOMPSON PRETTYMAN EGE, 1865–1883

> Rev. T. P. Ege, A.M., succeeded to the Presidency. The College continued, under his management, the good work begun by its predecessor. Students in large numbers from many states enjoyed the advantages offered.
> —*Irvingiana '07*, 15.

The death of A. G. Marlatt surely put Gorgas and the board of trustees in a bind; most of them probably figured that the dynamic and likable Marlatt would be their institutional leader for years to come. Since Marlatt died in the middle of the school year, a replacement had to be found quickly to ensure the longevity of the college, and it is quite probable that there was a quick search. The trustees would have been happy to find anyone to fill the post, even just to finish the end of the fall and entire spring terms.[32] In that sense, it seems quite sensible that Rev. Thompson Prettyman Ege (1835–1912), the principal at the Cumberland Valley Institute [C. V. I.] for young boys in Mechanicsburg, was chosen to fill the post. Ege had been the principal at the boy's preparatory school in Mechanicsburg since 1860, where both his father and his brother were educators. In addition to his principal position at the C. V. I., Ege had been an assistant principal at Cottage Hill College in York from 1858–59 and had done private tutoring for three years before that. Educated first in common and select schools and then at Bloomfield Academy, he achieved his A. B. [*Artium Baccalaurea*, a Bachelor of Arts, essentially] degree from Dickinson in 1855, and later an M. A. [*Magister Artium*, a Masters of Arts] in 1858, so the Methodist minister had the experience and qualifications necessary for running the college.

Born in Berwick, Pennsylvania on October 12, 1835, Ege's family had for many years been financially comfortable because of his great

---

32. During the first nine years of its existence, Irving had two educational sessions: The Fall which began the first week of September and ran through January, and the Spring which lasted from February until the end of June.

grandfather's iron works located in Boiling Springs and other spots across Cumberland County.[33] This family wealth quite possibly enabled Ege not only to accept the presidential position at Irving, but also to purchase the college outright from Gorgas, paying him $16,250 for the campus and Irving Hall in March 1865, making him the sole owner of the school. There is some doubt however, how much of this wealth had passed on down through the Ege family since the erection of the iron forges. Ege had borrowed money from his father Rev. Oliver Ege, who paid several of his debts, and whose will neglected to give any of his estate to Thompson, instead appointing his other son, Alexander H., as the executor.[34] It seems that the Ege money was tied up with Rev. Oliver Ege, who kept a tight hand on what trickled down to his son.

The purchase of the college by Ege raised some questions in the minds of the trustees, and President Ira Day, in particular. Being a Mechanicsburg resident and possibly knowing about Ege's financial situation, Dr. Day put forth an effort to have the property of the college transferred to its rightful owners, the board of trustees. At a special board meeting in March of 1865:

> The President [of the board] then stated that the Institution was about to change hands and it was necessary to prepare for the formal transfer which would take place immediately after Commencement [sic]. Rev. T. Ege, the purchaser of the College, then read the deed and explained his plan for disposing of a two-thirds interest by means of stock. It was moved that the Deed of Trust be given to the Board as security for the stockholders. Agreed to [by the board].[35]

Apparently, the plan to have the property taken over by the board was strongly encouraged by Mechanicsburg residents, as shares of Irving

---

33. T. P. Ege's great grandfather was Michael Ege, who constructed the Iron Works of the Carlisle Company at Boiling Springs just before the Revolutionary War. He also expanded the forges at Pine Grove Furnace and Mount Holly Springs and built Laurel Forge. Though Michael Ege enjoyed prosperity from his iron efforts, there is some question how much his fruits were enjoyed by his descendants. See Flower, Lenore Embick. *Irving College*, Mechanicsburg: Irving Alumnae Club, 1966, 11.

34. Flower, 12.

35. Irving College Board of Trustees Minutes, March 23, 1865.

stock worth $100 per share were purchased by 56 citizens of the borough. 100 shares worth $10,000 were purchased, some of them by the trustees, though Ege, "after five or ten years, [would] have [the] right to demand transfer from stockholders of stock by payment par value, all dividends [and] all dividends due or unpaid. If all be paid or taken by said Ege, trust shall be void."[36] The plan set in place was to ensure the longevity of the institution, but no one foresaw the devastating effects of Reconstruction and the economic depressions of 1873. These events caused a decline in the number of students coming to the school and must have forced many people to give up their stock (which was automatically turned over to Ege). Though official records do not indicate it, Ege may have retained most of the stock in this fashion, though the dividends were markedly less with the low enrollment. Ege himself still borrowed money, and during his tenure, several of the trustees put money into the school which they probably never saw again.

Though Ege came to Irving with a strong background and experience with educational institutions, he was not the administrator his predecessor had been. While 10 women graduated under Marlatt's last graduation of 1864 [see table 1.1], and 10 in 1865 during his half-year administration, the numbers slowly declined in Ege's tenure until they reached only 3 women by 1882. Marlatt averaged nearly 11 graduates and 76 students in attendance per year (according to data available), seeing a decline in both areas only during the early part of the Civil War (1861–63). This decline should be expected with a nation in crisis, though the numbers rose strikingly for the last two years of the conflict. Ege averaged almost five graduates and 45 students per year, but never matched Marlatt's double-digit number of graduates or achieved higher than 58 students per year (though the data is incomplete). The severe economic depression of 1873 financially prevented some parents from sending their daughters to Irving, and the graduation and enrollment numbers dwindled to almost nothing by the early 1880s. Very little source material exists from the latter half of Ege's tenure (1876–1882), suggesting that the school was not prosperous, and what evidence does exist (and what is mentioned in afterthought) neglects to mention anything positive. In the board of

---

36. Flower, 12.

trustees' minutes, Ege's annual reports gradually show the declining state of the institution:

> *June 22, 1869:* "though having had a hard struggle against discouragements hard times & losses,—yet he [Ege] had weathered the Storm and Still felt hopeful for the Future and intended to make every effort to maintain the Character & efficiency of the Institution."[37]
>
> *June 21, 1870:* No Presidential report mentioned.
>
> *June 21, 1871:* "Prof. Ege, then made his annual report, stating that the year had been a prosperous & happy one, being one of his happiest & best in the History of the College."[38]
>
> *June 19, 1872:* Ege showed increased prosperity of the institution.
>
> *1873–1875:* No Presidential reports mentioned.
>
> *June 21, 1876:* "The past year has been one marked with increased prosperity to the College, the attendance having nearly doubled that of the two or three preceding years."[39]
>
> *June 20, 1877:* ". . . although the number of pupils has not been as large as should be, owing, doubtless, to the continued depression in business, yet the year past has been a success."[40]
>
> *June 19, 1878:* Ege's Presidential report not mentioned.
>
> *June 18, 1879:* "Prof. Ege, Prest. of The College made his annual report, assuring the Board that while the number in attendance during the year was not as large as desired, yet considering the continued business depression, it was a successful year . . ."[41]
>
> *1880–1882:* No board minutes available

---

37. Irving College Board of Trustees Minutes, June 22, 1869. The scattered capitalization occurs in the original document.
38. Irving College Board of Trustees Minutes, June 21, 1871.
39. Irving College Board of Trustees Minutes, June 21, 1876.
40. Irving College Board of Trustees Minutes, June 20, 1877.
41. Irving College Board of Trustees Minutes, June 18, 1879.

Though Ege's reports were often sugar-coated to ensure the board that the condition of the institution was in working order, it appears that Ege was having problems with Irving. The lack of board minutes from the last four years of his tenure suggests a worsening condition that was either not recorded or destroyed. In reflections of past administrators in school yearbooks, catalogues, and publications, other presidents have glowing remarks stated about them during their stay at Irving. Ege's description in *Irvingiana '07*, the fiftieth anniversary annual, only states that he maintained the status quo at the college after Marlatt's death until it closed. A man who spent 18 years of his life at Irving, and received such a small fraction of commendation, raises at least some questions about his administrative ability.

TABLE 1.1. ENROLLMENT AND GRADUATION NUMBERS FOR IRVING COLLEGE, 1865-1882. A Comparison of enrollment and graduates during the administrations of Irving's first two presidents: A. G. Marlatt, 1856-1865, and T. P. Ege, 1865-1882. Both sets of data are taken from the Irving College Catalogues, which are not complete in this early period, and unfortunately are absent during the latter half of Ege's tenure. However, *Reports from the Commissioner of Education* through the U.S. Government are also used for Irving's size, though no reports existed before 1868, thus leaving the earliest statistics of Irving's size available only through surviving catalogues.

Year	Number of Students Enrolled at Irving College	Number of Graduates from Irving College
1856-1857	72[42]	0[43]
1857-1858	92	11
1858-1859	NA	14
1859-1860	70	17
1860-1861	NA	10
1861-1862	55	8

42. *The Weekly Gazette* from January 14, 1857, 3, reveals that Irving had over seventy students in attendance. 72 is placed here as an approximation.

43. Irving's first graduation did not occur until 1858. Since its opening in 1856, no student would have achieved the necessary requirements by 1857.

1862-1863	NA	6
1863-1864	NA	10
1864-1865	76	10
1865-1866	87	7
1866-1867	58	9
1867-1868	58	5
1868-1869	NA	2
1869-1870	49	6
1870-1871	47	3
1871-1872	43	6
1872-1873	39	6
1873-1874	38	5
1874-1875	43	3
1875-1876	36	4
1876-1877	43[44]	4
1877-1878	45	6
1878-1879	42	4
1879-1880	42	5
1880-1881	45	6
1881-1882	NA	3

There is some question about Ege's commitment to the idea of educating young women, since he had come from a boys' school to administer Irving. Ege's college catalogue of the 1875–76 school year raises some questions about where the school was going:

> The strong-minded sentiment, and the few colleges that are
> latterly stimulating young and tender girls to compete with men
> side by side, in studies and classes, or that are proposing a course
> of study as rigid and severe in order to equal the most advanced

---

[44]. The Board of Trustees minutes show Ege's annual report as having nearly twice the attendance of the previous two or three years.

colleges for men—we say it with all due respect—are doing more for the injury of future generations than any dozen institutions in the land.[45]

Even if the language inserted acted as a ploy for parents to send their daughters to Irving instead of Vassar or Elmira College, who were beginning to equal men's college curriculums in the 1860s, the message is clear that Irving would neither be co-educational nor upgrade its curriculum to offer courses that would endanger a woman's heath: "Pupils are too often required, by a process most irksome to themselves and to their teachers, to violate their natures and to delve in abstract sciences and studies when they should be led by a pleasanter and more profitable path."[46] Following some of the themes of Clark's *Sex and Education,* Ege and Irving accepted impressions that science and more abstract work would not be healthful for its young students:

> It is believed that under proper conditions a young woman may study earnestly and fearlessly, and, [*sic*] without detriment to her health, enrich her mind with learning's richest stores . . . But to do this she needs pure atmosphere, plentiful sunlight, generous variety of nutritious food, warm, simple and light clothing, careful protection from dampness and cold, judicious exercise in the open air, from eight to nine hours' sleep, and a restriction to six hours of actual study out of every twenty-four.[47]

Though these statements enticed parents and dispelled fears of unhealthy education for women, the progressive nature of the founding of the institution in a socially conservative area like the Cumberland Valley diminished by the 1870s under Ege, who may have indeed interpreted education for females as a back-burner issue, as he began to seek interests outside of Irving College. Despite his drawbacks as an administrator, Ege appeared to be well-liked by the student body, at least according to Mary

---

45. Irving College Catalogue, 1875–1876, 4.
46. Irving College Catalogue, 1875–1876, 4.
47. Irving College Catalogue, 1875–1876, 3.

H. Ashman, class of '81.[48] "Perhaps one of the most potent factors in his influence and the one which first springs to mind as I think of him, was the sweet, patient optimism which characterized his attitude amidst all the chances and changes of his private life and his work in the college . . . He was patient to a fault—patient *with our* faults."[49] Ashman describes his demeanor as friendly too:

> While he was gentleness itself, perhaps for that very reason every school-girl culprit trembled before his mild sway and knew that justice would be meted out. Yet merciful as well, was he, and lenient as a father when the offence [sic] permitted. Indeed his little government was of the patriarchal sort, and we all felt that the reproach on his kindly face was harder to bear than severe 'tasks' from 'another.'[50]

Other accounts offer fond memories of Ege:

> How vividly I recall his genial presence and kindly nature. Many times, when with an illy-prepared lesson we entered the recitation room, how artfully we contrived to lead him into a discussion, pro and con, on some favorite topic, or lapse into a reminiscent sketch, till the bell would sound, and we breathed a sigh of relief: our agony was over. He skillfully read, between the lines, our lack of application, and this very kindliness of disposition was enough to make us feel conscience-stricken. He was certainly *"Primus inter Pares."* [First among Equals][51]

> In his personality he was delightful. His fine countenance and gentle manner were unified by his sunny smile and the quizzical glance from over his spectacles which I am sure not one of his 'girls' will ever forget. Neither will they forget his enjoyment of a joke . . . especially his happy manner in the Latin class . . .

---

48. For each the students I have included graduation dates, or years of study at Irving to ensure understanding of the time period and of the students themselves.
49. Ashman, Mary H, '81. "President T. P. Ege," *The Sketch Book*, Vol. I No. 1, February 1895, 23–25.
50. Ashman, 23–25.
51. *The Sketch Book*, Vol. II Nos. 4–5 February\March 1896, 120.

> He was charming as a teacher, impressing with great force all he sought to impart and yet never wearying in his too often necessary repetitions to the dullard or slothful one.[52]

Ege's personality was quite the contrary according to Lenore Embick Flower, '04, as he "had not . . . the latter's [Marlatt's] gifts of personality, nor the warmth, and devotion to things vital for successful education . . . he was of medium height, rather heavy build and regarded by his contemporaries as pompous."[53]

Whether pompous or delightful, Ege administered Irving during a stagnant period which saw no growth in the school's campus or curriculum. By maintaining the status quo, Irving was forced to close by 1883: "the United States commissioner of education eliminated from his list of bona fide liberal arts colleges all Pennsylvania women's colleges except Bryn Mawr."[54] Despite a state charter and women students still coming to attend the school, Irving, a Division B school according to the U.S. Department of Education along with all other Pennsylvania schools but Bryn Mawr, had to close. The trustees certainly planned for changes or at least discussed them, but in either case Ege removed himself from them, leaving Irving to return to the Episcopal ministry in Germantown during mid-classes of the 1882–1883 school year. With the Department of Education breathing down the necks of the board and without a president to help institute the changes needed to upgrade the school's standards, the trustees had no choice but to close the school temporarily. Ege left not only Irving, but his father's church when moving to Germantown to become the rector of St. Peter's Church (1883–1888), and a professor for one year at Germantown Academy (1883–1884). Eventually Ege traveled to Gettysburg, becoming the rector of Prince of Peace Church for ten years (1888–1898), and his further travels took him through Philadelphia and New York until his death on March 31, 1912. Unable to find a replacement so quickly and with Irving College in poor financial condition, the trustees needed not only to implement changes within the

---

52. Ashman, 23–25.
53. Flower, 13.
54. Klein, Philip S. and Hoogenboom, Ari. *A History of Pennsylvania*, Penn State University Press: University Park, Pennsylvania, second edition (1980), 387.

college curriculum, but elect an educational leader to help enact them. Irving stood without students for five and a half years.

MARY KESSLER AND IRVING'S REOPENING, 1888–1891

> I never met a more indefatigable worker than President Kessler. Even when suffering from physical ills she would not relinquish more duties than she absolutely must
>
> —Clara Kast, 1895[55]

With Irving closed after Ege's departure of 1883, the school stood lifeless until into the picture stepped a woman with a zest for running organizations, even if it meant doing everything herself. Mrs. Mary L. Kessler (1843–1929), an experienced and well-traveled teacher who had taught at Chambersburg High School and Hagerstown Female Seminary in Hagerstown, Maryland, accepted the challenge of re-opening the school. Since Rev. Ege left for the Episcopal ministry, there appeared to be no significant attempts at securing a president by the trustees, or else they were unsuccessful. Kessler, who taught at Mercersburg Academy, Uniontown, Lehighton, Shippensburg Normal School, and Oxford Academy (New York), had the determination and the years of experience it took to be an administrator. *Greater America* magazine wrote a full-length history and description of the college in 1899, and said of Kessler, the "third President of the College," that "Her scholarly accomplishments and long experience as a teacher made this selection a good one. Mrs. Kessler added to the thoroughness and efficiency for which Irving has ever been noted."[56]

Born to a Lutheran clergyman, Rev. Benjamin Laubach on August 25, 1843, in Southampton Township of Franklin County, she was taught early on by her mother, Ellen Wunderlich Laubach, until she was old

---

55. Kast, Clara May, '95. "President M. A. L. Kessler, A. M.," *The Sketch Book*, Vol. I No. 2, March 1895, 59.
56. "Irving College, Mechanicsburg, Pennsylvania.: Its Marked Prestige and Growing Importance in its Chosen Field. The Higher Education of Women," *Greater America*, Vol. II, Nos. 10–11, July-August 1899, 1.

enough to attend the "well-known private school of Misses Pinner," in Chambersburg. Graduating from Hagerstown Seminary in 1861, she later taught there (1877–82), and at Lutheranville Seminary in Maryland (1883–86), before arriving at Irving. Kessler's husband, Rev. Christian Kessler, a German Reformed Minister, left her widowed and with a daughter, therefore Mary was forced to earn a living to support her family from an early age. Irving became the first administrative post for Kessler, but she was awarded the diminished title of "principal" simply because of her gender, though performing all the necessary duties of the president. But Kessler's abilities made her more than able to run the institution of her predecessor, and the "principal" title and possible criticism from outsiders (though none are recorded, it is possible they existed) may have fueled Kessler's fire to get Irving up and running again.

Kessler was a hard worker and, in many ways, extended her duties to keep the college running smoothly. Teaching mental and moral science, German, psychology, botany, and history, she supervised the chapel services, helped in the kitchen and with the housekeeping, as well as being principal. Clara Kast, an Irving graduate of 1895, said that "Mrs. Kessler was a very busy personage, much in demand here, there, everywhere."[57] Kessler excelled as a teacher, "[n]ot only scholarly, of remarkable general information, a thorough teacher—a *genuine teacher*—she was also well prepared to oversee domestic arrangements."[58] "She was as versatile as she was administrative. For example, when the cook failed to appear and the student body, though small [,] had to be fed, she would go from classroom to kitchen, quickly mix some tasty concoction and then be summoned, as often happened, to meet a prospective parent in the College parlors. At the end of the visit, she would go to another class 'leaving often in her wake a shawl hastily donned to protect her in the chilly halls.'"[59] Despite this apparent super-human drive, Kessler suffered from rheumatism, which often prevented her from being able to sit in a chair. But, this did not stop her completely. If her condition prevented her from making it down to the recitation rooms to teach class, Kessler

---

57. Kast, Clara May, 59.
58. Kast, Clara May, 59.
59. Flower, 15.

requested that all her students come up to her private room to receive their lesson. She was relentless:

> I never met a more indefatigable worker than President Kessler. Even when suffering from physical ills she would not relinquish more duties than she absolutely must... Always energetic herself, she had no sympathy for any who tried to shirk work, and woe betide the girl who came to class with a poorly prepared lesson and a lame excuse.[60]

Though she ran Irving as a very able administrator, she loved teaching first. She loved bringing subjects alive for her students, teaching "agonizing lessons" in psychology which "brought us to a full realization of the fact that we did not yet know quite everything."[61]

Kessler's hard work thrust Irving on the road to prosperity, although her constant and demanding attention to the school evidently wore her down. Enrollment increased again as 39 students came in 1889, 58 in 1890, and 70 in 1891, though all but seven had come from the Keystone State. But the endless teaching, administering to students, cooking meals, and cleaning the kitchen took its toll; Kessler resigned her position at the end of the 1890–91 school year. According to the board of trustees, Kessler regretted resigning as principal but

> the duties as such were too exacting and arduous for her to bear; That her health has been somewhat impaired by reason of the same and that she was obliged for this reason to relinquish the duties of Principal of the College; that her zeal and interest in behalf of the College would not be lessened as a teacher in the College...[62]

The responsibilities overwhelming her, and possible outside pressures to resign being uttered under the breaths of educational conservatives who

---

60. Kast, Clara May, 61.
61. Kast, Clara May, 60.
62. Irving College Board of Trustees Minutes, June 9, 1891.

believed that no woman should be the head of an institution, Kessler remained at Irving as a teacher only.[63] At the same meeting which Kessler resigned, the board selected their next administrator, E. E. Campbell, whose pleasant demeanor and excellent administrative ability would raise Irving to a new level.

IRVING'S GOLDEN AGE: E. E. CAMPBELL, 1891–1926

There's one consoling thing about the earth. Everything's attractive.

—E. E. Campbell, 1906[64]

The selection of a president to take the reins from Mary Kessler must not have been a difficult one for the board of trustees, as E. E. Campbell (he always referred to himself as E. E.) accepted the position in June of 1891. It is possible that when Campbell arrived as a geology teacher in 1890 with his previous administrative experience, and with a stature that appealed to the board, that by the end of the school year they planned on offering him the presidency anyway. Whether Kessler felt obligated to step down is unsure as it seems that the trustees approved of Kessler's performance as an administrator, though it seems likely that they preferred a male presence in the top slot. Kessler certainly ran herself ragged trying to keep Irving afloat, so the sources tend to favor a Kessler resignation influencing Campbell's appointment as president.

Edmond Ernest Campbell was born one of nine children to Rev. John Francis and Martha Catherine Campbell on January 21, 1859, in Waynesboro, Pennsylvania. His father being a Lutheran minister, E. E. moved to Shenandoah Valley, Virginia when he was just eight years old, but received education in "excellent public schools," until he eventually departed for Roanoke College in Salem, Virginia. E. E. achieved his A.

---

63. Kessler would die in Irving's closing year, 1929 at the age of 86. She was survived by her daughter, Mrs. Eleanor Coates in that year and buried at Cedar Grove Cemetery in Chambersburg. After leaving Irving in 1895, she taught and became principal of Soldier's Orphan Industrial School in Scotland, Pennsylvania.

64. *The Sketch Book*, Vol. VIII No. 6, March 1906, 14.

B. degree the same day that his father obtained his D.D. [Doctor of Divinity] from Roanoke in 1879. He started teaching, filling positions at graded and select schools until 1882, when he joined the faculty of Hagerstown Female Seminary in Maryland.[65] He filled the chair of Latin and Mental Science at Hagerstown, leaving in 1888 to accept a faculty position at Staunton Female Seminary in Staunton, Virginia. When he accepted a position at Irving in 1890, E. E. had been the principal of the Education Department at Tressler's Orphan's Home in Loysville, Pennsylvania, an establishment with which he kept a close tie while at Irving.

When Campbell moved into Irving Hall in the summer of 1891 as its new president, he brought a family of three with him. Married to Agnes Zufall of Meyersdale, Pennsylvania, E. E. had little Annie Catherine and Emma Nelle Campbell. With an overwhelming personality, a zest for talking with people, and an avid sense of humor, Campbell was a likable president, who interacted well with both the board and the students:

> [E. E.] liked dandelions and wore a dandelion in his lapel . . . He said that he remembered that Lincoln had said that he thought God must have liked the common people because he made so many of them, and [Campbell] said he felt that way about dandelions. And he always enjoyed them, a fresh one each day.[66]

With his arrival, changes transpired in the school and Irving began to see prosperity that it never witnessed before. Campbell purchased the school outright in 1898 from several board members who each had privately owned separate portions of the school individually and collectively, though never as a unit of trustees as required by the 1857 charter. These board members may have welcomed E. E.'s purchase, since it relieved them of any private ownership of the college, which had been a risky enterprise since Ege's administration. However, some board members probably questioned the premise of a proprietor-president since the trustees were to be the final word for the institution. Regardless of the controversies that developed from the ownership situation, the board

---

65. Hagerstown Female Seminary would eventually become Kee Mar College in Hagerstown, Maryland.
66. Oral History, Jane Campbell Beard, '29, April 12, 1994.

entrusted Campbell to "appoint and employ such additional teachers as may be required upon consultation with and concurrence of the resident members of the board."[67] E. E. announced plans of starting a kindergarten school at Irving, received a collection of minerals, shells, aerolites, and rocks from Mr. C. E. Brindle for use in ecology study, and increased the library holdings by subscribing to several newspapers and magazines, both religious and secular.[68]

Under Marlatt's and Campbell's tutelage, more and more students flocked to Irving for their education [see table 1.2]. Even though a national economic depression in 1893 hit businesses hard through 1897, Irving showed no sign of slowing as the college had its largest enrollment ever by 1894 [102] and continued to break that record in 1895 [110], 1897 [120], 1899 [123], 1900 [132], 1901 [142], and 1904 [143]. Irving graduated its largest class since 1860 with 17 students in 1899, a record which the school continued to set in 1902 [24], 1917 [30], 1918 [31], 1922 [35], and 1926 [37]. The data obviously states how much more successful E. E. was in comparison to his predecessors, enrolling over 100 students a year from 1894–1926 and over 125 in 19 of his 36 years. He graduated at least 13 students a year from 1896–1926, graduated 20 or more students 13 times, and thirty or more students 4 times.[69] Neither Marlatt not Ege came near these colossal numbers, as Marlatt graduated 86 students total, sending off 13 or more students only 2 times, while Ege handed out only 84 diplomas in 18 years, and never handed out more than 10 at a single commencement [see tables 1.1 and 1.3].

TABLE 1.2 STUDENT ENROLLMENT AND GRADUATION NUMBERS FOR IRVING COLLEGE, 1888-1929. This table is a comparison of the student enrollment and graduates of Irving College under the direction of five different administrators. Mary Kessler was principal from 1888-1891, E. E. Campbell was President from 1891-1916 and 1917-1926, M. H. Reaser

---

67. Irving College Board of Trustees Minutes June 9, 1891.

68. Campbell had the kindergarten school up and running in the early part of his tenure, though there is no evidence to suggest that it existed past 1891. According to his account books, E. E. was paid $5.00 for one child, possibly $10.00 for two and a $12.50 appears from one family which may have been a special rate for three children, though there is no proof of that fact. Campbell had seven names paying for the service in the fall term, four names for a second term over the winter, and eight for a spring term through June.

69. Though E. E. was officially not president of Irving from July 1, 1916–June 6, 1917, the 30 students who graduated in 1917 were essentially the result of Campbell's work.

was president from 1916-1917, Rev. Charles R. Trowbridge was acting president from 1926-1928, and Rev. Thomas J. Ferguson was acting president from 1928-1929. The majority of this information was attained from college catalogues, presidential annual reports in the trustee minutes, and student records. In case of the last three years of the institution, these records are not clear on Irving's enrollment [indicated by **]. In some cases, the numbers for enrollment appear to be lower than indicated from other more general sources [indicated by *]. See footnotes for further clarification.

Year	Number of Students Enrolled at Irving College[70]	Number of Graduates from Irving College[71]
1888-1889	34	0
1889-1890	39	2
1890-1891	58	4
1891-1892	70	6
1892-1893	83	6
1893-1894	78	5
1894-1895	102	6
1895-1896	110	10
1896-1897	108	13
1897-1898	120	18
1898-1899	119	17
1899-1900	123	15

---

70. The enrollment numbers were obtained first through the trustee minutes, then college catalogues, and when neither of these were available for usage, class records and reports from the U.S. Board of Education were used. The numbers for enrollment tended to be high (120+) when listed in the President's report to the trustees in the trustee minutes, the college catalogues varied from year to year, while the student records tended to be on the low end in enrollment numbers (100–108). For the purpose of this study, I used whatever numbers were available though I tend to think that for the starred years [*] that the enrollment is considerably higher. In most years E. E. recruited students until his space was full and most accounts state that the college was full or near full in most years. The doubled-starred enrollment numbers [**] indicate an approximation because no accurate record was available. The approximation for the last three years of Irving are based on the fact that the board and president pro term limited the enrollment to 125.

71. The number of graduates were obtained from the college catalogues which contained a running list each year. However, many graduates, especially the Campbell children, obtained more than one degree from Irving and therefore appear more than once in the numbers listed.

1900-1901	132	16
1901-1902	142	24
1902-1903	115	16
1903-1904	135	13
1904-1905	143	15
1905-1906	131	17
1906-1907	138	19
1907-1908	135	17
1908-1909	128	21
1909-1910	133	23
1910-1911	128	14
1911-1912	130	16
1912-1913	132	20
1913-1914	136	17
1914-1915	100*	17
1915-1916	125	21
1916-1917	100*	30
1917-1918	103*	31
1918-1919	102*	18
1919-1920	135	23
1920-1921	117	21
1921-1922	120	35
1922-1923	100*	24
1923-1924	125	22
1924-1925	124	19
1925-1926	139	37
1926-1927	125**	22
1927-1928	125**	20
1928-1929	125**	19

TABLE 1.3. IRVING COLLEGE GRADUATION NUMBERS BY ADMINISTRATOR. The following is a comparison of the number graduates per administrator in the number of years each oversaw Irving College. Two items of note concern the fact that Ege took over for Marlatt after his death midway through 1865, therefore the 10 graduates of that year really are of Marlatt's work, and the 30 graduates of Reaser's one year administration, and most of Trowbridge's 42 graduates are really to Campbell's credit.

Administrator	Number of Years at Irving College	Number of Students Graduated	Avg. Number of Graduates per Year
Rev. A. G. Marlatt 1856-1865	9	86	9.5
Rev. T. P. Ege 1865-1883	18	84	4.6
Mrs. M. A. Kessler 1888-1891	2	6	3.0
Dr. E. E. Campbell 1891-1916, 1917-1926	36	612	16.9
Dr. M. H. Reaser 1916-1917	1	30	30.0
Rev. C. R. Trowbridge 1926-1928	2	42	21.0
Rev. T. J. Ferguson 1928-1929	1	19	20.0

One part of this growing field of students joined Irving's Music Conservatory, which became the college's trademark through the hard work of Music Director Harry C. Harper. Not long after Harper's arrival in 1895, Irving built a first-rate Music Department in which most students at least took classes or piano lessons, even though they were not enrolled in the entire program. With the rapid interest in music among the students, Campbell fitted the college buildings with 21 upright pianos (including a baby grand and concert grand) by the time of the school's closing and constructed a music hall.[72] After the introduction of recorded sound, Campbell added a music library to Irving, purchasing an Edison Diamond Disc machine and a large library of phonograph records in 1922. In 1897, Campbell purchased a new pipe organ for Irving, which included a full set of pedals, 30 stops, and six combination stops running on a water motor. Irving never had an organ previously, due to its large expense, though the school had always sought one. This added another dimension to the music course, providing for pipe organ instruction and graduating students who went on to be church organists. Campbell probably paid for the organ out of his own pocket (the organ was valued at $1,000 after the school's closing) and purchased other needed items for the school in this fashion as he saw fit.

With the growing numbers of students through 1892, Campbell completed construction on Irving's first new building in 37 years, Columbian Hall, with a first-floor auditorium and numerous student rooms. The dorm space on the second and third floors doubled the possible occupancy for boarding students from 40 to 80, and because of its coexistence with the Columbian Exposition commemorating the 400th anniversary of Columbus's voyage to America at the Chicago World's Fair, the building was so named. Interestingly enough, the building currently reads "Columbia Hall" over the entranceway, though in college literature and student correspondence it is always referred to as "Columbia_n_ Hall." This is a surprising mistake if it indeed has existed since its initial construction. Campbell would never have allowed a mason to make such a grave error, but no evidence on the building exists that the masonry sign was tampered with or that a space for that missing "n" ever existed. No living student is aware of the name contradiction, as each assumed that the building had the correct name since the time they walked its halls.

The Columbian construction emerged as an important one for the school, since the introduction of a 650-seat auditorium finally enabled student concerts, plays, lectures, and most importantly, graduation exercises, to occur on campus. Though teas and small musical gatherings

---

72. The pianos that Irving had were in a mixture of conditions. By the settlement of Campbell's estate in 1929, two pianos were worth $200 together, another piano $250 on its own and another only $10. The 16 other pianos were worth $1,600 total and probably give a fair realization of the condition of most of the pianos at $100 a piece. The baby grand piano was priced at $250, and the concert grand piano at $500.

occurred in the first-floor parlor of Irving Hall, before the completion of Columbian in 1893, no space offered the room needed for a congregation of recital or commencement proportions. In the days before Campbell's growth, all major events were held either at the Methodist Episcopal Church in Mechanicsburg, or after 1866, in Franklin Hall, both of which stood across from each other on Market Street at the town square. Columbian Hall enabled more living space and allowed for enrollment to increase, though within 6 years the college was filling every room in both dormitories.

Possibly in response to the meteoric increase in student population and the decreasing space to hold them even after Columbian Hall was completed, E. E. built his first residence in Mechanicsburg, erecting a Victorian house on the other side of Main Street and the Cumberland Valley Railroad tracks. With Campbell's growing family, he needed a larger residence, as the presidential confines of Irving Hall were slowly outgrowing their usefulness. E. E. and Agnes had two more children by 1895, Clara Evelyn and William E., and by vacating their allotted space in Irving Hall, more students could be admitted. The profits E. E. started to see from the growth of his institution enabled him to devote some money to constructing a house. The house, named "Sunnyside" after Washington Irving's estate on the Hudson River, was completed either in 1894 or 1895 (records for the house are sketchy at best).[73] *The Sketch Book,* a monthly student publication of the college, stated that Sunnyside had the utmost in modern conveniences, with electric light instead of "smoky lamps," and "instead of chattering teeth and frozen fingers, when

---

73. Some debate has raged that Sunnyside had stood across the railroad tracks from Irving since 1855. However, there is no documentation that Marlatt, Ege, or Kessler lived in the building as no land deed mentions the building even after Irving's closing in 1929. The building was demolished in the mid-twentieth century after the federal government purchased the land for use as a Naval facility. The *Sketch Book* of April 1897 mentions Sunnyside "springing up," the February\March 1896 edition congratulates E. E. on the name for his "new residence," and the 1895-96 college catalogue also mentions the building though earlier publications do not. There is proof that two presidents, Marlatt and Campbell, lived in Irving Hall. One alumnae account from Marlatt's tenure reminisced in the October 1904 *Sketch Book,* mentions a student sneaking down to practice in the parlor "directly under President Marlatt's room" in Irving Hall, while the *Carlisle Sentinel* from October 21, 1895, mentions that E. E. was moving from Irving Hall to the Shellenberger property. Although no Shellenberger exists in any of the land deeds tied to Campbell, it seems probable that E. E. is moving to the Sunnyside property which originally was owned by Shellenberger, or E. E. is moving to the Shellenberger estate that is a transitory residence until Sunnyside is finished. However, seeing that the house was either completed in 1894 or 1895, the former seems likely.

the thermometer stands at zero, each room is heated to the warmth of summer," as E. E. had installed central heating.[74] It would not be long before Irving's boarding facilities were again at their maximum.

The dormitories had modern conveniences like electric light and heat as Campbell tried to care for his students in the best way possible. With a telephone connected during Kessler's term reaching Harrisburg, Lancaster, Reading, and Allentown in the east and Carlisle, Newville, etc. in the west, E. E. had a long-distance Bell telephone affixed by 1905, which apparently reached all other areas. Though there were not phones in students' individual rooms, telephoning, though probably frowned upon by the administration, was possible for long distances. Trains reached Irving eight to ten times per day, enabling day student attendance, trips to the theater and concerts in Harrisburg, and the convenience of traveling down the Cumberland Valley and eastward toward Philadelphia.

Irving continued its convenience for students with campus expansion and construction projects at the turn of the century. E. E. added an annex on the west end of Irving Hall in 1901, adding additional classrooms and a larger art studio. In 1902, the college completed Music Hall which extended southward on the east side of Irving Hall. Named for the growing Music Department which had 24 piano rooms for student practice, the basement had a complete steam laundry for 3,000 pieces daily and a storeroom for a second floor, 200-seat, 80 x 65-foot dining room. The modern, third floor kitchen, 16 x 22 feet in size, contained four large double-bottom, copper steamers which received steam through boilers located underneath Columbian Hall.[75] Attached with dumb waiters to transport food down to the second-floor dining area, Campbell affixed the kitchen with speaking tubes communicating with every floor in the building, cupboard space, and an annex for additional storage. At the double-door entrance to the dining room, a large laundry chute was installed, and the new addition also included a student club room, and two rooms for dorm space. Besides the kitchen, the top floor had a gymnasium, china and linen rooms, and extra space provided for the restoration of the students' reading room and library. With each new

---

74. *The Sketch Book*, Vol. III No. 5, April 1897, 148.
75. "Irving's New Annex," *The Daily Journal*, Vol. II No. 1, November 20, 1901.

building project, E. E. ensured that the rooms were well-ventilated, kept in excellent repair, of first-class sanitation, lit with electricity, heated by steam, and had hot and cold running water for each story and bathroom. Apparently, Campbell succeeded at trying to make his college presentable, as one magazine stated that Irving avoided the gloomy interiors which can create "depressing effects," as they are well papered, carpeted, and furnished in antique oak.[76]

About the time of this new construction, E. E. purchased four acres of land at the rear of the college where more than 150 shade trees were planted to beautify the surrounding campus. Campbell added a tennis court, an outdoor basketball court, croquet grounds, and even projected bicycle tracks (which were never built). With the completion of the annex in 1901, Campbell had an enclosed court between Columbian and Irving Halls, which he decorated with a rock fountain centerpiece, and later with geraniums and rhododendrons. He added pathways on campus, and enabled sidewalk construction and hedges around the perimeter of the campus.

The most ornate of all the projects around 1900 was the construction of a new campus residence for President Campbell. In 1907, he had nearly finished "a very handsome residence on the southeastern part of the College grounds, where he [would] be able to entertain faculty and friends. Its style of architecture is the Spanish Renaissance."[77] Why E. E. completed another residence just 12 years after building Sunnyside is not completely clear, though for him the physical closeness to his students and his entertaining of guests and parents on campus required a closer residence. Sunnyside suffered from a fire in 1901, though it did not burn to the ground thanks to students with buckets of water. But, considerable damage may have prompted E. E. to consider a new place of residence. The death of Campbell's first wife, Agnes, on February 23, 1896, not long after the building of Sunnyside, could have placed a damper on

---

76. "Irving College, Mechanicsburg, Pennsylvania.: Its Marked Prestige and Growing Importance in its Chosen Field. The Higher Education of Women," *Greater America*, Vol. II, Nos. 10–11, July-August 1899, 1.
77. *Irvingiana '07*, 23.

the house for him.[78] E. E. married a second time in 1897 and may have wanted the new residence for his second wife to call home. After obtaining the money needed to again build a fair-sized house with applicable entertaining space, E. E. finished his new residence, called "Argyle" after his branch of the Campbell Scottish clan, by the time the students returned to school in 1908.[79]

Campbell did not construct another residence hall at Irving, but when additional space was needed for boarding students, E. E. let out rooms in Argyle for students, a practice he had started while living at Sunnyside. If the dorm rooms would fill for the upcoming year, E. E. hand-picked selected students to live with him at Argyle. The students living there, though physically separated from the remainder of boarding students, participated in the normal events of social life at Irving: "we put on our pajamas and went to that feed at Argyle. Charlotte and I were the only two invited from Irving Hall! The rooms that the girls have over there are just darling, and [the] Campbells just let them do as they please."[80] Since the students who resided at Argyle arrived through special selection, they or their parents probably knew the Campbells well and thus required less monitoring than other boarding students. Either way, living in Argyle gave these special students something to cherish and be proud of.

Whether "Argyle" was built for his second wife or not, the death of Campbell's first wife and his second marriage certainly must have been a trial. When Agnes passed on in 1896, she left E. E. with four children and a college to take care of, which despite deep distress he exhibited over the death of his wife, left him in quite a predicament. According to a letter from Ella Bruton, a faculty member at Irving (1895–1897) who wrote E. E. in March after Agnes's passing, Campbell certainly mulled over important decisions: "As to your giving up the College—do not

---

78. Agnes was born September 2, 1866, and had twins born after Annie Catherine: Emma Nelle and Mary Agnes. Both born on December 30, 1889, Mary Agnes died as a toddler on February 24, 1891. Annie would go on to school at Radcliffe (for history), Bryn Mawr and Irving, while Emma studied at Drexel.

79. E. E.'s Argyle and Argyle socks are both named after the Argyle branch of the Campbell clan from Scotland. The socks are named as such because the tartan design adapted by this branch of the clan was the design used in that style of sock.

80. Diary entry from an unknown student, November 9, 1925. The "feed" is the same thing as a feast which is described in more detail in chapter two.

decide that yourself until the way is clear. This is the Lord's school and he will take care of it. Do not feel that the whole burden rests on you."[81] Campbell probably fretted over this decision for quite some time until he could determine what to do with his four children and 120 students. It seemed quite apparent he needed a wife. He found her on the campus of Irving as Lilly Grace Koser (1875–1966), the daughter of a Protestant Minister, who began working earlier that school year teaching shorthand, typewriting, penmanship, and bookkeeping after graduating from Irving's course in 1895. Nearly 18 years his junior, they married 22 months after Agnes's death, at a service presided over by Lilly's father in her hometown of Ardentsville, Pennsylvania. This could have caused quite a stir among the townspeople, for though Campbell was a Democrat and a bit more liberal-minded then the overwhelmingly Republican borough, marrying someone 18 years younger barely two years since your first wife's death could hardly be perceived as a symbol of mourning. There is no archival proof that the townspeople disapproved of the marriage, but it is quite possible that some of them scoffed at his second marriage, as afterwards he changed his membership from the Lutheran church in Mechanicsburg to the Zion Lutheran Church in Harrisburg. In Campbell's defense, he did need to find a companion and a caretaker for his children. He could not have been in any condition to run a women's college and a household of preschoolers. Why he wooed Lilly instead of someone more his age is unknown, unless he was so busy with Irving College that the only women he came into contact with were students and faculty. However, E. E. involved himself with Mechanicsburg in many facets, from the volunteer fire company to the health board. A great many people knew him, and it is uncertain how likely he would meet any single women his age. Regardless of the reason, it is apparent that E. E. loved both of his wives, and Lilly became not only vice president of the school, but like a mother to the students of Irving.

As he portrayed the father figure in Irving's small world, Campbell reached out into the community and became a well-known Mechanicsburg resident. The Lion's Club of Mechanicsburg, the Mechanicsburg Chautauqua Association, and the Mechanicsburg Board of Health were

---

81. Bruton, Ella. Letter to E. E. Campbell, March 2, 1896.

just the start of Campbell's involvement in the community. Standing on the Democratic platform, E. E. served a term in the state legislature as a representative from Cumberland County, though for only a short time. Apparently, it was customary for candidates to provide a few drinks for the stragglers who voted at the last minute of an election to ensure that they voted in the candidate's favor. Campbell, who detested drinking, would have nothing to do with such a practice, and it cost him at the voting poll that day; he was not reelected.[82] During World War I, Campbell took an active part in Red Cross Work, sponsoring Liberty Loan Drives and addressing patriotic meetings across the country. After changing his membership to the Zion Lutheran Church of Harrisburg, E. E. became the president of the Church Council of the Congregation and a teacher of the Men's Bible Class, a weekly vocation which he took very seriously. Campbell supported the Modern Woodmen of America, the Local Order of the Knights of Malta, and the Mechanicsburg Hook and Ladder Fire Company, where he enjoyed giving speeches at the annual banquets.

Enthralled at giving speeches, E. E. gave them every chance he could and was often called upon to do so. He was an ardent storyteller, and between him, Reverend A. R. Steck, and Dr. S. W. Herman (all three of them trustees), Irving students could hear fantastic stories as the three urged each other on. E. E.'s youngest daughter, Jane (Campbell) Beard, '29, described him as a family man, close to his children, who often had high standards for them to succeed in life. Not overly strict, E. E. was a genial person with a native wit and an overwhelming sense of humor. "He loved to disregard the dignity of his profession, at times, and to enter, whole-heartedly, into the spirit of fun,"[83] getting into snow-ball fights with students, or when watering the flowers, sprinkling the young ladies, even through their dorm windows. "Never did a girl enter his office or pass him in the corridor, that he did not have some cheery word to say to her."[84] He had generosity, charm in his conversation, and a twinkle in his eye even when reprimanding a student. "He was [a] wonderful, short, sunny man [,] and adorable."[85] A kind, stern, religious, and

---
82. Oral history with Jane Campbell Beard, '29, April 12, 1994.
83. *The Sketch Book*, December 1926, 24.
84. *The Sketch Book*, December 1926, 25.
85. Oral history with Marion Strouse Scharf, '18, May 18, 1993.

Irving's Administration, 1855-1957

understanding man, "if [E. E.] had something to say, he'd certainly tell you."[86] At the celebration of Irving's fiftieth birthday in 1907, students were already looking back fondly on Campbell's tenure. Attendance had increased under Campbell's direction "until every room was occupied and no more students could be received . . ." and with the new dorm construction, "again all rooms were filled."[87] Campbell had enticed many young women to attend the school, thus increasing enrollment, but Campbell was remembered for strengthening the school's departments too: "The Departments of Music, Art, and Oratory are in a most flourishing condition."[88] Sixteen years after first arriving at Irving, Campbell could celebrate his success with Irving at its 50th anniversary, since he was one reason the school reached that milestone.

With construction and new facilities being added to the college regularly during the beginning of Campbell's term, E. E. had created a fine educational atmosphere at Irving that was gaining attention around the state. Through his administrative methods, Campbell had established a school with a rigorous work schedule for a fair cost:

> The multiplication of schools and the resulting competition for patronage have induced many institutions to meet the demand for cheap schools by curtailing the cost of efficient teachers and generous provision for the comfort of students; but this is a competition into which Irving College does not enter. Dr. Campbell, the President, seems firmly impressed with the belief that there are enough patrons who appreciate a competent service and are willing to pay for it: to sustain a high-grade institution . . . There is no institution for the education of young women in Pennsylvania that surpasses Irving College, in the convenience, comfort and capacity of its buildings or in its beautiful and accessible location.[89]

---

86. Oral history with Pauline Hege, '25, October 15, 1993.
87. *Irvingiana '07*, 15.
88. *Irvingiana '07*, 15, 23.
89. *Greater America*, 1.

> From the moment you send for a catalog, and receive it with a personal letter from the registrar, you feel that a personal interest is taken in you. You will find that this interest continues throughout your college career and that our happiness and welfare are the personal aims of those in authority. Parents know that when their daughters are in *Irving*, they are safe and well taken care of, for this reputation is an established fact.[90]

According to Campbell, Irving had benefits over other schools:

> The courses in Music, Expression and Art have no superior in any college in our state. The Department of Public Instruction of Pennsylvania recognizes the good work done at 'IRVING' and issues to her graduates Professional and Permanent Certificates, enabling them to teach anywhere in the state without examination.[91]

After a trip to an educator's convention at Vassar College in 1897, Campbell received notice that Irving was indeed of merit: "[i]t gives me pleasure to inform you that your school was admitted to membership in this Association [Association of Colleges and Preparatory Schools] at the meeting recently held at Vassar College."[92]

With this protracted growth, Irving prospered and received more attention, and Campbell, being the owner of the school, also prospered. By 1901, the prosperity of the school and of Campbell was apparent to the trustees: "We believe that the welfare of the school would be promoted and its further growth and efficiency better secured and assured by vesting the property in the board of trustees rather than by continued individual ownership."[93] For years, the board members made efforts to turn the college property over to the members of the board, who according to the 1857 charter, were the rightful owners anyway. Like Ege before him, E. E. had purchased the college outright, but Campbell realized the

---

90. *Pennsylvania School Journal, Educational Review*, Vol. LXXVII, No. 3A, 26.
91. Campbell, E. E. Letter to Alumnae, June 30, 1914.
92. *The Sketch Book*, Vol. IV, No. 3, December 1897, 81.
93. Irving College Board of Trustees Minutes, June 4, 1901.

benefits of having the trustees in control of the property and was not entirely against it. However, E. E. could not be expected to just *hand over* a profitable institution that he paid for and made prosperous without proper compensation. He asked the trustees for about $50,000 for the college, an amount which the trustees initially deemed difficult, but feasible. Campbell felt that he should not "be expected to give up his present commercial advantage [Irving property] and opportunity without some special financial consideration in return."[94] The trouble with this transfer of property began after this initial meeting between E. E. and the board in 1901.

At the annual meeting in June, a special committee was appointed to investigate the financial matter and report upon it at the next meeting in 1902. The matter was deemed worthy enough to call a special meeting of the board for November 29, 1901. William J. Gies, a professor from Columbia University who married an Irving graduate (Mabel L. Lark, '97), joined the board in 1900 and would soon become E. E.'s rival on the issue.[95] He submitted a report for the committee that apparently was very exhaustive and had been amended several times before the board accepted it. The report stated that Irving's best interest lay in the board obtaining control of the college property, and that Campbell's asking price was nullified by the 1857 charter which gave the board exclusive ownership to Irving's property. The committee, realizing the tall task of raising $50,000 to pay E. E. for Irving, maintained that "Dr. Campbell entirely ignores the fact that the charter rights and privilege—the 'franchise' so to speak for his 'business'—belong to the Board."[96] However, with the addition of a new annex to Irving Hall and other improvements in process, at this November meeting E. E. made it clear that he had now wanted $60,000 for the college property. Campbell submitted actual real estate estimates for all the college property, [see Appendix A]

---

94. Irving College Board of Trustees Minutes, November 29, 1901.
95. Dr. William Gies went on to have an illustrious career, essentially becoming the father of modern Dental Education. He was a professor of biochemistry at Columbia University from 1907–1937, was the editor of the *Journal for Dental Research* from 1919–1935 and was the founder of the International Association of Dental Research. Two awards are given in his name, the journal *Science* published a tribute to Gies upon his death [see: "The Challenge to Dentistry" by Theodor Rosebury, vol. 126, issue 3282, Nov. 22, 1957] and his "Gies Report" published in 1926 established modern standards for the profession.
96. Irving College Board of Trustees Minutes, November 29, 1901.

which included not only the land and buildings but extraneous items like pipe organs, pianos, and other furnishings. The committee found fault with the estimates given (thinking them too high), and recommended an estimate of $35,000, not including the annex to Irving Hall which was currently under construction. Citing Campbell's private earnings from Irving from 1898–1900 at about $10,000 each year [see Appendix A], the committee reiterated:

> The purpose of the Board is naturally one of a benevolent character and Irving College was always intended for the greatest good to the greatest number of students. This purpose is entirely defeated and the Board put to shame when financial profits are gathered by any one concerned in the administration of its affairs. Salaries commensurate with amount and character of service rendered are entirely deserved but no properly regulated college administration ever converts a surplus of its funds into private wealth; "profits" are rather transformed into material evidences of collegiate progress and the institution grows in usefulness with their increase and proper use.[97]

The November meeting ended with no transfer being consummated, but that did not prevent William Gies from inflating the issue. Gies, now spearheading the Committee on Transfer of Title, reported again on the situation at the 1902 annual meeting, bringing forth several resolutions in response to Campbell's reluctance to give up the college property. "Whereas the owner of the property in which Irving College has been conducted does not see fit to transfer and convey the said property to the Board on terms satisfactory to the Trustees . . . it is hereby:

1. Resolved by the Trustees of Irving College that Dr. E. E. Campbell be and he is hereby elected President of Irving College for the academic year 1902–03 and that the President's salary for the same time be made $1800.00.

---

97. Irving College Board of Trustees Minutes, November 29, 1901.

2. Resolved also that the owner of the college property be paid a rental of $2700.00 for the use by the Trustees of the said property for the academic year 1902–03.[98]

The adopted resolutions also established an executive committee which "shall conduct and manage all the affairs of the College on behalf of the Board except such as are included in the duties to be exercised by the President, as prescribed by the Charter and By-Laws."[99] Though these resolutions went into effect, no property changed hands. With E. E. owning the college, being a board member, and many of the trustees befriending him (including Board President, Rev. A. R. Steck), no transfer occurred, though Gies tried his hardest to wrestle Irving away from Campbell. In 1903, the board questioned E. E. on whether he would accept $45,000 for the college or the salary and terms put forth by the committee in 1902; E. E. declined both.

Letters of correspondence between Gies and Campbell have survived from 1906–1908 mainly concerning the purchase of Irving from E. E, though communication between the two men may have occurred sometime before and after those two years. In 1906, Gies tried to involve Andrew Carnegie, Helen Gould, and other New York City elites in purchasing the school to put it on a non-proprietorship basis, in order to place the college with the trustees. At the annual meeting in June, Gies put forth suggestions for the board to pay E. E. the $60,000 in various ways, but all motions to do so were lost. When not at board meetings, Gies wrote three-to-six-page letters to Campbell almost twice every month concerning the issue, which appeared to grind at Campbell, as at times the communication between the two became very strained, though still polite. It appears that both were quite frustrated with each other: Gies with E. E. not giving up the school on his terms, and E. E. with Gies nagging him at every turn. A letter from Board President A. R. Steck to Campbell showed that Gies's constant pressure was affecting him:

---

98. Irving College Board of Trustees Minutes, June 3, 1902.
99. Irving College Board of Trustees Minutes, June 3, 1902.

> As to Prof Geis [sic]: If you know what is good for yourself and Irving, you will <u>never again</u> permit the subject of purchasing Irving come before that Board to be kicked and cuffed about like a football. <u>Keep it out</u>, as you value your peace of mind. Lose no time in telling Geis [sic] so . . . You know your <u>price</u>. You know the institution is your own property. <u>He</u> knows both facts also.[100]

Whether Carnegie or some other contingent was going to purchase Irving or not is a mystery, though Steck thought that Gies had the connections to make it happen. However, by 1903 the board appeared ready to bury the issue and most members became disgruntled with Gies's attempts at prolonging the issue:

> I read it and reread it—that is Dr. G's [Gies's] communication and I said—'What on earth is he striving to accomplish'! [sic] He is a 'mystic' an enigma to clear-headed people. I'm amazed at his presumption and gall . . . He signally [sic] failed in his former projects—in disrupting the Board and the college . . . He knows well that what he stood for in the board fell through with a thump.[101]
>
> —Board Member Charles S. Trump

> Dr. Gies' letter is certainly modesty in the green. I have no desire to misjudge any man, but with the facts in evidence before me I can come to but one conclusion and that is that Gies is insane on his own importance. For one educated man to sit down and write another educated man a letter of the nature and character such as Gies wrote you is not only bewildering but staggering . . .[102]
>
> —Board Member W. A. Shipman

Gies is no longer mentioned in the board minutes after 1910, and no mention of his resignation is ever put forth in the recorded minutes, possibly because everyone was glad to see him leave. With the departure

---

100. Steck, A. R. Letter to E. E. Campbell, March 13, 1906.
101. Trump, Rev. Charles S. Letter to E. E. Campbell, December 23, 1907.
102. Shipman, W. A. Letter to E. E. Campbell, December 2, 1907.

of Gies, the ownership question died with the board and Campbell coexisted as president and proprietor.

No matter who officially owned the college, the health of the institution was always an ardent concern for Campbell, and he took pride in the fact that his students never got sick. At every board meeting, E. E. made a health report about the college: "the health of the students to have been most excellent—no disease in the buildings throughout the session..."[103] "Colleges in many places have been closed by diphtheria and scarlet fever and greatly interrupted in their work by other diseases. Not so here."[104] Edward S. Wagoner, President of the Board of Health for Mechanicsburg in 1901, commented that "in all the years this institution has been under Prof. E. E. Campbell's management and proprietorship, this board has had no occasion to deal with a single case of contagious or infectious disease located within the college walls..."[105] E. E.'s record at the school was nearly spotless as his relentless efforts to prevent disease from spreading on campus worked well. In the last 40 years of the institution, only three students died on campus, apparently from conditions outside of Campbell's control. Twice in the spring of 1919, a student died from a typhoid fever epidemic that ravaged through Mechanicsburg's water system, with 36 cases and ten deaths in town and four cases on campus alone. Elizabeth Coffman of Liverpool, Pennsylvania fell ill with dysentery, high fever, and sickening stomach, passing away on campus on March 25, just four days before spring vacation. Coffman's death on campus was the first ever in Irving's 63-year history, as students were sent home early for spring vacation with a letter detailing the events that transpired. Exactly one week later, Mary Moore of Pine Grove, Pennsylvania died from the same ailment, and luckily the two remaining student cases on campus recovered soon after. Dr. Campbell spoke at both funerals of the students and "the parents of these two girls were outspoken in their appreciation of [Irving's] care and solitude for both girls."[106] In memory of Coffman and Moore, the entire school planted memorial trees on campus and held beautiful services in

---

103. Irving College Board of Trustees Minutes, June 4, 1900.
104. Irving College Board of Trustees Minutes, June 1, 1909.
105. "Buildings Inspected," *The Daily Journal*, Vol. II No. 2, November 21, 1901, 1.
106. Irving College Board of Trustees Minutes, June 3, 1919.

commemoration. The third student who died during Campbell's tenure was Miss Harriet Johnson of Tamaqua, Pennsylvania, who died of acute diabetes on Valentine's Day 1923 at the college infirmary after being ill only two days.

Campbell emphasized health for two reasons: to keep his students safe and to have parents have full trust in him to care for their daughters. Mothers and fathers feared sending their daughters to college after Clark's *Sex and Education* made headlines with the public, stating that too much education was damaging to females, causing sterility and illness. Campbell kept such a close eye on the health of his students to refute the claims in *Sex and Education* and reassured parents with his impeccable health reports for the school. Campbell certainly convinced a few parents with his active part in the town's health, becoming president of the Mechanicsburg Health Board after the disastrous outbreak that befell the water system. Campbell wanted his students safe. E. E. wanted his college to be like one large family, having parents entrust their daughters to him, as if at college *he* would be their father, enforcing a strict but loving atmosphere. For the most part, Campbell created this environment of love and discipline and cared for many of the students as if they were his own children. The college catalogues discouraged parents from sending any sweets through the mail, since it curtailed studying through the large conglomeration of girls who gathered to eat the goodies. Also, if parents *had* to give their daughters spending money, E. E. requested that it be deposited with him, and he would distribute the extra money as he saw fit.

The student experience with Dr. Campbell as this "father-like" figure began very early on with the process of their coming to Irving. Campbell interviewed nearly every student before their entrance into the college, not only to introduce himself and orient the pupil, but also to ensure the parents that their child would be taken care of. "In earlier years, he [E. E.] would do what he called canvassing . . . if someone might be interested in sending a daughter, he would call on their home during the summer, and talk to the families, and the girl, and explain about the college . . ."[107] "[E. E.] did that with all of his admissions. He visited every home . . . [He] only had so [much] room for so many girls at the school, so he

---

107. Oral History with Jane Campbell Beard, '29, April 12, 1994.

could be very particular."[108] Being able to choose all the students who walked Irving's halls, he "judged the students by the home atmosphere" when recruiting them in order to achieve the best selection of students.[109] "Inasmuch as the College receives only a limited number of students, it is advisable that application for rooms be made early. Rooms are assigned as applications are accepted."[110] While it appears unlikely that Marlatt or Ege practiced this exhaustive interviewing process, Campbell enjoyed getting to know the students and parents, as his outgoing and pleasant personality helped to spread a good word about the school. E. E. often contacted alumnae inquiring whether they had any daughters old enough or knew of any young women interested in a college education at Irving. Word-of-mouth was a popular way for students to hear about and attend Irving, as many students' sisters, cousins, and neighbors attended the school through the stories that present and former students disclosed.

This system worked well for E. E., and it enabled him to attract women from all over the east coast, and even other countries [see Appendix B, table 1]. Whereas Irving students in the first few years of its opening tended to come solely from Pennsylvania and surrounding southern states, after the Civil War more Midwesterners and New Yorkers traveled to the Mechanicsburg school. Witnessing students from 26 states, and countries such as Norway, Canada, Cuba and Puerto Rico, Campbell had obtained a wider influence for the college across Pennsylvania and out of state than ever in its earlier years.

Because Campbell canvassed the students and had a successful school running at Irving, he could afford to be particular with the students he wished to accept, therefore maintaining Irving as a small college. The perfect Irving student was "one who would cooperate with other people . . . work along with other people and not try to make waves [or] be a disturber. [He strived for] a harmonious type of atmosphere . . ."[111] Since Campbell did not initiate any other building projects on campus after 1902, the size of the boarding students could not grow beyond the 80 that roomed in the dormitories and the few that stayed at his residence.

---

108. Oral History, Mary Lu Shaffer Heinz (1925–1927), May 12, 1993.
109. Oral History, Marion Strouse Scharf, '18, May 18, 1993.
110. Irving College Catalogue, 1905–1906, 10.
111. Oral History, Jane Campbell Beard, '29, April 12, 1994.

While other colleges grew and built additional buildings and facilities, Campbell maintained the status quo at Irving after the early part of the century. By 1927's commencement, Hood College (1897) and Wilson College (1868), both of whom were founded after Irving, had surpassed Irving's degree recipients per year, graduating 90 and 75 respectively, compared to Irving's 24 that year. Other schools which had grown larger offered more to the women students. Wilson had 17 buildings to house its 400 residents, while Beaver College in Jenkintown, though founded three years before Irving, had a gymnasium in addition to the swimming pool and athletic fields that Irving had. The schools, though they were graduating more students with B.A.'s than Irving, appeared not to have the variety of degree possibilities that Irving did. At that 1927 graduation, Hood College handed out 64 B.A.'s and 26 B.S.'s in home economics, while Wilson awarded 72 B.A.'s and 3 B.S.'s. Of the 24 Irving graduates, 3 received an A.B., 5 a home economics degree, 8 a secretarial certificate, 1 a degree in voice, 5 a degree in piano, and 2 a degree in the dramatic arts. Despite its small size, Irving's degrees were diverse.

To say that everything under E. E.'s control ran smoothly is not entirely correct; Campbell did have his problem students and faculty members. Students were under such rigid time constraints and strict supervision that discipline was not usually an overwhelming issue. But when it did come up, E. E. took care of it: "Some students who had been in attendance last session and who were not making a very good record, and whose influence was not particularly desirable, were asked not to return."[112] In response to a "tense atmosphere" among the students in 1919, two additional students were expelled to alleviate the problem. However, these random occurrences creep up in any school, even one with the effervescent Dr. Campbell, who was overall well-respected by the students and faculty alike.

One faculty member did stir up trouble for Campbell, however. At the board meeting of 1901, Campbell submitted an unusual request, asking the board for the dismissal of Professor C. F. Kloss because of his disloyalty to the president and Irving College. What exactly brought about this action from Campbell is not entirely clear, although Lenore Embick

---

112. Irving College Board of Trustees Minutes, June 1, 1909.

Flower, '04, perceived Kloss to be in a plot to remove ownership of Irving College from Campbell. According to Flower, "teaching... was not [Kloss's] primary concern," as he apparently interviewed students, talked to faculty about salaries, and planned on viewing the college financial records to determine just how successful Irving and consequently Campbell, was. Kloss placed all the financial information in the hands of the board by the next annual meeting. Kloss apparently sprung William Gies and his crusade into action, and they may have been working together in an effort to remove Irving from Campbell's ownership. No sources ultimately prove this fact and even Flower neglects to mention names in her recollections. Although the board's resolution was for Campbell and Kloss to "reconcile their differences," six months later Kloss handed in his resignation, relieving E. E. of any faculty headaches.

These headaches with Kloss, in addition to the constant nagging about his proprietorship of Irving, may have made Campbell uneasy about staying at the institution any longer. After the turn of the century when the ideas of vesting Campbell's property with the trustees surfaced, E. E. began looking into selling the college to the Lutheran Synod to be run as a Lutheran College for women. One Saturday afternoon, the Lutheran Synod adjourned to visit Campbell and the faculty for a reception at Irving, which thoroughly impressed the Synod, who were "both surprised and gratified to find it in such fine condition and the pupils so well cared for."[113] One Lutheran minister even stated: "Why this is like home, and a parent should have no compunctions of conscience in sending his daughter to this finely equipped school to be educated."[114] Despite the impression Irving made on the Synod, Campbell could not convince the Lutherans to purchase the school, estimated at probably the same price he quoted the board of trustees:

> I can not [sic] but feel that the Lutheran Church has ignored and lost the greatest opportunity that it has ever had to establish a college for young women under its own auspices. It is with real

---

113. "A Visit to Irving College," Unknown News Clipping, c. 1900–1925.
114. "A Visit to Irving College," Unknown News Clipping, c. 1900–1925.

regret and disappointment that I see the institution pass out from under our own church auspices.[115]

The benefits of securing the Lutheran Synod as the school's owner would ensure funding and support for years after E. E. Campbell's administration. Since the school had loose ties with the Lutherans anyway, a formal affiliation surely must have been on the Synod's members' minds as well as Irving administrators. Even the State of Pennsylvania suggested this move forward:

> The way is now open for you to continue your work for the public schools. My only advice is, do well whatever work you undertake and ultimately get the Lutheran Church to take over the college for the purpose of making it one of the regular institutions under the United Synods. In the long run, no school can live unless it has backing of that sort.
> —Nathan C. Schaeffer, State Superintendent of Public Instruction[116]

Campbell's offer being refused, the Lutherans would not again bargain with Irving College until after Campbell's death, though it appears that other attempts were made. Gies apparently tried wooing Andrew Carnegie and other New Yorkers to purchase the school, and Marion Strouse Scharf, '18 was contacted by Lenore Embick Flower, '04 about a purchaser: "she'd [Flower] call me over when Dr. Campbell was having difficulties. She called me and asked if I would contact Vance McCormick [,] who was a very prominent man in Harrisburg, and ask him if he would buy Irving College."[117] Though a variety of attempts were made, no interested proprietor purchased the college before Campbell's death.

Though most people involved with Irving attributed its success to Campbell, some resistance to the president existed. Possibly because of

---

115. Irving College Board of Trustees Minutes, May 30, 1916.
116. Schaeffer, Nathan C. Letter to E. E. Campbell, July 22, 1918.
117. Oral History, Marion Strouse Scharf, '18, May 18, 1993. A prominent businessman, McCormick was mayor of Harrisburg from 1902 to 1905, was best known as the president of the company that published *The Patriot* and *The Evening News*, arguably, the two most important newspapers in the area.

the pressure applied by the board and particularly Gies and no success in his efforts to secure a purchase from the Lutheran Synod, Campbell announced his retirement from the institution to take effect after commencement on July 1, 1916:

> After having expressed my desire on different occasions to see "IRVING" become an institution for the education of our young women under the auspices of our own Lutheran Church, and having received no substantial encouragement at any time from parties who should be interested, and having a desire to be relieved from further responsibility of conducting the institution on my own responsibility wholly, it is with real regret that I notify the Board that I have disposed of all my rights in the IRVING COLLEGE property . . .[118]

Campbell put his college up for sale, and Dr. Matthew Howell Reaser, head of the Beechwood College for Girls (Beaver College) in Jenkintown, Pennsylvania, acquired the property, succeeding Campbell as Irving's next president.[119] Campbell announced that the new administration of Irving College extended beyond Reaser, as E. E. remained unaware of the details, though Irving would be officially turned over October 1, 1916. Campbell reassured the board about the change in command:

> Doctor Reaser promises to continue the institution largely along present lines, and hopes to enlarge considerably the attendance of students and expects to add other departments . . . He expects to have the usual number of old students return in the fall. An aggressive campaign is now on for new students.[120]

---

118. Campbell, E. E. Presidential Report, Irving College Board of Trustees Minutes, May 30, 1916.

119. Beaver College, which originally was located in Western Pennsylvania in the town called Beaver, moved after 72 years to Jenkintown in Eastern Pennsylvania merging with Beechwood College located there in 1925. According to the *Pennsylvania School Journal*, Beaver College was the third oldest women's college in the country chartered on December 28, 1853, after both Georgia Female College and Elmira College in New York, even though several other colleges were founded before, though perhaps of lesser quality, even in Pennsylvania [see Appendix C, table 1]. Beaver College would later change its name and now exists as Arcadia University.

120. Campbell, E. E. Presidential Report, Irving College Board of Trustees Minutes, May 30, 1916.

Reaser purchased Irving with a strong educational background and years of experience under his belt. Born in Leavenworth, Kansas in 1864, young Reaser moved to St. Louis at age 10 and attended college at Washington University until his junior year when he moved with his father, Dr. J. G. Reaser, to Fulton, Missouri, where he finished his A.B. at Westminster College. After also receiving his Ph.D. from Westminster, Reaser went on to teach at the Carthage Collegiate Institute until he accepted the presidential post at Brookfield College in Brookfield, Missouri in 1886. Raising enrollment in five years there from 30 pupils to over 200, Reaser made the school self-supporting and secured funds for its operation, establishing himself as a top-rate administrator in the process.[121] Because of his success at Brookfield, Oswego College for Women in Oswego, Kansas elected him president of their college, which he accepted in 1891. He had more than doubled the enrollment at Oswego, but suffered from repeated attacks of malaria, forcing him to give up education temporarily in order to recover. After a two-year hiatus, Reaser returned to take the helm of Lindenwood College in St. Charles, Missouri, a position which he held from 1893 to 1903. Erasing a debt of $12,500 and securing an endowment of nearly $10,000, Reaser continued his successful collegiate administration, increasing enrollment every year and "[improving] the property in every way."[122] From 1903–1911 Reaser assumed the presidency of neighboring Wilson College in Chambersburg, where he continued his success by completing the campus chapel building, spending $4,000 on athletic grounds, doubling the campus size with another 25 acres, building roads and sidewalks, installing the first telephone exchange, constructing two student club rooms and a new presidential residence, and setting aside $500 each year for adding new books to the library. Under Reaser, the entrance requirements at Wilson steadily increased: "until now in all subjects—Latin, Mathematics, Modern Languages, History, English, Science—they are up to the standard set by leading women's colleges."[123] Reaser increased the number of electives in

---

121. Tanner, Amy E. "President Reaser, *The Pharetra*, Vol. XVI [actually XVII], No. 1, October 1903, 3–5. *The Pharetra* was the student literary publication of Wilson College.

122. Tanner, 5.

123. Lloyd, Nettie Hesson. *Wilson College, 1870–1910: Forty Years of Wilson as told by her Presidents, Faculty and Students.* Chambersburg: Repository Press (1910), 88.

each department, had his A.B. graduates recognized and accepted into graduate programs of other prominent schools,[124] and abolished the Preparatory Department to raise the college standards. In 1904, Reaser graduated 15 students and employed 24 faculty members; by 1910, Reaser graduated 59 students and employed 34 faculty members. Increasing enrollment as at other schools, Reaser administered 276 women in 1906, which he raised to 365 by 1910. Faculty salaries increased under his tenure and student self-government arrived in his first year after several years of debate and petitioning by Wilson students. Resigning his post at Wilson after graduation in 1911, Reaser accepted the presidential post at the Beechwood College for Women in Jenkintown, Pennsylvania. Five years after arriving in Jenkintown, Reaser purchased Irving outright from E. E. Campbell. Almost immediately, changes resulted as Reaser announced that Rev. N. L. Euwer would be named Associate President, the "directing head of the institution [who] will report to the president."[125] Reaser relayed to the trustees from the outset that:

> [it] is the purpose of the new administration to place the title of the property in the Board of Trustees and have the Board of Trustees assume financial responsibility. Under this arrangement doubtless the members of the present Board will feel disposed to tender their resignations.[126]

Five days after E. E.'s resignation, every member of the 1916 Board resigned, giving up their power to new board members who were apparently associated with Beechwood College. M. H. Reaser became President of the Board though President of the institution as well, and Rev. N. L. Euwer became Associate President of the Board, though Associate President of the college. Even though Campbell had been a trustee during his tenure, he was never the Board President and did face opposition, despite his control of the property and the presidency. However, with the complete changeover in ownership, Reaser now controlled everything.

---
124. Columbia, Radcliffe, Cornell, and the Universities of Wisconsin and Chicago all accepted Wilson graduates into their advanced degree programs.
125. "Irving College Head Quits," News Clipping, June 1916.
126. Campbell, E. E. Presidential Report, Irving College Board of Trustees Minutes, May 30, 1916.

In appreciation of Campbell's efforts as President, Katherine Wheelock of the faculty, and an Irving graduate herself in 1892, presented E. E. with a "handsome loving cup," provided to Wheelock by the Pittsburgh Irving College Club. "Tears mingled with smiles" at the ceremony as Campbell "eulogized the Irving girls for loyalty and spoke of his deep and abiding love for the institution."[127] As Campbell packed up his family and moved to Washington, D.C., Rev. Euwer moved into Argyle as the new administrative head. No literature from the school nor any living graduates remember Reaser, possibly because Euwer interacted with the students from Argyle while Reaser presided over both colleges from Jenkintown. There is speculation that administrators from Beechwood only wanted control of Irving for its charter of unlimited degrees since their own school could not grant such degrees in their programs. This assumption has some support as within one year, Reaser tended his resignation, and the influence of Beechwood College was gone. The former board consisting of President A. R. Steck, C. R. Trowbridge, Rev. S. W. Herman and company retained their trustee posts and elected Campbell as president for the 1917–1918 school year. Why Reaser and his cohort evacuated Irving after just one year is unknown, though many graduates speculated that the Beechwood administrators could not "make a go of it" with Irving and decided to dump the idea of controlling both colleges. It seems quite apparent that Reaser wanted out of the Irving situation rather early in his administration, as his name appears in neither the 1916–1917 nor 1917–1918 college catalogues, nor in any college publication or annual, allowing for his brief tenure at Irving to be easily forgotten. Though the Irving property does change hands from Campbell to Reaser and back to Campbell officially, the Beechwood head may have known by the winter holidays that his plan to control Irving's charter was not going to work. With no former Board members or Irving administrators at his disposal, and only Euwer, a religion, philosophy, and education professor new to Irving's faculty in 1916 before his Associate President promotion, Reaser may have bitten off more than he could chew trying to run two institutions. Campbell repurchased the college

---

127. "Loving Cup for Dr. E. E. Campbell," *Harrisburg Telegraph*, June 2, 1916.

Irving's Administration, 1855–1957

property from Reaser and retained the Presidency on June 6, 1917, at the close of Irving's commencement services.

Because of only a one-year presidency, it is not surprising that Matthew Reaser is absent from most school literature and student memories. However, it is interesting that Reaser also appears to be a forgotten piece from Wilson College memories, despite the widespread success that he had there. In one student publication, Reaser is mentioned as having a hospitable nature and entertaining numerous students and faculty at his residence. However, Reaser could have been an excellent administrator who enjoyed raising endowments and enrollments for colleges, but simply avoided becoming attached to any one college for any length of time, seeing better opportunities for himself ahead. Regardless of his motivations, Reaser, though a successful administrator at multiple schools, pulled out of his Irving project allowing for the return of E. E. Campbell.

Despite a few incidents, it is quite obvious that Irving was a success story for Campbell and being a school administrator may have been E. E.'s calling in life. However, Campbell could not run Irving forever, though aside from his brief retirement in 1916–1917, it appeared that he might indeed do so. He was a man who enjoyed life and the company of others, and indulged in food and social gatherings (though not alcohol) enough to add weight steadily to his small frame until complications resulted:

> For the first time in my life illness befell me. The first day of January found me in bed with bronchitis. After a couple days I was out of bed and around in the house. On January sixth after a strenuous day I retired a little fatigued and about 2:30 A.M. awoke to find myself having a serious attack of heart failure. The doctor came quickly to my relief and after three injections and two doses of heart stimulants my heart responded and the crisis was passed. The attack was not due to any organic heart trouble but to functional trouble. Since then I have had to move cautiously and must still do so. From January sixth till after Easter I was absent from the College though in touch with it at

all times. My weakened heart muscles will require time and quiet for their upbuilding.[128]

The heart failure E. E. suffered in January 1926 confined him to a bed for two months and though he recovered and returned to his post, recuperation lasted only so long. His heart, not strengthening as planned, failed Campbell again as he suffered a second heart attack at midnight on August 3. Becoming unconscious, and growing steadily weaker, Campbell, who had taken an automobile ride with his family just two days before, died on August 4, 1926, at Argyle with his family by his side. "The heart attack was a recurrence of the trouble which almost caused his death during the winter months, and he had not fully recovered from this illness."[129]

Though his names were written incorrectly on the memorial program (his name is listed as Ernest Edmond Campbell), a private funeral was held at 1:30 P.M. on August 7, with a public service just 30 minutes after in Columbian Hall. While the bell above Irving Hall tolled in memory of its president, E. E.'s close friend and Irving's board president, A. R. Steck presided over the public service:

> . . . as a disciplinarian he [E. E.] had few equals, his tact, sympathy[,] appreciation of the problems of the student, his good humor and his penetrating insight of the questions that came before him as a college president, made him a man of unusual power and usefulness. Doctor Campbell insisted that education was in order to service and that character found its roots in faith in God and Christ, and that the hundreds of young women who came to Irving College returned after graduation to their homes, with a stronger and more intelligent faith in all things great and beautiful.[130]

---

128. Campbell, E. E. Presidential report to the board of trustees, Irving College Board of Trustees Minutes, May 31, 1926.
129. "Irving President Dies," *The Harrisburg Telegraph*, Vol. 96 No. 183, August 4, 1926.
130. Steck, A. R. at Campbell's public funeral. Reprinted from a news clipping in Irving College Board of Trustees Minutes, September 8, 1926.

Dr. Campbell's reputation as an educator was state-wide and it was largely the result of his indefatigable efforts that Irving College assumed the place in the educational world which it holds.[131]

Campbell was buried at Chestnut Hill Cemetery just about a mile south of Mechanicsburg.

THE LAST GRASPS AT LIFE, IRVING AFTER E. E., 1926–1940

[T]he small classes, close relation between faculty and students, excellent food, home-like atmosphere, carefully chosen faculty, and lovely class of students—all combine to make the Irving girl one of the happiest of all.
—*Pennsylvania School Journal, Educational Review*, 1928. [132]

With Campbell gone, the board of trustees needed to find a suitable replacement and quickly for the upcoming school year. It was decided that Reverend Charles W. Trowbridge, the recording secretary of the board, was to be acting president until another could fill the position. Trowbridge, who lived on the corner of Chestnut and Main Streets with his sister-in-law just a block from campus, walked to campus during his short stint as president. A tall and slender person, he wore a black hat at kind of a rakish angle and a black coat, reminding Betty Boffemmyer Stram, '29 of Pennsylvania Governor Gifford Pinchot.[133]

With no permanent replacement selected for two years and Trowbridge frequently hospitalized in 1928, Dr. Rev. Thomas J. Ferguson, D.D., also of the board of trustees, was chosen as acting president until the next educational leader for Irving could be found. Ferguson, who had been the pastor of the Silver Spring Presbyterian Church since 1878, was born in Dry Run, Franklin County, was educated at Westminster College

---
131. News clipping, August 6, 1926, Mary Shope's '26, Stunt Book (1922–1929).
132. *Pennsylvania School Journal, Educational Review*, Vol. LXXVII, No. 3A, November 15, 1928, 27.
133. Oral history with Betty Boffemmyer Stram, '29, April 22, 1993.

and at Western Seminary, and even served in 1910–1911 as a member of the state legislature. It seems evident at this point that with no purchaser for Irving in sight (and no president), the end of the college was near, though in the trustee minutes of 1927, any notion of the college closing was "baseless." Though both Trowbridge and Ferguson maintained the same policies and practices put in place by Campbell, when E. E. died, so did the strong personality of the presidency of Irving. Though Trowbridge was a likable and interesting man, neither he nor Ferguson, who was staider and more conservative, could replace the outgoing, dominant, and dynamic E. E. Campbell. "There were two presidents that . . . came after Dr. Campbell that I didn't . . . well, of course I respected him all right, but [they were] not a Dr. Campbell to us girls at all."[134] Irving was not the same without Campbell at the helm.

While the trustees searched for their next permanent president, the Lutheran Synod made one more attempt at obtaining the college in 1928 when looking for a site for a denominational college. Though the Lutherans initially turned down Campbell's offer for the college in 1916, after his death they reconsidered to purchase Irving at his quoted price. In what appeared like the last chance for the future of the college, the Lutherans began to close in on the deal with the Campbell heirs to purchase not only the college grounds, but to initiate expansion, by purchasing a nearby farm owned by Margaret Blackburn. The final negotiations for the transfer were to take place in Philadelphia, where members of the Synod's committee on the purchase were to meet. Dr. S. W. Herman, of Irving's board of trustees, secured with Miss Blackburn that she intended to sell her land located just south of the school as long as her mansion house on the land remained kept up by the Synod and that Blackburn and her mother could live in the house until their deaths, if so desired. After traveling to Philadelphia to speak with the committee on the sale, Herman regrettably found out that Blackburn had visited the committee that morning, informing them that she had changed her mind about selling the land. Though the Blackburns seemed to enjoy the arrival of the Irving girls each fall, their last-minute reluctance to sell prevented the Synod from purchasing the Irving property and the Irving

---

134. Oral History with Catherine Steck, '18, October 16, 1993.

girls from coming back that fall of 1929. The Lutherans eventually chose their college site in Washington, D.C.

By graduation 1929, rumors circulated that the school might not reopen, and students were notified over the summer not to return to Irving in the fall. Lilly Grace Campbell and the First Bank and Trust of Mechanicsburg, the executors of E. E.'s estate (worth over $18,000), made the final decision to close the school and put the property up for sale. Irving faculty were advised a month earlier to start looking for work, while Mae Noss, a college dining hall server, did not even find out about the closing until she read it in the newspaper.

School authorities declined to comment when the school closed but issued the following statement to the press:

> To settle an estate which has remained open for three years, Irving College, Mechanicsburg, Pennsylvania, wil [sic] not be open for reception of students for the session of 1929–1930 . . . This is one of the few colleges in America that has full State recognition without having raised any endowment.
>
> Since the death of Dr. E. E. Campbell, who was the president thirty-five years, Irving College has been continued under the general direction of his former policies. The standard set during his presidency has been maintained and advanced under the successive presidencies . . . The enrollment for the coming session would have included students from ten states of the Union. The members of the Alumnae Association are living in every state in the Union and in foreign countries.[135]

The news shocked students over the summer who largely had been ignorant about the school's state of affairs. With the stoppage of the 1929–30 school year, the alumnae convened to initiate the reopening of the school, a similar practice that would save Wilson College some years later. Meetings were held in the fall by the various alumnae groups of the school in order to secure funds to reopen the school. The quoted cost to rejuvenate the school was $80,000, with an $800 option price to

---

135. News Clippings from Mary Shope's '26, Stunt Book (1922–1929).

be paid at the outset. The $80,000 would pay for the property cost of the school and help to update the library and fix up the buildings (especially the heating system) to put the college back in working order.[136] The Pittsburgh Irving College Club (PICC) decided on using their general treasury fund for the school's reopening to help the former students purchase the school and establish a board of trustees with members from each alumnae club. Suggesting involvement from the Chamber of Commerce, three men spoke on behalf of Mechanicsburg, for establishing an endowment fund and a board of trustees, incorporating some town members. The PICC initiated a fundraising drive selling *The Mirror* magazine at $1.50 per sale with 50% of the magazine cost acting as profit for the school, but within a month this sale was discontinued. The Central Pennsylvania Irving College Club gave three benefits, one in Mechanicsburg, one in Harrisburg, and a card party in nearby Camp Hill, to raise money. By late November 1929, the alumnae had secured the $800 option price, obtaining $240 from the Alumnae Association treasury, $140 from the PICC, $140 from the Philadelphia Irving College Club, $140 from the Central Pennsylvania Club, and another $140 from the Altoona Irving College Club, which borrowed their money from their scholarship fund. Letters went out to all alumnae to give $150 a piece to reopen their Alma Mater, but with the onset of the Depression, this goal was unreasonable. Even if 400 of the 687 alumnae could offer $100, totaling $40,000, the local bank (probably the First Bank and Trust) would have lent $20,000 to help the open the school. But even this was unreasonable for most people. Before long, community groups began to pledge their support of Irving, with the Mechanicsburg Lions' Club, the Mechanicsburg Chamber of Commerce, and the Ministerial Association (representing Mechanicsburg churches) sending representatives to Alumnae meetings to "support any movement toward opening the college."[137] The State Department of Education declared that it was behind the resurrection one-hundred percent, and notified the alumnae that if the college reopened and maintained a class A college ranking

---

136. Apparently, the heating system was really in disrepair, as certain rooms could not even be heated in the winter.

137. Irving College Alumnae Association Minutes, special meeting, November 23, 1929.

(interestingly, a classification it never achieved before) the charter would be valid. A valid charter would excuse the graduates from having to raise the $500,000 endowment that was required of all colleges chartered after 1895. It was decided by the alums that $5,000 would be spent for a professional, country-wide fund-raising campaign, lasting six weeks to raise about $150,000. It was suggested by a Mr. Hockenberry, who was to front the campaign, that the majority of the money should come from Mechanicsburg through alumnae and local businessmen. Before long, a larger campaign organizer, the Ketcham Company from Philadelphia and Pittsburgh was consulted, who suggested a $25,000 contribution from the town and most of the money from the alumnae themselves. With a $7,000 fee to provide their services for a 6–8-week campaign, which rose to $8,000 by the next alumnae meeting, a Mr. Hall, who had worked with Beckley College, informed the alums that he could raise the $8,000 cost for alumnae to get started. Hall, who had an interest in music and in reestablishing Irving's widely respected music conservatory, wanted to have some official authority along with the president and trustees of the college, should he raise the money. He predicted that if Irving achieved $100,000 in five months, the school could reopen in September. Signing a contract with Ketcham to begin the colossal campaign should $8,000 be raised to pay them by March 3, the alumnae appeared satisfied that an ardent effort for Irving was underway. An emergency meeting of the Alumnae Association would be called when Hall raised his promised $8,000. However, the Chamber of Commerce stated that it could not underwrite the campaign, and no emergency meeting was ever called. As 1930 dragged on, no meetings of the Alumnae Association ever commenced, and it appears as though the consequences of the Great Depression had taken effect. No money existed for a reopening.

Some questions arise as to exactly why the college closed. According to Carol June Bradley, who delivered a paper on the college's history in 1952, the college closed due to a lack of an endowment, which in its 73-year history, the school never raised. Lenore Embick Flower 04, claims that the onset of the Depression shortly after its closing prevented any reopening after the state no longer accredited the school's graduates for public school instruction. Other sources point to competition from other schools in the area, the declining enrollment, and the general fix-up that Irving desperately needed. The answer is a combination of all these points, and no one factor caused the school to close. First of all, the state would not recognize Irving's graduates due to its inadequate library and lack of an endowment, therefore expansion was needed, expansion which could not occur after the Depression hit. Even though the alumnae donated a number of books in 1929, a major addition to the library holdings and probably a separate library building was needed. According to Jane Campbell Beard '29, her mother and the other Campbell children regretfully made the decision to close Irving since it needed financial support, and the available money was tied up in E. E.'s estate. The First Bank and Trust, who was also part executor of his estate, felt that the college couldn't continue and suggested to the Campbells to close out the estate and the school. How much competition hurt Irving's situation is not evident by the full load of students that attended Irving in the last few years of its existence. Since the board instituted a cap of 125 students after E. E.'s death, dropping the enrollment from its highest at 139 in 1926, the graduating classes were 22, 20, and 20 in the three commencements after E. E.'s passing, certainly not a downward spiral [see Table 1.2]. However, Campbell and The Board of Trustees maintained Irving as a small school after its rapid growth at the turn of the century, while other local schools like Wilson College in Chambersburg grew to have enrollments two and three times that of Irving.[138]

Living Irving graduates who were interviewed in the 1990s, have varied views on why the school closed, though many reveal that the reasons were not disclosed while they were students or alumnae. Marjorie Wise Mohler '27, claimed that the school closed because the remaining people in charge of the institution could not administer the school without Dr. Campbell. Pauline Hege '25, claimed that a lack of management and lack of funds closed the school, while Ruth Hoy Diffenderfer '26 said the school was lacking in students, losing them to local schools like Wilson College and Albright College. Mary Baylor Havely '29, believed that the Campbell heirs knew that Irving could not continue, even though

---

138. In 1927, Wilson College graduated 75 women (72 BA, 3 BS), Hood College in Frederick, Maryland graduated 90 women (60 BA, 26 BS in Home Economics), while Irving graduated 24 (3 AB, 5 Home Econ certificates, 8 Secretarial certif., 1 voice student, 5 piano students, and 2 dramatic art students).

the students thought it would go on forever. Her opinion of the closing stated that the school emptied its pockets from paying the high-priced faculty. Though the school needed money in 1929, it was most likely not caused by the faculty salaries.

How much blame can be put on the Campbell heirs is questionable, though they were certainly the easiest scapegoats for the blame. Lilly Grace Campbell was vice president of the school essentially since her marriage to E. E., and Paul Campbell worked in the college office in its later years handling the finances, grade reports, and student transcripts, so the Campbell family certainly knew *how* to run the school. With E. E. dying in 1926 and the school closing just three years later, it is obvious that he had a tremendous impact on the college not shown in presidential reports or financial statements. He had a well-liked personality and had close ties with the community, alumnae, and his students. The finer points of running Irving may not have been passed on to the heirs simply because they were part of the finer points of E. E. himself.

The Board of Trustees was reporting that alumnae had failed in reopening the school as early as 1929, but the Campbells remained hopeful that someone would buy the school property. Lilly Grace wrote the board consistently with little hope: "I regret to say that I have not heard of anyone interested in any plans to finance a reorganization of Irving, so I have no good news to present to the Board of Trustees."[139] Newspapers reported that several area schools tried to consolidate with Irving in order to gain the strong charter, but any offers that were made were not consummated. In 1936, though the Campbells sold Argyle to be used as Seidle Memorial Hospital, the rest of the college remained vacant. For Irving, things seemed to go from bad to worse: Rev. Trowbridge died in 1937, Rev. Ferguson died in 1938, and Columbian Hall suffered a horrible fire on May 6, 1938. Local police perceived the $30,000–40,000 damage to be linked with an arsonist that had struck local areas before, as the building was literally destroyed.[140] One last lead for Irving's resurrec-

---

139. Campbell, Lilly Grace '95, letter to the Irving College Board of Trustees, read at the meeting of the board, June 11, 1937.

140. Because of the extensive damage due to the fire, the roof and entire third floor was removed, leaving only the first two floors and flat roof that is present today.

tion appeared in February of 1940, when a letter arrived for Paul Campbell from Bernard E. Stansfield, an insurance agent in Mechanicsburg:

> I have had correspondence with A. Emerson Howell, Attorney at Law, Honesdale, Pa., with regard to purchase of Irving College, and I am enclosing the last letter from him in which he asks a question concerning the library which I can not [sic] answer. . . . He does not say who his client is naturally, and I am wondering if you know any folks in or about Honesdale, Pa., who might be interested in Irving? We certainly should follow every lead to the best of our ability and will do so.[141]

The client is never revealed, and the sale, once again, is never consummated. By June 1940, Lilly Grace suggested to the board that it may be best to consider no more future for Irving. With the effects of the Depression still affecting the greater populace in 1940, the board agreed with Mrs. Campbell and made motions to remove the sign from over the gate and discontinue the annual board meetings until further notice. A huge rummage sale was held in 1941 to sell off the many contents of the college buildings that had not been moved since Irving was vacated 12 years earlier. Coffee pots, kitchen utensils, beds, and college china were all sold off to the highest bidder at a two-day auction. An estimated 500 people attended, purchasing desks, chairs, and Irving memorabilia. The academic gown of Dr. Campbell, "went [with] the colored hood, emblematic of Dr. Campbell's degree," for just 65 cents.[142] With the furnishings gone, with the board of trustees gone, the exoskeleton of the school was sold to a management company which converted both Columbian and Irving Halls into apartments, the same usage they receive today. By World War II, the campus and any ideas of higher education in Mechanicsburg were absent, but in 1957 the state provided a Pennsylvania historical marker along Main Street in front of the former entrance to the school commemorating Irving, the state's first college to grant degrees of the arts and sciences to women.

---

141. Stansfield, Bernard. Letter to Paul Campbell, February 17, 1940.
142. "Campus filled as Furnishings are Placed in Auction," *The Daily News*, September 18, 1941.

Solomon P. Gorgas, the founder of Irving College.

Washington Irving, noted American author for whom Irving College was named, in his study.

Pennsylvania historical marker at the entrance to the former Irving College on East Main Street, Mechanicsburg, Pennsylvania.

Rev. Thompson Prettyman Ege, D.D., Irving College President and author of the Ege family history and other works.

Irving's Administration, 1855-1957

A post cover from the time of President T.P. Ege, showing an engraving of Irving College as it looked post Civil War.

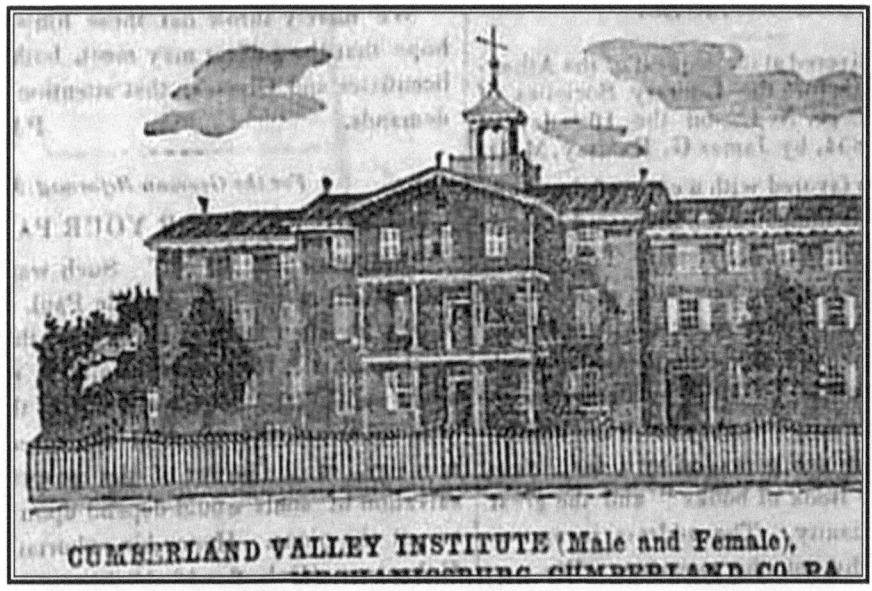

The Cumberland Valley Institute in Mechanicsburg, Pennsylvania. Rev. T.P. Ege first taught at this institute and later became President of Irving College.

A run on a bank during the financial panic of 1873, from *Frank Leslie's Illustrated*. The financial hardships during the late 19th Century led to the closure of Irving College in 1883.

Mary Kessler, 'Principal' of Irving College from 1888 to 1891.

Dr. E.E. Campbell, fourth President of Irving College, ca. 1890 when he came to Irving as a geology professor.

Irving's Administration, 1855-1957

View of Columbian Hall from the west with Irving Hall just behind, ca. 1900–1920.

View of the front entrance of Columbian Hall (complete with ivy supposedly from Washington Irving's Sunnyside) from the south side.

The college president's residence, Sunnyside, named after the home of Washington Irving. This home was located north of the college, across the railroad tracks, near the current Simpson Library.

View of Irving College in the early 20th Century. Irving Hall on the left, Columbian Hall on the right.

Argyle, the president's residence at Irving College located on Simpson Street. It was purchased by Seidle Memorial Hospital after the college closed and the building was torn down in 1991.

The Campbell family during the summer of 1901: L-R Annie, Josephine, Lilly Grace, William, Clara, E.E., Paul, Emma.

Dr. William Gies, former Irving College trustee who went on to become the 'Father of Modern American Dental Education.'

Dr. Matthew Reaser, former President of Wilson College and Beaver College and Irving President from 1916–1917.

Rev. Charles W. Trowbridge with the class of 1927.

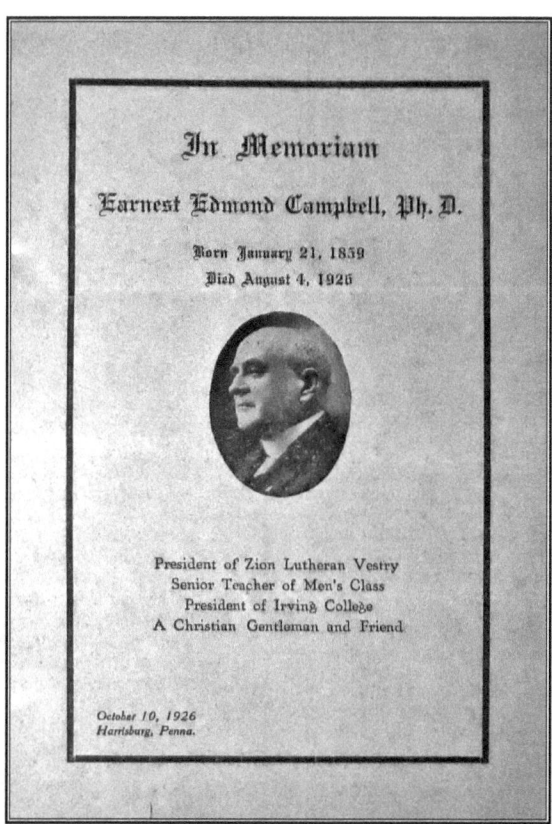

Memorial program for Dr. E.E. Campbell in 1926. His death was a huge blow to Irving College.

The campus of Beechwood College, which merged with Beaver College and is today Arcadia University. Dr. Matthew Reaser unsuccessfully attempted to merge Irving with Beechwood in 1917.

IRVING COLLEGE CLOSES; PROPERTY PLACED ON SALE

Widow of Late President to Discontinue School Almost 75 Years Old

Irving College, Mechanicsburg, almost 75 years old, will not reopen its doors next month and the property may be offered for sale.

Final decision to discontinue the school was announced to-day by Mrs. E. E. Campbell, widow of the late president, Dr. E. E. Campbell, and the First Bank and Trust Company, Mechanicsburg, executors of his estate.

Teachers of the last year were advised about a month ago that discontinuance of the school was contemplated in order to give them an opportunity to locate elsewhere.

Founded in 1856

Irving College, which was founded by Solomon Gorgas in 1856, has always been a privately owned institution and has been carried on continuously since its opening with the exception of five or six years early in its history. At the time of its incorporation it was given the right to grant degrees.

The first president was the Rev. Dr. A. G. Maillet, a Methodist minister. He was followed by the Rev. T. P. Ege. In 1891 Dr. E. E. Campbell purchased the college and carried it on till the time of his death in 1926. Dr. Campbell served a term in the State Legislature as the representative from Cumberland county.

Dr. Ferguson Acting President

During the years, 1926-1927, and 1927-1928, the the Rev. Dr. Thomas J. Ferguson was the acting president. Dr. Ferguson retired over a year ago after serving for fifty years as pastor of the historic Silver Spring Presbyterian Church.

About a year ago, when the Lutheran Church was looking for a site for a church college for women, the purchase of Irving College was considered but was given up for the new college to be erected in Washington.

During the past few months an effort has been made to get the

IRVING COLLEGE TO CLOSE DOORS

(Continued)

alumnae of the college to take over the institution.

Issues Statement

Mrs. Campbell, the widow of the former president, Dr. E. E. Campbell, issued a formal statement in which she said: "To settle an estate which has remained opened for three years, Irving College will not open for the reception of students during the 1929-1930 term."

Declining comment on reports that enrollment figures had prompted the closing, Mrs. Campbell said the future of the college depends upon action of the alumnae. Graduates of the college, she indicated, had been a party to the decision to close the school.

"Irving," the statement said, "has been one of the oldest colleges for women in the land. It was chartered by a special act of the Legislature in 1857 to confer all degrees. It is one of the two colleges in America which has had full State recognition without passing an endowment."

She said the policies of the former head, Dr. Campbell had been maintained and improved by his successors, including Dr. P. J. Ferguson, present acting president.

News clipping article on the closing of Irving College in 1929.

News clipping article detailing the fire at Columbian Hall on the former Irving College campus in 1938. The fire damage resulted in the removal of the entire top floor.

A modern view of Irving Hall, which was purchased and converted into apartments after the closure of the college.

CHAPTER TWO

STUDENT LIFE, 1856–1929

The atmosphere in the College has been elevating, wholesome, Christian. There is a home-atmosphere in the College that we believe is peculiar to "IRVING". The greatest and most lasting and far-reaching good done in the College is not that of the class room. I verily believe—indeed I know—that the greatest good the students here receive is the womanly development of Christian Character. Those of us who jealously regard this opening and developing of lovely Christian character get our truest compensation just here.
—E. E. Campbell on Irving, 1922[1]

THE EARLY YEARS, REV. MARLATT'S TENURE

In the nine years that he presided over Irving College, A. G. Marlatt tried to create a pleasant, healthy, and educational atmosphere for students to live, learn and grow while spending their four years at Irving. Student rooms had registers for heat and ventilation and large windows on each floor that provided views of the outside world as well as fresh air and a cooling breeze in warmer weather. The college emphasized

---

1. Campbell, E. E. Presidential Report to the Irving College Board of Trustees, within the Board of Trustees' minutes, May 29, 1922.

adequate, spacious rooms where "only two students occupy the same room."² Bathrooms were not personal to each room, but numbered at least one per floor, and the shower and "plunge" baths contained hot and cold water. Students enjoyed modern conveniences for healthful living even if those conveniences existed on a small scale in town. Running water was surprisingly convenient for Irving students as the borough laid pipe down East Main Street where the campus stood in April 1857, while many other parts of the borough probably still imported their water. Irving required the boarding students to furnish their own towels, a pair of sheets, pillow slips, and "if convenient," a silver fork, napkin ring, and teaspoon.³ By 1875, the college catalogues even suggested for students to bring an umbrella, overshoes, a waterproof cloak, and a balmoral skirt.⁴

Settled in their comfortable school-year home, the students (and townspeople) looked forward to the highlight of the year, the Commencement exercises, which Irving held the last week of June. The week consisted of the Baccalaureate service on Sunday morning, the anniversary address before the Irvington Society (the student literary organization) on Tuesday evening, and Commencement held on Wednesday evening. The college held every event at the Methodist Episcopal Church at Main and Market Streets, due to the lack of any adequately large campus space. The first commencement in 1858 was well documented and the ceremony included all student speakers aside from the prayer, benediction, and conferring of degrees. The salutatory address by Marietta Barbour Mullin '58, opened the proceedings, welcomed the parents and guests, and thanked the board and faculty, while the valedictory address by Margaret Rebecca Goslin '58, closed the student speakers with additional thanks, farewells, and encouragements. Several of the student essays at the first commencement dealt with the idea of women, education, and their place in society. Mary Elizabeth Miley '58, talked about the benefits of educating women and how the cultivation of their curiosity about life

---

2. Irving College Catalogue, 1857–58, 11.

3. Irving College Catalogue, 1867–68, 13.

4. A balmoral skirt is a white skirt which was unsuitable for most of the school year and therefore appears to be used as rainwear for the students.

was as important as a man's. Mary Olivia Buttorf, '58 explained how women had a place among the "Earth's Benefactors," and great people:

> We know that history is fond of recording the deeds of the sterner sex, and that although woman's whole life has been one of self-denial, and of earnest endeavor to accomplish that which directly tends to elevate, and ameliorate the condition of humanity, yet when works of usefulness are spoken of, too often her name is not heard."[5]

Though Buttorf's words were strong, they probably did not resonate off her fellow graduates as much as feminists of the time would have liked, since many of the ten speakers chose to speak on less gender-related subjects like "Idol Worship," "The Inner Life," and "The Language of Music." In points that will be further explored later, the women who chose to attend Irving leaned more toward a conservative view on life and would have agreed only in part with Buttorf's words. The prominent speakers touched upon the women's education issue at the inaugural commencement, as Rev. Herman M. Johnson, D.D. of Dickinson College in Carlisle, gave the Baccalaureate sermon on "The True position of Woman is the Problem of the Present Age," stressing the importance of women's education to alleviate this dilemma. The anniversary address to the Irvington Society, "Woman's Mission," presented by Rev. Dr. D. W. Bartine of the Philadelphia Methodist Conference, also concentrated on women's education.

In addition to the speakers, music was provided by the Keystone Cornet Band (the local town band), a vocal piece sung by student Fannie Laetita Porter '58, and awards of honors were administered to the students. A Classical Honor was given for excellence in the ancient languages and literature, and Mathematical, Musical, and Deportment Honors were given for excellence in those areas.

Commencement weeks during Marlatt's tenure resembled each previous assembly, as the seniors wrote and recited 10–12 essays and performed interspersed musical numbers. Over the years, the essays shifted

---

5. *Irvington Annual*, Vol. I No. I, 1858, 10.

from the importance of women's education to more subjects of student interest, resembling the true backgrounds and feelings of the graduates. Interestingly enough, at the Baccalaureate service in 1859, Rev. Conway P. Wing, D.D., a prominent speaker and author in his own right, gave a sermon that included what was to become the college motto for Irving.[6] Speaking from Psalm 144, verse 12, Wing recited: "That our daughters may be as cornerstones polished after the similitude of a palace."

One of the earliest student organizations established at Irving was the Irvington Society, a literary group that met every Friday evening to improve composition, elocution, and criticism. The group would frequently sponsor lectures and set aside the Tuesday before Commencement for their annual address delivered by some prominent local speaker. During T. P. Ege's tenure, a $1 entrance fee was added to belong to the society, which also included monthly 10¢ dues allowing for society privileges and its library. All of the fees and dues benefited the society library and reading room, which the society supplied with the best quarterly and monthly magazines and daily and weekly newspapers for use in discussion. This student organization would eventually evolve into the Ivy Leaf and Olive Branch Societies in 1869.

Other than the literary society, there were few organized events to distract the students from their studies. The graduating class of Irving published *The Irvington Annual,* whose object was to "stimulate the students to excel in literary composition, and at the same time to furnish them with pleasing *souvenirs* of their college days."[7] The *Annual* essentially resembled a synopsis of the Commencement exercises of that year, containing all the student essays and addresses held that June. Reported to be published every July first, the *Annual* may have seen its last printing during its second year as the upcoming Civil War put a halt on two graduation ceremonies, enough to possibly reduce interest in the publication.

Along with the annual publication, the college frequently sponsored music and literary soirees, which received large attendance from people in the community. The *Weekly Gazette* reiterated how the audiences received the productions:

---

6. Wing would go on to publish *History of Cumberland County* in 1879.
7. *Irvington Annual,* Vol. I No. 1, 1858, 44.

> highly entertaining and amusing, and the young ladies acqunted
> [*sic*] themselves in a very creditable manner, reflecting great
> credit, alike on themselves and the Institution . . . These soirees
> are a commendable feature, and tend greatly to the improvement
> of pupils by imparting and cultivating that affability so essential
> in the education of youth.[8]

The performances of colloquies, essays, and music educated the students to "improve the young ladies in composition, elocution and music, and to enable them to acquire that ease of manners and polished address, which so eminently marks the accomplished lady."[9] The performances were part musical numbers and part essays, which incorporated traditional music and literature with original works by the students. Soirees often contained several dramatic performances from one-act scenes to a medley of dramatic parts from larger works. A standing-room only crowd at an Irving soiree held on Friday night, March 13, 1863, witnessed what must have been a sight to see with the play "Uncle Sam and his family" performed by the entire student body. One student portrayed Uncle Sam and:

> the balance of the class, [portrayed] the loyal and seceding States,
> and several other characters. After the young ladies representing
> the seceding States, had made their complaints, and expressed
> their intention of withdrawing from the family circle, several
> others representing different nationalities, made their appearance,
> expressing their willingness to assist their adopted parent, . . .
> who were followed by all the loyal States, in rapid succession,
> all announcing their intention to assist in preserving order in
> the family circle; and before whose indignant glances and just
> denunciations, the refractory spirits appeared to quail, even as
> their prototypes will yet do, and that ere long.[10]

---

8. *Weekly Gazette,* Vol. II No. 21, April 9, 1857, 3.
9. *Weekly Gazette,* Vol. II, No. 4, February 26, 1857, 3.
10. *Cumberland Valley Journal,* Vol. VIII No. 9, March 19, 1863, 3.

The piece was a phenomenal hit "and [was] received with marked applause."[11] Other original dramatic performances included "The Seasons," where each of four students represented the four changes in the year, "extolling the beauties and advantages she possessed," and the "Restored Captive," a drama about a Native American chief.[12] Some of these early soirees included original student pieces, though many of them came from classical composers, and may also have included the song "Silver Spring." With words written by J. Dewitt Hyers, and music by F. W. Haas, the song "Silver Spring" was dedicated to the teachers and students of Irving College in 1860. Though the sheet music's lyrics talk exclusively about the Silver Spring of the Cumberland Valley and never even mentions the school, the sheet music does feature Irving Hall on its title sheet and the writers apparently did dedicate the song, despite the lack of newspaper accounts.

With soirees only held semi-monthly for students, the college also brought in outside lecturers and provided other entertainment. The Irvington Literary Society usually invited missionaries and literary scholars to speak, but the school also planned outdoor events journeying on trips to the woods, or the country, having dinner waiting for them upon their return.

For many trips, the school had the benefit of easy access to the Cumberland Valley Railroad, whose "facilities of coming to and going from the institution [were]ample and speedy."[13] The rail which connected Harrisburg with Carlisle, Mechanicsburg, and Chambersburg with Martinsburg, West Virginia, had conductors that provided the young ladies with polite service stopping along Trindle Road right by the campus. This railroad provided an expedient source of transportation for the Harrisburg and Carlisle day students, or even Mechanicsburg residents, who could take a quick trip to the other end of town. This convenient rail service allowed for day trips into the city of Harrisburg for shopping and

---

11. *Cumberland Valley Journal*, Vol. VIII No. 9, March 19, 1863, 3.
12. *Cumberland Valley Journal*, Vol. VIII No. 9, March 19, 1863, 3.
13. *Weekly Gazette*, Vol. III No. 8, January 14, 1858, 3.

entertainment, which failed to occur as often as the students would have liked and *never* without a chaperone.

The train did provide an interesting meeting with General Robert Anderson, the defender of Fort Sumter, in December of 1861, just eight months after the firing of the Confederate forces upon the fort. Anderson, who was returning from Carlisle to Harrisburg via the Cumberland Valley Railroad, traveled on the train with several Irving students, who planned to disembark at the campus. As the train stopped,

> a crowd pressed around the platform, eager to grasp the hand of the brave soldier, identified with the early history of the rebellion, all of whom were gratified. About a dozen of the students of Irving . . . were taken into the car in which the General was, the conductor kindly consenting . . . The young ladies who were introduced to him appeared highly delighted and honored by the introduction, and he appeared no less delighted than they at meeting so many handsome ladies. On the arrival of the train at the College, all the students and the President and his lady were standing on the green, and when it stopped, Prof. R. D. Chambers, who was on board, introduced President Marlatt to the General. The train moved off amid the waving of handkerchiefs, the General standing on the platform until they were out of sight.[14]

Anderson's passing through Mechanicsburg gave the students the first sight of the American conflict in their backyard. While the Confederate States fielded the main stage for the war, the Cumberland Valley remained rather quiet other than the occasional flag-raisings and parades of local boys leaving town: "I Remember the gallant Mechanicsburg boys, gathered on the campus to give us a last serenade before marching on, as they and we thought, to speedy victory."[15] Early on in the war, Irving went on with plans as scheduled much to the surprise of the local news: "Although many of the female academies in Pennsylvania have been

---

14. *Cumberland Valley Journal*, Vol. VI No. 50, December 5, 1861, 3.
15. Kennedy, Mary E. "Reminiscences of '61," *Irving Sketch Book*, Vol. I No. 4, May 1895, 42.

obliged to close in consequence of the present agitation, which affects educational as well as business enterprises, we are happy to know that this Institution has so far weathered the storm, and will this year graduate a very promising class of young ladies."[16] Even though Irving went on as usual, apparently in 1861, the school did not have an official Commencement: "our President told us he thought it best [that] we should quietly assemble in the parlor, there to receive our longed-for diplomas. Alas for the girl who was looking forward to her public appearance before a crowd of admiring and appreciative friends!"[17] Irving did not close up shop, but some events changed because of the war.

Though the students did not witness the Civil War directly in these early years, having students from the South at the college must have created some tension. Before the Civil War (as opposed to the later years of the nineteenth century), more young ladies from the South came to Irving for schooling. But as Mary E. Kennedy '61 remembers: "Girls who had always been harmonious, now began to take sides; presently we would come across a Maryland girl in the corridor, gaily singing 'Maryland, my Maryland.'"[18] The valley continued its quiet observance of the War Between the States until the Summer of 1863, when General Jenkins crew of Confederate rebels marched up the Cumberland Valley, burning Chambersburg, threatening Carlisle, and entering Mechanicsburg on June 28. Though the June 1863 Commencement was still on schedule, while the seniors dressed in their graduation gowns, President Marlatt canceled the ceremony, came to each prospective graduate individually, gave each her diploma, and told them all to leave for home immediately; the Confederates were in Chambersburg.[19] Though Mechanicsburg became the northernmost advance for the rebel army, the Confederates passed through the town peacefully since the townspeople cooperated with their demands for food and shelter. The rebels would leave the town and the area shortly after the occupation and engage at the Battle of Gettysburg that July. Commencement exercises returned with unequaled attendance in 1864, "Perhaps owing to the fact that our

---

16. *Carlisle Herald*, Vol. LXI No. 30, June 21, 1861, 2.
17. Kennedy, Mary E. "Reminiscences of '61," *Irving Sketch Book*, Vol. I No. 4, May 1895, 42.
18. Kennedy, Mary E. "Reminiscences of '61," *Irving Sketch Book*, Vol. I No. 4, May 1895, 42.
19. Oral History with Phoebe Ringwalt, '64, as appearing in: Flower, Lenore Embick. *Irving College*, Mechanicsburg: Irving Alumnae Club, 1966, 10.

citizens were deprived of this delightful annual treat last year by the rebel invasion, and that they have such a warm feeling for the institution and all connected with it, they viewed the exercises from a slightly prejudiced stand-point."[20] Though the Confederates never threatened Pennsylvania again, some parents probably second guessed sending their daughters away to college while the war still raged. Mrs. S. W. Regester: "was an Irving girl in '61 and '62, although the civil war [sic] kept me from being a graduate. My parents did not like the idea of my being so far from Baltimore when the bridges between there and Irving were being burned, and so they would not let me return."[21]

Despite the local scare that the Civil War must have caused, President Marlatt maintained a stringent student life. His personality enabled a very close and friendly relationship with the townspeople. Though the school curriculum offered little time for anything but class work, as one student reiterated about Jennie L. Anderson, '60:

> she practiced the piano in the parlor, and at 6 o' clock in the morning. She had to guess at the time frequently. One time she went to practice in the parlor directly under President Marlatt's room, and soon he came to the door and said, 'Jennie, is that you? Do you know what time it is?' She said no. He said it is just one o'clock.[22]

With little time during the day due to busy class schedules and music practice, students found whatever means were necessary to finish their work or practice their pieces.

Though students felt "trapped" in their rooms studying, the local Keystone Concert Band often stopped by to serenade the young girls: "The ladies of Irving Female College had the pleasure of a rich treat on Saturday evening last, in the shape [of] a delightful serenade from the Keystone Concert Band."[23] This situation occurred more than once: "The young ladies of Irving Female College were favored with a very delightful

---

20. *Cumberland Valley Journal*, Vol. IX No. 19, June 29, 1864, 3.
21. "From the Girls," *Irving Sketch Book*, Vol. II Nos. 6–7, April\May 1896, 169–170.
22. *The Sketch Book*, Vol. VI No. 9, October 1904, 12.
23. *Weekly Gazette*, Vol. II No. 16, March 5, 1857, 3.

serenade from the Keystone Concert Band, on Saturday night last, and on Monday night a number of families and fair ones in town enjoyed a similar treat."[24] Robert Brunhouse in his book *Miniatures of Mechanicsburg* also noted this rendezvous:

> After traversing the principal streets the [Fire] Company [and the Keystone Cornet Band] proceeded to Irving Female College, where they were received with waving handkerchiefs and a perfect shower of magnificent wreaths, constructed by the ladies of that institution in honor of the occasion. Before leaving the College grounds the Band performed several very beautiful airs which was followed by "Three Cheers, for Irving Female College" which was responded to with a hearty good will by all present, making the welkin [*sic*] fairly ring, with their joyous shouts, after which the Company marched up to the Church where the lectures were held, and proceeded to decorate it with the numerous wreaths and garlands which they had received, giving to the place such an appearance of joy and gaiety as was quite foreign to its natural somber and gloomy look.[25]

Regardless of the workload, either Marlatt or the borough residents ensured that entertainment for the young students was also part of the curriculum.

SIMILAR PATHS, EGE'S TENURE, 1865–1883

> Last night after having retired, we suddenly heard the sweet strains of music. Of course all ran to the windows to listen to it, and perceived it to be the 'Mechanicsburg Band,' who kindly serenaded us. May they soon visit us again.[26]

---

24. *Weekly Gazette,* Vol. II No. 19, March 26, 1857, 3.
25. *Weekly Gazette,* May 4, 1858, 3.
26. Irving College Monitress' Journal, November 19, 1872.

Like when the Keystone Concert Band played for the young women while Marlatt was president, the Mechanicsburg Band also serenaded the students, symbolizing the similarities of student life from Marlatt's term of office to Ege's. Though expanding services and technology provided telegraph, mail, and express and expanded rail facilities, the life on campus in 1877 resembled that of 1857. The descendants of the Irvington Literary Society—the Olive Branch and Ivy Leaf Societies—were in constant competition and served Irving as the only student organizations the young women could join. The two competing organizations constantly fueled a mutual but pleasant rivalry in order to incite excellence in "composition, elocution, and literary criticism."[27] Each would have its own separate sponsored program during Commencement week, and throughout the year would hold literary entertainment every other month.

No other new organizations developed after the arrival of Ege, and with the discontinuation of the *Irvington Annual* after a few years, soirees were probably the only events that kept the students socially sane. Ege helped continue the popular soirees, arranging about one per month. One soiree staged on December 20, 1866, was the first event in Mechanicsburg's newly built town facility, Franklin Hall. Though the music and literary event owned the prestige of breaking in the new town hall, Franklin stood unfinished: no plaster on the walls and no glass in the windowpanes, which the borough boarded up for the occasion. Only a three-legged stove placed on the stage heated the patrons of the soiree, and though the temperature outside reached about zero degrees Fahrenheit, many townspeople arrived to show their support. Irving entertained another soiree with The Cumberland Valley Institute in 1872, which may have been established through Ege's ties with the young boys' school in Mechanicsburg. Many times throughout Ege's tenure, events were planned with the C. V. I.; the Institute's boys would come to Irving for dances, or as in 1872, the Irving girls came to the Institute for an oyster supper.

Irving students warmly greeted this greater contact with boys and the occasional soirees, but the small amount of available free time did not mean that the young women did not get into trouble. The president and his faculty, though they resided in one building, could not

---

27. Irving College Catalogue, 1869–70, 13.

be everywhere at once. Therefore, Ege first instituted the novel idea of student monitors. Though resembling "narks" more than a student government, each student took her turn at monitoring the other students to make sure they attended chapel, were in bed at "light's out," and showed their faces appropriately at any other scheduled times. The monitress, as this student monitor was called, reported the occurrences during her shift in a journal that each student used perpetually. Surprisingly, the entries did not expose deviant girls, but instead talked of the events of the day: the weather, upcoming vacations, and arrival of new students. Later Irving heads adopted these beginning ideas of student government and expanded them to allow the students more voice and control.

Ege installed a system of merits (instead of demerits) to help maintain obedient and respectful young women at Irving. Each student began the year with fifty good conduct marks; for every week that the student did not receive detention or lose a good conduct mark, a mark was added to the fifty. Had any apple-polishers attended Irving, under Ege's system the student could have received eighty-four marks, though any act of negligence or disobedience subtracted marks from the total. Any detention that a student received, subtracted two conduct marks. From the monitresses' journal entries that exist, students tended to be quite obedient and respected the strict rules put in place, as few suspended merits were recorded.

Though students looked forward to the upcoming breaks, not all of the boarding students went home. When Christmas, Thanksgiving, and Easter neared, many of the students from faraway states stayed at Irving, attending church services with the faculty who remained. It was not unusual to have new students come to Irving around Christmas or Easter, and according to the monitresses' journal of 1872, new students were coming in throughout the year. Students left mid-term for various reasons during Ege's administration, probably due to the cost of school and the economic depressions that afflicted the country in the late 19th century. This mid-term departure became such a problem that Ege instituted a one-year term for students instead of two equal length terms. With the number of students leaving and arriving at Irving, it could have been somewhat disorienting and distracting for the small student body and the faculty.

One stabilizing force that did come out of the Ege era was the Alumnae Association. Suggested by board member Levi Kauffman at the trustee meeting in 1878 in order to boost alumnae interest in the college, twenty graduates met the following year to organize the association. That first association of 1879 represented 11 classes, all but one which had graduated under Ege, and planned to hold an annual meeting during each Commencement week; it was a tradition which lasted longer than the institution.[28] Upon paying dues all graduates were members, and the organization established its purpose "to preserve unbroken, or reunite, the ties of college life, and to perpetuate our interest in our Alma Mater."[29]

KESSLER, EEC, AND IRVING'S REBIRTH AND GROWTH, 1888–1929

> That the Faculty are all ears, the Seniors all nerve, the Juniors all mouth, the Sophomores all nose (knows) and we fear that the Freshmen will become all eyes, gazing at these freaks of nature.
> —Facts learned by the Freshmen class of 1904[30]

When Kessler and Campbell arrived at the end of the nineteenth century, many new student activities and programs emerged, resembling the number of societies and extracurricular activities of present-day colleges. Of the student organizations that existed at Irving, nearly all of them formed after Irving's reopening in 1888. Many of them had individual society mottoes, colors, flowers, and yells, and many also elected officers and collected dues.

---

28. The initial association had representatives from the classes of '60, '68, '70, '71, '72, '73, '74, '75, '77, '78, and '79. The first officers were: Mrs. Kate Zacharias, president; Miss E. Power, vice president; Miss B. Painter, secretary; and Miss Emma Stayman, assistant secretary. An alumnae association of some degree has lasted from this initial point into the 1990s; in August of 1996, about six former students gathered for their annual meeting.
29. Irving College Alumnae Association Minutes, Articles of Association.
30. *Irvingiana '02*, 46.

Maintaining the literary atmosphere that Marlatt instituted, the Gorgas Literary Society (named after the college founder), developed out of the early literary organizations. Providing readings of expression and extemporaneous debate, the society required the power of self-command in front of an audience and ran the annual celebration of Washington Irving's Birthday on April 3. Having 52 members in the 1902–1903 school year, the society eventually was absorbed by the Eta Nu Society, which formed in November of the following school year.

Originally organized by the class of 1904 as a "fraternity" with the seniors forming the charter members, Eta Nu was a sorority that involved its members in a variety of interests and discussions. Any student in the regular college course was eligible for membership, and their Saturday meetings (offered twice a month) covered topics in an open forum ranging from situations in foreign countries to the make-up of Congress. Eta Nu had a question box, from which important subjects of the day would be drawn for discussion from student suggestions. The organization held a mock presidential election in November 1904, initiated club pins in 1905, and "[t]hrough the kindness of Senator [Boies] Penrose," received daily copies of *The Congressional Record*.[31] With "the purpose of the Eta Nu Club . . . to develop in the members, and among the other students an intelligent patriotism and an interest in the questions of the day," the society numbered 19 in 1904, 11 in 1912, 29 in 1915, and 21 in 1917. Though instituting Greek letters upon its inception, Eta Nu resembled more of a literary society initially, though developing many characteristics of a sorority (such as pins) very quickly.

The first sorority at Irving was Phi Rho Mu, which began as a literary society in the 1893–1894 school year. With well-prepared debates that were "good and not too long," the society acted similarly to Eta Nu.[32] Any Irving student was eligible for membership, with the majority approval of the established members and a $1 initiation fee. Conversely, any member could be expelled by a 4/5 vote of the members "if she has proven grossly derelict to her duties."[33] The sorority had six officers,

---

31. *The Sketch Book*, Vol. VII No. 4, January 1905, 6.
32. "The Phi Rho Mu," *The Sketch Book*, Vol. I, No. 2, March 1895, 71–72.
33. Phi Rho Mu Constitution and By Laws, 1894.

including two chosen by the Sorority President: a critic and a chaplain, who respectively "criticized" the performances of the society and opened the exercises with prayer. During their six regular meetings, Phi Rho Mu divided into two groups and discussed and debated topics. Each question at hand was eventually decided by the Sorority President and two associate judges, while appointed Commissioners on Queries from each division submitted the three questions for debate. Absent members received a 5¢ fine for every missed meeting and needed to obtain permission from the critic to leave the meeting for the bathroom. Emphasizing an "acquaintance with parliamentary usage, readiness of expression in extemporaneous debate, and the power of self-command in the presence of an audience," Phi Rho Mu also held an annual celebration on April 3, probably in competition with Eta Nu.[34] "We are saving up our best for the annual celebration on the 3d *[sic]* of April, and will show an appreciative public what we can do with a question of international interest."[35]

With the appearance of Eta Nu and Phi Rho Mu, Irving's infiltration of sororities grew in number through the early 1900s, though only Eta Nu and Phi Rho Mu essentially maintained an educational purpose. Kappa Epsilon was a small sorority with six women which apparently only lasted for the initial year of 1903. All the students involved were officers of interesting titles (Superintendent of Motive Power, Assistant Superintendent of Motive Power, Clerk to Superintendent, Conductor, Motorman, Register), and the "aim" of the organization is simply stated as "to do the people."[36] Epsilon Epsilon Sigma was founded initially in October 1904 with six women who would spend the evening together and celebrate members' birthdays. Epsilon Delta, who held banquets during the term, Phi Delta Psi, and Theta Beta Gamma all appeared by 1909, though none of them appeared to have had specific purposes other than for socialization. Beta Beta was organized by 1903, Sigma Sigma Epsilon by 1907, and Sigma Gamma Kappa, whose motto was "Eat Drink and be Merry," originated by 1907.

---

34. "Irving College for Young Women," *The Sketch Book*, Vol. I, No. 4, May 1895, 159.
35. "The Phi Rho Mu," *The Sketch Book*, Vol. I, No. 2, March 1895, 71–72.
36. *Irvingiana '03*, 73.

Though little documentation remains of any kind of initiation process among Irving's sororities, it is evident that they occurred. Marion Strouse Scharf, who was a member of Eta Nu during her years at Irving as a high school-equivalent prep student (1914–1918), faced an initiation into the organization which normally only accepted college level Juniors. She remembered putting on bibs with several of her classmates and swallowing great amounts of an unknown, horribly tasting liquid.[37] Henrietta Thomas (1909–1911), had an initiation experience for her induction into Eta Nu, though not quite so harsh as Scharf's. Receiving a small envelope which contained an invitation for Thomas into the Eta Nu Club for the final initiation, it seems quite possible that the modern bidding and selection process for women in sororities occurred at Irving as early as 1909 (if not earlier). For her final initiation, Thomas had to spell, pronounce, and make a five-minute speech on the word "melanobricheous."[38]

Sororities, which grew in number at other colleges in the early 1900s, have been tolerated to the present day by administrations who faced constant pleading by students for more independence, more student rights, and more men on campus. Campbell, however, only allowed sororities when he thought they had educational benefit, as Eta Nu's and Phi Rho Mu's debates and discussions first did. The growing number of social sororities on campus, with initiation practices and exclusive memberships, was not tolerated by Campbell, and in 1910 he and the faculty put an end to them:

> For the past few years the Sorority feature of the school has become more and more manifest, and with it, clannishness and selfishness also. Not being willing to sacrifice the prevailing characteristic of "IRVING" in its student-body, i.e., cordial good

---

37. Since Marion attended Irving after the demise of the social sororities, it is interesting to note that she went through an initiation for entrance into Eta Nu. Eta Nu was allowed to continue probably because of its literary focus, but that does not mean that they stopped any initiation practices. It seems quite probable that most sororities had initiation ceremonies of some sort and possibly even hazing, though not documented.

38. Melanobricheous appears to be a medical term formed out of medical root stems as no medical dictionary lists the term. *Melano* refers to "black," *brich* a "rear-end," and *eous* "of or pertaining too." Eta Nu probably constructed the word out of its stem to add to the challenge for Thomas.

fellowship throughout the student-body, the faculty met the evening before the arrival of students in September, and after a full discussion passed a resolution forbidding the Sororities to initiate any new students. The President of the College called together, the first week of the session, the students in the college representing the Sororities, and explained the situation and read the resolution and asked them to receive it in the spirit in which it had been passed. There was a full and fair discussion of the situation pro and con, some tears shed and suggestions made, but a general acquiescence finally on their part. The spirit of the resolution has been faithfully and loyally respected, and no new students have been initiated into these sororities. With the graduating class of this session nearly all of the Sorority girls are connected. Thus this troublesome and perplexing problem has been solved without hurt and without any unkind feeling.[39]

Though sororities were defunct, Campbell had allowed so many other student groups that students had plenty of ways to involve themselves in campus activities. Eta Nu continued as the campus literary organization, probably because of its educational influence.

Along literary lines, the student publication called *The Sketch Book* began its monthly circulation in 1895 and lasted (though with intermittent interruptions) until 1929.[40] Named after one of Washington Irving's famous works, *The Sketch Book's* early issues acted as a means of communication for Irving students, informing parents and alumnae of the clubs, classes, and social life on campus. Though an informational source, before too long, students were encouraged to submit literary works to *The Sketch Book*, as an award of $1 was given to the writer of the best story submitted in January 1905. Published by the senior class of each school year, *The Sketch Book* staff usually consisted of 12 students who acted as editors or subject writers on athletics, music, elocution, art, and exchanges. The publication received exchanges with other college

---

39. Campbell, E. E. Presidential report to the board of trustees, Irving College Board of Trustees Minutes, May 31, 1910.

40. *The Sketch Book* in its original run lasts almost interrupted from 1895–1898, then starts from scratch in 1903, 1911, and 1926.

publications of the time, though mostly area colleges like *The College Mercury* from Gettysburg College, *The Mercersburg Monthly* from Mercersburg Academy, *The Susquehanna Journal* from Susquehanna University, and *Dickinson Union* from Dickinson College.[41] Though a fun outlet for student creativity, students still agonized about the production of the monthly, as seniors passed on advice to the upcoming juniors: don't make your first issue longer than 20 pages, don't publish more than five stories an issue, and don't get angry with the printer ("That's hunting trouble").[42] Two poems in the publication stated exactly how the editors and writers perceived the outcome:

> **A School Annual**
> This SKETCH BOOK is a great invention—
> The school gets all the fame,
> The printer gets all the money,
> And the staff gets all the blame.[43]
>
> **Result of Putting Out the Sketch Book**
> Sleepless nights, restless sleep, classes cut, exams flunked,
> Rotten grades, tempers lost, patience strengthened, awful weather, Sick photographer, impatient publishers, inquisitive students, doctor bills,
> Final Result—NEVER AGAIN![44]

The Sketch Book had to be done on the students' free time: "In short, don't worry about the 'Sketch Book.' It won't be half the cause of worry those 'awful' class essays and 'terrible' speeches will be."[45]

The content of the student publication remained mostly educational or social in nature, usually avoiding any controversial issues. "The

---

41. Some exchanges existed with high school publications like with Mercersburg Academy and *The Academian* of Harrisburg Academy while some existed with other female colleges like *The Newbury Collegian* from Newbury, SC (which at the time was considering going co-educational) and *Wellesley Magazine* from Wellesley College. Some of the exchanges were relatively far representing such states as Kansas, Massachusetts, Wisconsin, and Ohio.
42. *The Sketch Book*, Vol. VIII No. 6, March 1906, 8.
43. *The Sketch Book*, 1923, 90.
44. *The Sketch Book*, 1923, 90.
45. *The Sketch Book*, Vol. VIII No. 6, March 1906, 8.

Autobiography of a Secondhand School Book," "Africa in the 20th Century," "Hawthorne as a Romancer," and "A Trip to Mars" typify the kind of work students wrote for *The Sketch Book*. After the publication returned after a long absence in 1926, it became almost strictly literary, leaving behind its informational roots. To say that absolutely no controversial issues entered the conservative halls of *The Sketch Book* is untrue, especially with "Some Points of View on Women's Suffrage" written by Wellesley professor, Maude Thompson. But articles of that nature were rare and tended not to be written by the students.

Other student publications existed on campus; a yearbook was published sporadically (1901, 1902, 1903, and 1907). The *Irvingiana*, as it was called, involved student literary works, and essentially acted as *The Sketch Book* with pictures. Though containing faculty information and pictures of all the active groups on campus, the yearbooks were expensive to produce and with *The Sketch Book* published regularly, there may have been little interest in yearbooks after the first few appeared. Meant to be the junior class's contribution to the school, the last *Irvingiana* was in 1907; a lack of subscriptions from students and alumnae forced *Irvingiana '08* to go unprinted.[46]

The students did have their own newspaper, but it did not exist very long. On September 28, 1928, the first edition of *The Blue and Yellow Streak* (named after the school colors—a light blue and a bright yellow), appeared covering similar sorts of events to the previous *Sketch Books*. Publishing activities and social events every week, the newspaper appears to have died by Christmas 1928. One 10¢ issue shows the result of a mock presidential poll (though women could vote by this time) giving Hoover a 61-vote edge over Alfred E. Smith. With only two issues surviving today and only four known to have ever existed, lack of interest, lack of free time, or printing cost all could have been factors in its demise sometime in 1929.

The conservative students who walked Irving's campus participated greatly in the local YWCA (Young Women's Christian Association) chapter which opened on campus under great support of President Campbell.

---

46. Due to lack of interest, despite letters written by the *Irvingiana '08* staff to alumnae, they received only 15 of the 150 needed subscriptions.

The first mention of the YWCA on campus is in 1900, though its predecessor, The Christian Endeavor Society, existed several years before that. The Christian Endeavor Society, which had 43 members in 1897, had a different member lead the service every Sunday. When it evolved into a YWCA chapter in 1900, it adopted the similar Sunday evening format with topics such as "Secrets of Happiness," "Self or Christ," and "What it means to be a Missionary," introduced and discussed by the members in attendance. With elected officials, it was not long before the YWCA planned most weekend social receptions, dances, and outings, making membership almost a must for any young woman needing social acceptance or weekend entertainment. Many of the events raised money for needy causes such as missionary work, a blind person in India, the Tressler Orphans' Home (in Loysville, Pennsylvania), or sending a member to the Summer YWCA Conference. The organization had 61 members in 1911 and by 1913 nearly all boarding students were members. Campbell emphasized the work of the YWCA and often measured his success by their number of members. "The College YWCA exerts a most wholesome influence in the institution," Campbell mentioned quite often in his reports to the board which followed along with the purposes of the organization (see table 2.1). At the beginning of the year, old members entertained new members with a bonfire and marshmallow roast, and just before Christmas break a Christmas Pageant replaced the vespers service that Sunday night. The organization sponsored basketball, tennis, aesthetic dancing, croquet, Saturday evening entertainments, parties, and an annual formal dance. Though the YWCA offered so much, as the 1920s wore on, fewer students joined as E. E. noted: "[d]ue to changing values in women, [the] YWCA is doing the best they can[,]" being held together by its frequent dances, which more and more students wanted, and "not being too critical of conduct."[47] Despite Campbell's fears, by 1926 50 members were initiated and in Irving's last year, nearly every Irving student was a YWCA member.

---

47. Campbell, E. E. Presidential report to the board of trustees, Irving College Board of Trustees minutes, June 3, 1924.

TABLE 2.1. PURPOSE OF YMCA AT IRVING COLLEGE. This information is taken from the YWCA's Student Handbook published in 1923.

- To lead students to faith in God through Jesus Christ.
- To lead them into membership and service in the Christian Church.
- To promote their growth in Christian faith and character, especially through the study of the Bible.
- To influence them to devote themselves in united efforts with all Christians to making the will of Christ effective in human society and to extending the Kingdom of God throughout the world.

Because of the strong influence that the Music Department had at Irving with its director Harry C. Harper, many musical clubs formed. The Clionian Society, who incorporated vocal solos, speeches, and instrumental solos for their meetings and planned recitals for their guests, was one of the first musical clubs, appearing in *The Sketch Book* in 1898. Mr. Harper first directed a Glee Club in 1902, which averaged about 30 members through 1915, and he also directed the Trio Club (1901–1902) with 4 each of first sopranos, second sopranos, and altos. The St. Cecilia Music Club (c. 1912–1915) subscribed to the leading music magazines, having a library of over 100 volumes devoted to the subject of music, while the Lyric Club, organized in 1921, received active membership mostly from the voice students with 39 members in 1922. The Lyric Club acted as an advancement from a mere glee club striving to "bring to its members an actual and intimate acquaintance with the various musical forms and periods of music development, thus adding to and supplementing the more detailed and theoretical work of the Appreciation Class."[48]

Though music obtained the highest popularity at Irving, sports clubs also existed, though much later in Campbell's tenure. Basketball and tennis were the most popular sports as the college constructed grass courts on campus for both teams. Each basketball team, sometimes organized one per class, had roughly 6–10 players, while the tennis club had 34 members in 1901, 24 in 1903, 32 in 1907, and 13 in 1921. Teams

---

48. *The Sketch Book*, 1922, 41.

formed, tournaments were set up, and rivalries between teams and classes developed. The basketball team received requests to play other schools, such as that of Lebanon Valley College in 1905, but due to lack of practice and the fact that the only court was an outdoor one, requests during the winter months (when basketball is usually played) had to be declined. Despite the court handicap, Irving did play the Dickinson College girls once during the 1910s.

Competition in tennis ran rampant at Irving, as it is rumored that the students looked forward to tennis tournaments since it was the sport that the women most liked having the boys watch them play. Students held popular fall and spring tennis tournaments where the winner received a "loving cup," the runner-up, a can of tennis balls.

Before long, sports were so popular at Irving that an Athletic Association was even inaugurated, electing managers of teams and captains of squads. A greater interest in physical activity grew with the addition of a small, nonregulation pool in the basement of Irving Hall about 1917. The college organized a Red Cross swimming test with beginner, intermediate, and lifesaving classes offered regularly. Swimming became very popular during the winter months.

Besides basketball, tennis, and swimming, students organized baseball teams in 1927, and Irving apparently had field hockey, archery, and soccer. All of these available athletic competitions were not akin to Irving alone as many schools developed organized sports teams and clubs during the "golden age" of college athletics (1900–1930). As women in sport became more acceptable into the twentieth century, tennis, basketball, field hockey, and other sports began to appear on college campuses and influenced intercollegiate competition, though Irving was for the most part limited to Mechanicsburg.

Student government, which existed in a mild form under the Ege tenure with monitresses, existed to a greater degree under Campbell. The Student Senate went into effect in the 1893–1894 school year, but when first suggested the administration felt some reluctance as to its practicability to women college students.[49] However, after its application, it became more useful and influential as "the decisions of the senate, in all the cases

---

49. "The Student Senate," *The Sketch Book,* Vol. I, No. 1, February 1895, 35.

of discipline that have been before it, have been so just that no appeal has yet been taken to the faculty, and no fault has ever been found with its judgments by the students or faculty."[50] With its members elected by the students, the senate maintained a high moral standard, relating all disciplinary action to the faculty. The elected students acted as modern-day resident assistants in dormitories, and the system was revised with the institution of a student government in 1916. Responsible for monitoring students during quiet hours, study hours, afternoon walks, after lights out and in chapel and church, any Irving student could be a member of the government after a short probation period. Compulsory meetings were held to discuss disciplinary action of students and those members who did not attend faced a 10¢ fine. The President of Student Government carried out the regulations (see table 2.2) of the association and acted as the head captain of fire drills, which she called at her discretion. Acting as an additional arm of Dr. Campbell, the student government followed regulations that he had in place previously. Lights out were at 10:00 PM, no student was allowed beyond a two-block radius around campus, and chapel attendance every morning was mandatory. If any student deviated from these rules, a House President from the dorm (which were divided into a number of houses), a monitor at chapel, or another government member reported to the president of the association, who decided the action against the perpetrator.

---

50. "The Student Senate," *The Sketch Book*, Vol. I, No. 1, February 1895, 35.

TABLE 2.2. REGULATIONS FOR STUDENTS MAINTAINED BY THE STUDENT GOVERNMENT OF IRVING COLLEGE, 1916. Obtained from the Students' Government Association's *Constitution and By-Laws*.

QUIET	WALKING
1. No Boisterous Conduct in College Halls. 2. Students must be in class, in their rooms, the library, or YWCA room during recitation hours. 3. Quiet maintained between retiring bell (9:45 P.M.) and rising bell (7:00 A.M.). 4. Every student must be in room during study hour (7:00-9:00 A.M.). 5. Quiet every week day except Mon + Sat 8:15 A.M.-12:30 P.M., 1:15-4:15 P.M., and 7:00-9:00 P.M. 6. Music students can practice with special permission 6:30-7:30 A.M. in one of the southeast practice rooms.	1. Daily walks from 3:15 P.M.-dusk in groups of three or more any day with proper registration. Seniors may walk in groups of two. 2. College walk is around campus and two squares on Main Street including Hoover's store. 3. Strolling, idling, or promenading is not permitted with this walking privilege. 4. Country walks can be taken with permission of Preceptress. 5. Sunday walks can be 1:00-2:00 P.M. or 4:00-5:00 P.M. 6. No student can walk alone without permission, nor visit any eating place except "Bobb's."
CHAPERONES	**LIGHTS**
1. No student can attend an evening entertainment without a chaperon. 2. Long country walks must have a chaperon. 3. Students visiting the doctor, dentist, photographer, or railroad station must have a chaperon.	1. Lights out at 10:00 P.M. 2. Students must turn off light when leaving a room. 3. Students may study after lights out in class room 2 in Columbian Hall until 11:00 P.M. with permission of house president.

DINING ROOM	CHAPEL ATTENDANCE
1. No loud talking. 2. No books in dining room. 3. No letters opened or read. 4. Respect for faculty. 5. Students may not speak to a servant unless presiding teacher or senior is absent. 6. No calling from table to table. 7. Students excused from Dining Room by tables. 8. Leaving Dining Room requires permission from teacher.	1. Monitor from each class reports absences to Student Government President. 2. All students must attend and be prompt. 3. No studying during Chapel.
	CHURCH ATTENDANCE
	1. Maintained on the honor system. 2. All students must register before leaving for church. 3. Students may be excused from church due to illness with permission of nurse.

Other smaller student groups existed on campus under the Campbell tenure. The Magazine Club (appr. 1911–1918), who received *Harper's Monthly, Review of Reviews, Ladies' Home Journal, The Red Cross Bulletin,* et. al., supplied the students with current literature and provided volumes for the library. Sponsoring lectures from time to time, the club issued a collection of Irving College songs written by alumnae and students, the first collection of its kind in the school's history. With the growing interest in acting, students coordinated a Dramatic Club with elocution teacher Miss Alice C. Hartley in 1909, though interest in drama was evident years before. The club appeared sporadically until Irving's closing, putting on performances in Columbian Hall, the Technical High School auditorium, and at Gettysburg and Dickinson Colleges.[51] The Owls (1903) were a cooking club whose motto was "We meet to Eat," the Education Club (1919) met once a week to "formulate, present and listen to programs on subjects of educational interest," while a small number of students who represented the southern states established the Southern Club.[52] Other clubs that existed were the Bicycle Club (1901–1902),

---
51. The Green Room Players were another dramatic organization which put on plays in the late 1920s.
52. The Owl's club is present in: *Irvingiana '03,* 72. The Education Club is presented in: Irving College Catalogue 1919–1920, 61.

Chafiney Dish Club (1901), the Epicureans (1901–1902), a Croquet Club (1902), The Sunshine Club (1907), The Smilers (1912), The Friday Club (1893), and the General Culture Club (1907).

Many of these student groups helped to plan activities on campus as the college calendar soon became full of afternoon teas, Sunday trips, and dances. The biggest celebration of the college calendar was certainly Commencement Week. Commencement 1890 was "crowded almost to suffocation . . . [as] our [townspeople of Mechanicsburg] in large numbers wended their way to the College, to be present at the Commencement exercises," for which *two* students graduated. In 1891, the news of Irving's commencement took up four of the six columns on the front page of Mechanicsburg's *Saturday Journal,* so the event caused quite a stir in town. Commencement Week resembled the end of the year festivities of past years involving students in Baccalaureate (Sunday) and Commencement services (Wednesday or later), which occurred at Trinity Lutheran Church in Mechanicsburg and at the college chapel in Irving Hall until Columbian Hall arrived in 1893. Processing in black gowns, the students received their diplomas from Dr. Campbell, who himself wore a purple and gold hood, while the Secretary of the Faculty dressed in master's regalia of crimson and white. Students continued to wear black gowns through the graduation of 1929, though it appears that they wore different color tassels on their mortar boards to signify a different curriculum of study. Music and collegiate study students certainly must have been differentiated in this way, using one color for a Mus.B. degree and another for an A.B., though colored tassels certainly could have signified elocution, domestic science, and preparatory students as well.

Tuesday evening students presented musical and literary entertainment with receptions following, while the board of trustees held their annual meeting earlier in the day. The annual congregation of the alumnae met Wednesday morning while the evening brought Commencement with essays read by students, songs sung by college choruses, and recitals performed by music students. As Campbell continued as President, additional student entertainment was offered either at Commencement or during the week. The class of 1896 introduced the initial Junior Class Entertainment in 1895, as audiences witnessed music selections, a

"Christmas Suite," and the play *Pygmalion and Galatea* at Franklin Hall. A farewell song was sung to the class of 1901 at their Commencement, while President Campbell added a President's reception during Commencement Week, which had hundreds of people calling on Campbell in 1905 with an orchestra, refreshments, and decorations of many beautiful Japanese lanterns. An address to the YWCA became an annual event as outside speakers (usually ministers) spoke to the members on Sunday evening. The 1905 Commencement Week visitors attended the senior class play, an oratorical contest, and Music Department recitals for graduation. The class of 1906 even put on a Junior Burlesque:

> Dressed in gowns of black and holding lighted candles, the Juniors were found seated on the porch of the college, while from a large scroll was read the past achievements of the class and what great things had been accomplished. The solemn march was then taken up to a shady part of campus where the scroll, caps and gowns and other class paraphernalia were consigned to the flames and the yells of the about-to-be Seniors . . .[53]

The week of Commencement in 1908 included a tennis tournament, a matinee musical, and a mock faculty meeting presented by the members of Eta Nu, who impersonated different Irving teachers.[54] The activities of Commencement Week grew throughout the early 1900s during the school's growth spurt and Campbell maintained the aforementioned activities through the 1920s. One of the week's most interesting events took place the Monday before Commencement. Class Day, as a student exercise, first appears in college printings in 1898, though it may have started with Campbell's promotion to President. Traditionally, senior class prophecies, poems, orations, and junior class responses filled the day's events. Any class yells, cheers, symbols, or colors coincided with the college's light blue and bright yellow colors. These class traditions consisted of a large part of the day's ceremony and by 1900 included

---

53. "Forty-Ninth Commencement of Irving College," *Saturday Journal*, Vol. 46, No. 43, June 10, 1905, 2.
54. Interestingly, according to *The Sketch Book*, Vol. IX, No. 7, June 1908, 16, it is quoted: "It is strange however that so few of the Faculty were present to see themselves as others see them."

the tradition of planting a class tree on campus. Similar to Wellesley's tree planting and Smith's Ivy Day, students maintained the tradition of dedicating a class plant in 1929, when State Botanist, Dr. E. N. Gress, witnessed the planting. Though at other schools this ceremonial planting occurred annually, it was sporadic at Irving, as occasional class gifts would be shrubs or trees.

Other years had different Class Day activities. Class Day 1904 took place as a farce with students portraying different members of the faculty, while in 1906 the senior class read their last will and testament, bequeathing a bottle of nourishment to the juniors, a beautiful candlestick to the sophomores, and blue baby slippers to the first-year students. The last Class Day in 1929 not only had the State Botanist in attendance, but was ushered in by a class breakfast, followed by a senior skit at 8:15 in the morning, special chapel exercises at 10:30, and eight ushers who marched across campus to dedicate the shrubbery. The students christened 1929 Class Day chapel exercises as "Moving-Up Day":

> [a]t this time all the classes will move up to the seats which they will occupy next year, the Seniors taking their place with the Alumnae. The Juniors will receive with dignity and ceremony the honor of gracing the three front rows so nobly filled by the present Senior Class. It will be a sad occasion for the Seniors when they will be moved away from their beloved seats never to return.[55]

Students also expected the bonfire of the 1929 Class Day to be a tradition carried out by future Irving girls:

> each member of the Graduating Class throws into the fire some article representing a latent wish or hope whether it be congratulatory to the College or not. It must be a grand feeling to throw it away and get it out of your system and then leave your Alma Mater with only the happiest memories.[56]

---

55. *The Sketch Book*, 1929, 23.
56. *The Sketch Book*, 1929, 23.

The class of 1929 added traditions to Class Day in hopes that they would be carried on in the future, but unfortunately they stopped that particular spring when the college closed.

Before Commencement occurred in June, students looked forward to the May Day celebrations that commenced every May 1st. These very elaborate and creative pageants involved a variety of dances and chants, and most importantly, the crowning of the May Queen, who was chosen by her classmates. The pageants' stories ranged from sleeping flowers awakened by the sun and rain to the finding and crowning of the Queen of May, though the topics usually dealt with the rebirth of Spring. Each pageant incorporated the current students' own ideas, although they all usually involved finding the May Queen, crowning her, and dancing around the May pole. The Saturday afternoon program started appearing in college literature about 1917, though it originated a few years before that. Twelve students participated in the 1918 May Day, some as raindrops, some as violets, while others portrayed a wild geranium, a spring beauty, and the sun. In contrast, 75 students shared in the 1925 festivities as Italian dancers, Russian haymakers, little gossips, black nags, or queen attendants, who told "of the man in the moon who comes to earth to seek Spring. After much wandering he finds a queen whom he crowns Queen of the May."[57] The 1929 May Day pageant had all of its costumes made by Mary Baylor Havely '29, a home economics student who, rather uniquely, enrolled for an accelerated program and graduated in three years. As part of her special enrollment requirements, she was required to make all the outfits for the May Day festivities and finished them without the aid of a pattern.

"May Day was quite a thing," said Ruth Hoy Diffenderfer, '26, "... So help me ... we never got it right ... I think if we'd have practiced for six months we wouldn't have had it right. But that was the social event."[58] Marion Strouse Scharf, '18 remembered:

> I took part in my sophomore year [1916] in the Maypole dance and still remember wearing a hoop skirt with my Colonial

---
57. News Clipping, Mary Shope's, '26 Stunt Book, 1922–1929.
58. Oral History, Ruth Hoy Diffenderfer, '26, June 9, 1993.

costume. . . . We were dancing around the May Pole and then [we] did a curtsey. My heel got caught in my hoop, and I couldn't get up. I got hysterical. Here I was on the ground, trying to get my heel out of my hoop. Finally someone came to the rescue, and the dance could be continued. It couldn't be continued until I got on my feet again.[59]

Regardless of the mishaps, May Day celebrations brought a sense of excitement to Mechanicsburg.

Other celebrations occurred on campus commemorating certain holidays. As previously mentioned, the Eta Nu and the Phi Rho Mu societies took an active part in Washington Irving's birthday on April 3rd. 1895's debate, "Resolved, that the defeat of China in the Present war would be Beneficial to China and Advance Civilization," corresponded with vocal solos, two Tuscan folk songs, two essays, an instrumental duet, two readings, and an instrumental solo. The celebration was not completely dominated by the sororities. The 1895 celebration had a special treat in addition to the debates, the music, and the college chapel decorated with society colors, palms, and other tropical plants; it had young men to share the refreshments with. "Indeed 'the 3d' is a great event in our school year—an oasis—our day of days. . . . We will hear no retiring bells that night."[60] With 600 in attendance in 1895, another 200 showed for the follies of 1897 as schoolwork was suspended for the Saturday, April 3rd in order to prepare for the festivities that evening. Though the day was de-emphasized further into the twentieth century, 1916 had a broadened celebration on Irving's birthday, since it included the observance of the Shakespearean tercentenary.

In addition to Washington Irving, the beloved George Washington also received commemoration at Irving College. His birthday was a reason for celebration in the minds of the students. February 22, 1895, brought about a different result much to the students' chagrin:

---

59. Scharf, Marion Strouse, '18. Typed reminiscences of Irving, 1982. Oral history with Marion Strouse Scharf '18, May 18, 1993.

60. "Our Annual Celebration," *The Sketch Book*, Vol. I, No. 2, March 1895, 73.

> Some of the members of our [campus] were particularly anxious to see the president in his office the day before Washington's birthday. We wanted a holiday, but all our wishing was in vain as Mr. Campbell was many miles away. We sent him a telegram but alas, it was a case of the letter that never came. School went on just the same. Quite an idea of our president, to travel while such an important question is pending.[61]

Most of the birthday celebrations included receptions or half-days of school, though 150 attended a dance planned for 1918 and it was a welcome sight for the students on campus. Somewhat sporadic over Campbell's tenure, celebrations on Washington's birthday probably owed their origins to incessant student pleadings. A mid-winter reception in 1906, where students decorated each corner of the recitation room for each class, occurred on February 22nd during time off from school, though Washington's name is absent.

As was obvious from the May Day festivities and Commencement Week, dramatics were important among the student body of Irving, and plays were performed regularly during each school year. Though established plays such as Alfred Lloyd Tennyson's *The Princess* and Shakespeare's *As You Like It* were produced many times, the class play of 1904 evolved from the pen of Mary Lenore Embick Flower '04, involving the adventures of Dr. Campbell and other faculty at Irving. The students played female and male roles, often using make-up, long coats, and hats to depict men in dramatic productions. With most of the plays in Columbian Hall, it was not always easy as Ruth Hoy Diffenderfer, '26 describes:

> We didn't have any stage on either side of [the organ in Columbian]. It was just a stage with no dressing rooms, . . . and to get from one side of the stage, if you're going to be off for a while, you had to go all the way around the outside of Columbian Hall and come in the other side. . . . what they used to do is put a step ladder up to the window in back, and you'd

---

61. "The Twenty-Second," *The Sketch Book*, Vol. I, No. 2, March 1895, 73–74.

climb up the step-ladder and crawl in the window. And if you wanted to change your clothes there was a class room. I think it was Miss Hade's English classroom where we would dress.[62]

The Girls of 1776, A Bachelor's Romance, Six Pomegranate Seeds, and *The Heart of a Clown* were just a few of the performances that students portrayed from 1904–1929.

Because of the influence of music on campus, student and faculty concerts occurred quite regularly. Soirees similar to the literary and musical offerings under Marlatt and Ege appeared under Kessler and Campbell with the reopening of the school after 1888. Musical recitals became a common feature with Campbell, not only at the end of the year for graduation from the music course, but even occurring throughout the year. Six Irving seniors traveled to the United Brethren Church of Duncannon in 1905 playing a concert (with a number of encores) to benefit the Thaddeus Stevens Memorial School. The Irving College Glee Club played at Mentzer Hall at Dickinson College in 1913 and sang at the York High School Auditorium to benefit the city's poor residents. Columbian Hall saw a combined concert with Irving and Dickinson College students with a much-awaited half-hour reception afterwards (many of the Dickinson students missed the train home that night, having to walk). Though student concerts occurred on a regular basis, music students received a special treat when the faculty performed occasional concerts. But the most important concerts for the music students remained those for graduation, as their final grades depended upon a good performance, which was surely nerve-racking in front of parents and friends. Despite the stress, the recitals provided an evening's entertainment and another excuse to put off work until another night.

Some social gatherings on campus involved no grades, as students planned parties and clubs planned receptions for sheer enjoyment. Receptions offering a variety of refreshments from cake to fried oysters were sponsored by individual classes or certain student organizations and tended to honor other campus classes or the faculty. The gatherings presented music, lectures, and occasional interesting oddities like mesmerism

---

62. Oral History, Ruth Hoy Diffenderfer, '26, June 9, 1993.

(hypnotism), but usually involved conversation and eating. Planned parties took on a variety of forms. The junior and freshmen classes gave a "Progressive Novelty Party" in 1902, playing games which awarded a handsome, Gibson calendar to the winner and a booby prize to a losing teacher. A "tacky party" thrown by the choral class volunteered a bean race, humorous songs by the vocalists, and tacky refreshments like "doughnuts, cheese and all-day suckers."[63] In keeping with its job to provide weekly entertainment, the YWCA would sponsor parties, including card parties with prizes for winners of bridge, 500, spades, and diamonds.

Halloween parties appeared the most frequent over Irving's years with Dr. Campbell. One party featured "[s]ee-saws, cider kegs and an old farm wagon . . ." ghost stories, and a chapel dimly lit with great pumpkin lanterns and decorated with corn shocks, straw pies, autumn leaves, and ears of corn.[64] An elaborate party sponsored by the classes of 1910 and 1912 required both classes to dress similarly to each other, constructed a maze that "having once got in, you were lucky if you got out very soon," exhibited the ghastly appearance of Blue Beard's wives in the art room, and entertained events which included a "caldron containing fortunes," a tub for bobbing apples, fortune telling, a barn dance, and "John Brown's Body" march.[65] Classes planned Halloween parties nearly every year.

Although students looked forward to parties, most of them contained no men with which to socialize or dance. Therefore, students surely treasured formal dances the most of all events. Though cherished, dances were only held about twice a year and tended to be very strict. If any student wanted a particular boy on campus, he had to meet Dr. Campbell and the preceptress first for approval. Ruth Hoy Diffenderfer '26 had a brother who attended Dickinson College, and it was often her job to have her brother round up young men interested in going to a dance at Irving and take them down to meet Dr. Campbell and the preceptress. "All girls had to wear long dresses and long white kid gloves. . . . A chaperone was always present when girls had dates and the doors to the parlor had to be kept open. Only special permission from parents would permit

---

63. *The Sketch Book*, Vol. IX, No. 4, February 1908, 9.
64. *The Sketch Book*, Vol. VI, No. 1, November 1903, 7.
65. *The Sketch Book*, Vol. X, No. 2, December 1908, 5–16.

any student to leave the campus for a date."⁶⁶ While Miss Sarah Elizabeth Trump presided as preceptress at Irving, the student legend maintains that she called Dickinson College and "ordered" the number of boys she wanted to come and attend the dance; Dickinson staff would round up the number and send them on the train to Mechanicsburg as asked. The appearance of these new faces on campus garnered by Trump surely caused great excitement and anticipation among the students, causing many of the boys to linger in Mechanicsburg past the 10 o'clock train, the last to Carlisle until the next morning. Those who missed it, walked the 11 miles back to Dickinson.

The preceptress kept a firm hold on activities such as dances. Betty Boffemmyer Stram '29 said that "when they had dances, [the students] had to show [the preceptress] the dress they were going to wear, and if it wasn't just right, they couldn't wear it."⁶⁷ During the dance, the preceptress kept a close eye on what transpired; holding hands, the placing of arms around each other, or leaving the dance floor with your date called for immediate dismissal. Though males often attended Irving's organized dances, many times men were absent even from proms: "Anna was my man. She was very cunning and took good care of me. A grand good time. All the men [women dressed as men] looked very clever and the girls looked sweet. It was the real thing. The girls received a white carnation and the men a black (chocolate) cigar, which they all smoked."⁶⁸ Women at single-sex colleges often had to make do; at Smith, sophomores welcomed freshmen students at an annual Freshman Frolic, where each sophomore acted as a cavalier to her assigned freshmen, sending flowers, calling, dancing with her, and taking her to supper.⁶⁹

Though most dances that the students attended occurred in Columbian Hall or on campus, the students did attend social functions outside of Irving's walls. One incident had the students traveling to Mercersburg Academy for a mid-winter dance: "[the] girls had a delightful time and returned home Saturday evening, tired but very expressive of the

---

66. Scharf, Marion Strouse '18, Typed Reminiscences of Irving, 1982.
67. Oral History with Betty Boffemmyer Stram '29, April 22, 1993.
68. Henrietta Thomas's Memory Book, 1909–1911. In addition to this 1910 Junior Prom having no men, neither did the Junior Prom of 1912.
69. Horowitz, 162.

kindness they received from the Mercersburg boys."[70] Students often attended football games at Pennsylvania male colleges, as trips to Gettysburg and Dickinson Colleges are often mentioned in *The Sketch Book* and the college calendar listings in the *Irvinigana*. Since some of the students may have had boyfriends at these other schools, it was not unusual to see weekend trips home to visit them.

Other kinds of activities with a social atmosphere surfaced on campus. Dr. Campbell occasionally gave dinners or outings for the students, inviting a class over to his home, taking a hayride, or making a day trip to the mountains to gather chestnuts. Other colleges sent delegates to Irving for entertainment, such as a men's vocal choir from Dickinson, or glee and mandolin clubs from Franklin and Marshall.[71] The YWCA sponsored movies by the late 1920's, many clubs would sponsor lectures or prominent speakers, and the college even set up art exhibitions of student work or traveling art.[72] Displaying the racist beliefs existing in the time period, the junior class held a "coon wedding" on November 24, 1900, inviting a large number of faculty and guests to the ceremony that they performed. Twenty-four students were involved in the wedding which had a traditional wedding party, with students portraying African American ushers, flower girls, an organist, a minister, and guests. The "reception" involved all those present for eating and a cake walk, where "the cake was awarded to 'Mammy Cloe' and 'Old Black Joe.'"[73] Though this appears to be the only incident of its kind, it certainly displays the attitude and stereotypes of the time and shows that probably no African

---

70. *The Sketch Book*, Vol. VIII, No. 12, 20.

71. According to *The Sketch Book*, Vol. IV, No. 5, April 1898, 140–41, the glee and mandolin clubs from Franklin and Marshall made their fifth straight appearance at Irving in 1898.

72. The films sponsored by the YWCA tended to be offered every month featuring an 8–10-minute cartoon, and a 30–55 minute main feature which could be a helpful hint film for health or the home, or relating scenes of foreign lands. Some prominent lecturers came to Irving in 1908 alone; Professor Surface, the State Economic Zoologist lectured about bird species, while Mr. MacFarland, the President of the American Civic Federation, titled his lecture "Crusade Against Ugliness," in talking about cleaning up Mechanicsburg. Two exhibits in 1898 (one in February and one in June) displayed student artwork and was accentuated with music on violin and piano. Two traveling exhibits passed through Columbian Hall in 1912: an exhibition of hand painted Japanese Calendars by L. Nakaide of the University of Chicago, and the Turner Art Exhibit of Boston, showing 200 pictures of ancient and modern art, which was sponsored by the magazine club.

73. *Irvingiana '02*, 114–115.

Americans attended Irving nor made up a large part of Mechanicsburg at the turn of the century.

Holidays that intersected with the school year often were reasons for celebration. Keeping with the annual Halloween influence, the students had a ghost parade in 1905: "[s]ome few minutes before study hour was over a great majority of Irving beds were torn apart and the sheets wrapped around their owners. Masks and horns were procured by those who could get any such thing."[74] As soon as the 9:15 study hour bell rang, the students ran for the stairs and out to the basketball field, where a bonfire of corn stocks started. The students danced around this fire, and as it died out the "ghosts" proceeded to campus yelling, stopped at the northeast corner, and continued to yell at the gate and the tennis court.

Other holidays did not provoke such strange behavior. The students attended prayer meetings during Lent in the college parlor, hunted colored eggs on the Saturday before Easter, and consumed a "big dinner" at Dr. Campbell's residence over Thanksgiving.[75] Campbell had a traditional dinner for students on his own birthday with a large birthday cake, while after his death, Dr. Campbell's birthday was remembered with "a simple and dignified memorial service" in chapel.[76]

As mentioned earlier, presidential campaigns often brought about excitement on campus even before Women's suffrage in 1920. Students held mock elections on campus from time to time, though no documentation suggests that they were meant as protests or as part of the suffrage movements, as at Vassar. The 1908 campaign saw a grand parade put on by the junior class, led by the "Prohibitionists" and students representing Eugene W. Chafin and Carry Nation, followed by the "Republicans" with William Howard Taft, Teddy Roosevelt, Helen Taft, Alice Roosevelt Longworth, and "Nick" Longworth, and the "Democrats" brought up

---

74. *The Sketch Book*, Vol. VIII, No. 1, November 1905, 8.
75. E. E. often had a Thanksgiving dinner for students at his house. Since most local students went home for the holiday, or at least the holiday meal, Dr. Campbell would have students who could not travel home to his house for the annual feast.
76. *The Sketch Book*, March 1928, 2.

the rear with William Jennings Bryan, Ruth, and Kern.[77] The students representing the candidates gave speeches at their respective areas of campus (in the case of the Democrats, the side porch), and were cheered by their parties. The process was quite thorough with a registration process three days before the election involving girls 12 and over. The November 3 election was held in a school room with the election return coming that evening: Taft, 49 votes; Bryan, 43; and Chafin, 2.

Special occasions arose from time to time for which Irving girls participated, especially if something transpired downtown. Irving students most likely partook in Mechanicsburg celebrations like the Centennial in 1876 or Mechanicsburg's 100th birthday celebration in 1907. The most notable event involved the senior class of 1901 and the new trolley line constructed between Boiling Springs and Mechanicsburg. The seniors, all in caps and gowns, proceeded downtown to witness Miss Jane Hufford '01, their Class President, drive the first spike of the trolley line:

> After a few introductory remarks, our worthy President
> notwithstanding the smallness of her stature, drove the spike
> with several determined blows, applauded by all the students and
> bystanders. How well her strokes contrasted with the weak and
> feeble blows of the town burgess (who drove the second spike),
> the crowd that witnessed can testify.[78]

A thrill of a lifetime for Jane Hufford, this event further shows the close link between the town and the college.

Dr. Campbell treated the students to occasional trips traversing the area around the school. In addition to gathering chestnuts in the forests

---

77. Eugene W. Chafin (1852–1920) was a temperance leader and the 1908 presidential candidate on the Prohibition ticket. Carry Nation (1846–1911) was an American temperance leader who led violent demonstrations against liquor production. Alice Roosevelt Longworth (1884–1980) was Teddy Roosevelt's daughter and a social figure who married Nicholas Longworth (1869–1931), a politician from Ohio and Speaker of the House from 1925–1931, in 1906. William Jennings Bryan (1860–1925) was the Democratic Presidential Nominee and he strongly supported John W. Kern (1849–1917) of Indiana for the 1908 vice-presidency, though neither were elected. Ruth Bryan is William's daughter who married Major Reginald A. Owen of the British army, and Kern Bryan is his son.

78. *Irvingiana '02*, 105. This yearbook account appears a little far-fetched, though because of the close ties between the school and Mechanicsburg, it is not out of the realm of possibility that an Irving student performed this feat. However, the accounts in the yearbooks, especially relating to one's own class, tend to be exaggerated and efforts of achievement heightened, therefore this account may be exaggerated from what actually happened.

nearby, Campbell escorted several classes to the Carlisle Indian School, to Harper's Ferry, West Virginia, and various stops up and down the Cumberland Valley Railroad. A student trip in 1907 to Gettysburg had the young ladies admiring the monuments and getting their picture taken by the cannon that fired the battle's first shot. Pictures in one student's photo album show Irving girls visiting Mount Vernon in Virginia.

Upperclasswomen found time for initiation of the first-year students, a ritual that existed on other campuses as well as at Irving. Initiation could be sweet like at Wellesley where underclasswomen arrived at the first Sunday breakfast of college finding flowers on their plates left by the upperclasswomen, or it could be more devious as when sophomores at Wellesley tried to rob the freshmen class secrets (class motto, flower, etc.) before their unveiling on Tree Day. At Irving, Marian Claire Fisher '27 mentioned freshmen rules and freshmen week sporadically in the annotations of her hymnal as an upperclasswoman.[79] Apparently, the rules forced upon the freshmen lasted from the end of September until Thanksgiving, probably requiring the first-years to perform certain tasks at the sophomores', juniors', and seniors' beckoning. One such incident required the freshmen to get up at 6:00 A.M. and march around the "senior's block" with Marian and probably other seniors. Marian even mentioned an "Initiation week—ears showing and wearing hats," which probably required the freshmen to place hats on their heads all day with their ears sticking out.[80] At any of the schools the initiation process involved fun and not necessarily humiliation or intimidation, as is often associated with college initiations today.

Lest it appears that all Irving students did was extracurricular, it is important to understand how strict the curriculum and culture was, and how large a workload these students had; it is surprising that they even had time for outside activities. Often taking seven classes a term in addition to elocution and any music lessons, the students frequently commented on having too much work:

---

79. Often during chapel services, Irving students would write notes to each other in their hymnals, since talking was prohibited during the service. After writing messages, the students would switch their hymnals and read what each other had written. The hymnal of Marian Claire Fisher, '27, exists in the Irving College Collection, with annotations that provide and excellent glimpse into student life beyond school studies.

80. Fisher, Marian Claire, '27. Hymnal Annotation, October 26, 1926, 311.

A Sophomore's Idea of Education

Ram it in, cram it in	Scold it in, mold it in,
Student's heads are hollow.	All that they can swallow,
Slam it in, jam it in,	Fold it in, hold it in,
Still there's more to follow.	Students['] heads are hallow,
Hygiene and history,	Those who've passed the furnace through
Astronomic mystery,	With aching brow will tell you
Algebra, histology,	How the teachers rammed it in,
Latin, Etymology,	Jammed it in, crammed it in,
Botany, Geometry,	Rubbed it in, clubbed it in,
Ram it in, cram it in,	Rapped it in and slapped it in
Still there's more to follow	When their heads were hollow.[81]

Students memorized certain pieces of their lessons and came to class prepared with knowledge of the lesson or else: "If you didn't have . . . what [Adele Eichler] had assigned . . . memorized and do it verbatim, she would have a hissy."[82] Naomi Hade, who taught English at Irving from 1924–1926, enjoyed incorporating a lot of memorization, but she gave poems which students had to take apart and write their own opinions, offering a great opportunity for independent learning. Alberta Roach, an English teacher who immediately followed Hade and continued through the school's closing, "would put on the blackboard each day quotations from somebody which she thought was something to think about. . . . [W]e would learn that quotation—it was often something short—but I remember one was a quotation from Sarah Teasdale: 'Spend all you have for loveliness, and never count the costs.'"[83]

Because of the large amount of homework and busy extracurricular schedules, students tried to study at night when they were supposed to be asleep. A master switch turned out the lights at 10:00 P.M., cutting the breaker to all of the student rooms in order to prevent late-night studying

---

81. *The Sketch Book*, Vol. I, No. I, February 1895, 36.
82. Oral History, Ruth Hoy Diffenderfer, '26, June 9, 1993.
83. Oral History, Jane Campbell Beard, '29, April 12, 1994.

and ensure proper sleep. Despite their lack of electricity from 10 P.M. to roughly 7 A.M., many students tried their luck at studying anyway. Mary Baylor Havely '29 would sit on her wastepaper basket at the window to try and read by the light coming in from outside in order to get her work done.[84] Pauline Hege '25 tried similar methods to get work done:

> "I used to go [study] after you were supposed to be in bed.. Up the hall we had two or three [bathrooms]. This one bathroom, it was sort of up on a landing and you could go in there, and of course, you [would] lock the door. . . . you weren't allowed to study after [light's out] [so] . . . sometimes, you would get a flashlight, and put an umbrella over your head, study under this, because you weren't supposed to do that. But I used to sneak up to that bathroom at night, and get in the bathtub and study. Especially music . . . [since if one bathroom was occupied, a student would use another bathroom elsewhere, leaving Pauline undisturbed]"[85]

The students broke the "light's out" rule not only by studying, but also for social reasons. The package of forbidden goodies from home brought the students together for impromptu "feasts," so for gatherings during these late hours it seems likely that many students sneaked around for the thrill of not getting caught, should they be so lucky. Marian Claire Fisher '27 mentioned a number of times about having fellow students sleep in her bed with her probably to sit up and gossip with the sheer thrill of breaking the rules, as she mentioned several different women.

Though some of the students could be mischievous as times, they were often too busy to get involved in much trouble. The favorite pastimes of the seniors, as presented by the junior class of 1908, display sleeping, reading, studying English, studying Geology, and plugging and grinding away among the free time activities of the studious seniors.[86] However, the juniors also wrote that the senior class enjoyed talking, spooning,

---

84. Mary actually sat with a pillow in-between her and the wastebasket and still received an impression from the ring on the bottom of the basket.
85. Oral History, Pauline Hege, '25, October 15, 1993.
86. Grinding is college slang for a student who is industrious which characterized the seniors who tended to have heavier schedules and more work than the underclasswomen. Plugging also follows in suit, describing someone who works steadily.

flirting, running errands for music director Mr. Harry Harper (who was quite a handsome young man while at Irving), writing letters, losing books, walking up Market Street, dreaming and star-gazing.[87] Although the juniors were making fun of the seniors with these characteristics in *Irvingiana '07*, Irving students of all classes worked and studied steadily, enjoying the same interest in young men and love at that age.

Regardless of the workload and studying time of students, the Irving girls did occasionally have to face the wrath of the preceptress or Dr. Campbell. "The policy of the school as to discipline is to appeal to the noble quality of the girls and to trust to their honor instead of continuously being on the watch and that result is admirable,"[88] from Campbell's administration sounds similar to the issue during Marlatt's tenure: "The discipline is mild but firm. Students are taught to observe the regulations of the institution from love, and not from fear. There is one great rule, by which the conduct of all is measured, viz.: 'Do not act which a *young lady* would be ashamed to acknowledge.'"[89] Though for 65 years, Irving's instituted form of strict discipline on the student body was an everyday fact of life for the young women, by 1909 the air had begun to relax, despite E. E.'s objections:

> We are living in a day when the children dictate to a great extent to home government. Parental discipline is in a state of "Innocuous Desuetude." This makes the exercise of wholesome discipline in College more and more difficult. "IRVING" is known, everywhere that it is known, as an institution where discipline is maintained. Indeed parents who seem least able to exercise proper discipline at home are most anxious to send their daughters here. We have steadily refused to yield our position, and are holding onto the traditions and are maintaining under occasional fire, our vantage ground. It has been necessary to expel one student during the session, because of her unwillingness to submit to the college regulations. She was a young woman over

---

87. Spooning here refers to being physically affectionate.
88. Irving College Board of Trustees Minutes, June 7, 1892.
89. Irving College Catalogue, 1857–1858, 17.

whom her parents seem to have but little control. In spite of the manifestation of this spirit of unwillingness to submit cheerfully to college regulations, the year has been pleasant.[90]

By 1910, many women's colleges eased up on their student regulations following Bryn Mawr's example of student self-government which they adopted in the 1890s. The easing up on college rules diminished the seminary regulations that had been the starting point for student control since the 1820s.[91] The condition worsened for Campbell through the 1920s:

> The matter of exercising wholesome discipline becomes an increasingly difficult problem from year to year. Discipline in the home has greatly relaxed—parents have given way largely in the home to the whim of their children—and children have substituted their own wills in many cases for that of their parents. This is naturally reflected in the College.[92]

As automobiles, jazz music, and bob haircuts began creeping into student's minds, E. E. found it more and more difficult to enact the type of discipline that he and Irving had grown up with to ensure well educated and proper young ladies.

> The bobbed-haired—partly-dressed "flapper" dreams only of the exciting movie—the gay dance—the entrancing cigarette and anything that thrills. We have grown to rather like the bobbed-hair, bobbed-dress, bobbed-conventionalities—so that many [m]others have been brought around not only to approve these things in their daughters but in many cases go the daughter at least one better. It is becoming rather difficult to secure teachers not bobbed in several respects.[93]

---

90. Irving College Board of Trustees Minutes, June 1, 1909.
91. Horowitz, 149.
92. Irving College Board of Trustees Minutes, June 3, 1924.
93. Irving College Board of Trustees Minutes, June 3, 1924.

It has been more difficult than usual, perhaps, to maintain good discipline and order. The lack of proper home restraint and discipline, the demoralization incident to the moving picture show, and the demoralization as a result of the world war, are all having their baneful effect on family life, and those in position of authority all recognize that the air is surchargered [*sic*][94] with the spirit of unrest, unwillingness to do the things that should be done, and at the time and the way they should be done. All institutions from the high school to the College and University feel the same lack of proper regard for order. It has been necessary for us to dismiss two students and to place others under restriction of privileges. The spirit is not malicious, but mischievous, often deceitful, and generally daring.[95]

In the 1920s, college life for students turned outward from campus organizations to activities outside the college: motion pictures, automobiles, and men.[96] Though students still filled the organizations in place, the location of the college drama shifted to dating, dances, and social events where men were present.[97] With "unpleasantness" in regard to discipline at Irving in the 20's, Campbell's problems stemmed deeper:

> Students now-a-days want more privileges, more liberties, really more license. They not only insist on movies and still more movies but movies that thrill—they want entertainment and must have it. To be real happy they must also have frequent dances—dances with thrills and frills: the "frills" now are the cigarette and some thing to drink. And these are the girls of the present Christian homes . . . Our apology is that we find it a little disconcerting to get on happily with the "Modernist" girl from a Christian home when she insists on smoking, drinking, swearing

---

94. Surchargered here means to be overburdened.
95. Irving College Board of Trustees Minutes, June 1, 1920.
96. Horowitz, 284–285.
97. Horowitz, 284–285.

and vulgarity—and so we have had to separate ourselves from some of them this session.⁹⁸

Many of these "modernist" girls may have been suspended or denied admission but since "[g]irls were just beginning to bob their hair ... if you followed the trend, you were sent home for two weeks."⁹⁹

Smoking became a key regulational issue for the students in the 1920s. Since no one knew of the health hazards from smoking in the early 1900s and cigarettes resembled an outward sign of feminine sensuality, women often defied college rules to smoke.¹⁰⁰ Though some earlier college catalogs encouraged smokers not to apply to Irving, as the school approached the 1920s, Campbell was successful at keeping it out of his sight, but there was little he could do from keeping it out of Irving completely.

> We had a door that opened out on a balcony, and [my roommate] would open the door, put up an umbrella and cover it with a blanket. It provided a shelter for a smoke. All was well until one of [the] teachers walking along the hall one night, smelled the smoke. She was polite enough to knock on the door which gave the smoking female a chance to get into bed, but when the door was opened the fumes had not cleared. Naturally, my roommate was campused.¹⁰¹

One student story passed down had students smoking in their rooms, but when preceptress Miss Sarah Elizabeth Trump (1920–1929)¹⁰² (who detested onions) was heard coming down the hall, the deviating students

---

98. Irving College Board of Trustees Minutes, June 3, 1924.
99. News Clipping, Hagee, Dorothy. "Days at the Morn'," August 19, 1967.
100. Horowitz, 289.
101. News Clipping, Hagee, Dorothy, "Days at the Morn'," August 19, 1967. To be "campused" meant that the student was not allowed to leave the campus whatsoever for a month (not even the two-block radius).
102. An interesting biography about Miss Trump and the preceptress job in general came from the 1923 *Sketch Book*, 22: "Our nurse when we are ill; our giver of punishment and reward, when we deserve it; our teacher of etiquette at all times; our college mother, who gives her time to our wants, desires, and troubles, when our own mothers are far away."

would quickly eat onions to deter her from entering their room to investigate.

Day students had things a little easier as they could gingerly go off campus and smoke somewhere no one could see them. "[I] [s]moked down [at] the railroad tracks," Ruth Hoy Diffenderfer '26 mentioned, "if [they] found out that we had smoked, or anybody could prove we were smoking, that's it[!] . . . you were out." The administration asked students to leave if they caught them smoking but smokers sneaked outside or smoked out the dormitory windows until they did get caught. Bryn Mawr only allowed smoking at a designated area after ten years of debate, and after Wellesley instituted a smoking ban in 1918, students crept to the edge of town to light up.[103]

As with the regulations that prohibited smoking, the administration watched student behavior with a careful eye when men were on campus. In the 1800s, men were allowed on women's college campuses only for special occasions like festivals or the several dinners and recitals to which Ege invited the Cumberland Valley Institute boys. But by the 1920s, Campbell and other women's schools gave in to the constant student desire for men to make frequent appearances on campus. Though dances were the high point of year with students inviting dates onto campus, Irving students could not walk off the dance floor or out onto the campus grounds with their dates, so very little happened other than dancing: "If we got a kiss hello that . . . would be about the best for the night."[104] Ballroom dancing with men arrived at many women's colleges throughout the turn of the century, as Smith added men to their prom in 1894, Vassar in 1897, Wellesley in 1913, and Bryn Mawr sponsored its first mixed sex Tea Dance in 1929.[105] Irving probably brought ballroom dancing with men to campus early, accepting the liberal notion with Campbell's arrival as President.[106] Other than the dances and occa-

---

103. Horowitz, 289–292.
104. Oral History, Mary Baylor Havely '29, May 9, 1995.
105. Horowitz, 288.
106. With Methodists squarely against dancing, neither Marlatt or Ege probably would have allowed it, and Kessler probably did not face the issue as few dances and receptions of the like with boys occurred under her. Though officially ballroom dancing could have come to Irving in the early 1900s or 1910s, Campbell's emphasis on student extracurricular activities and social atmospheres may have allowed it in his first year.

sional concert performances by Dickinson College music clubs, men (other than faculty) generally were not on campus. No young man was allowed in a student's room; instead, the student received her visitors in the college parlor, which became a semi-regular occurrence for some. Even if students scheduled prearranged visits, if the student and her date wanted to walk downtown, a chaperone escorted them to the movies, the store, or whatever their pleasure. Though the chaperoning probably alleviated all monkey business on dates, some chaperones were lenient: "[I] saw Grant last night on [M]arket [S]treet. Miss Eicleler [sic] is a peachy chaperone—left us by ourselves. Came home at 12:30."[107] Alcohol became a danger with men from time to time when college boys visited campus: "Several of the Dickinson boys were drunk at the dance on Sat. night[,]"[108] though it probably was not a constant fear of the faculty due to the limited visits by large male groups. Occasionally men apparently sneaked on campus, possibly with the aid of a student, while some students crept out to go meet dates. One such incident involved Marjorie Wise Mohler's, '27, brother Robert, whom all the students at Irving found very handsome. One student sneaked across the street and waited in the vestibule of his house hoping to see him and declare her interest in him. Unfortunately for her, Dr. Campbell later learned about her charade. He prohibited the students from walking on the side of the street which Robert lived since it stood within the two-block radius that the students could travel from campus. Despite the harsh restrictions placed upon Robert's admirers, many students were free of this problem as some students had boyfriends from home that they saw on occasion, and the Irving day students generally did not fall under many of the regulations that Campbell instituted.

Irving erected regulations that mirrored other women's colleges. Campbell and his predecessors greatly frowned upon shopping and many women's colleges did not allow it at all. Students accepted guests in the college parlor and nowhere else; after students began on-campus dating in the 1920s, all dates even took place in the parlor. Wesleyan College in Cincinnati placed stringent rules on students that Campbell and other

---

107. Fisher, Marian Claire, '27. Hymnal Annotation, October 30, 1926, 156.
108. Fisher, Marian Claire, '27. Hymnal Annotation, c. 1922–1926, 225.

administrators were persuaded to lessen by the early 1900s. Similar to Irving with a rising bell, lights out at 10:00 P.M., and no visits to the city without parental consent, Wesleyan also prohibited nicknames to be used between students (which did happen at Irving); no walking, riding, or corresponding with men "other than [their] father, brother, uncle or guardian"[109] and no calls on the Sabbath except in an emergency. Irving and Wesleyan both required daily exercise, all student clothing to have student names, all expensive jewelry to be left at home, no letter writing during designated times (dining and chapel for Irving, on the Sabbath for Wesleyan), and mandatory church attendance on Sundays. Mary Sharp College in Winchester, Tennessee also prohibited student shopping purchases (except with parental permission) and like Irving, requested that any spending money that parents wished to send their daughters be deposited with the president for disbursement at his discretion.

One rule from Campbell warned parents against sending packages of goodies to their daughters, since mass congregation and deterred studying resulted. Regardless of the rule, many students received food from home and gathered Irving friends for a celebration called a "feast." "Tomorrow is the girl next door's birthday, and her mother sent her a monstrous angel food cake, a big box of apples, and a box of home-made fudge. Pauline just brought us each two pieces and then we went over to her room to get a piece of birthday cake."[110] Once a student picked up a package from the mail containing cookies or cakes, a gathering developed in order to make short order of the available treats. A student poem from 1901 best describes a feast:

A Midnight Feast
The light bell had rung, and good-night had been said,
And teachers and pupils had all (?) crept to bed—
The third floor of Columbian Hall, was teacherless that day,
"When the cat's away," you know the mice will always play." [sic]
First, one ghost then another, gilded from her door,
Till six ghosts gathered round a feast spread on the floor.

---
109. Woody, 199.
110. Diary entries of unknown student, October 3, 1925.

> So they reveled and they feasted, and made no noise at all,
> Yet fearing every moment to hear outside, a call.
> Pleasantly the time sped by—some flash-light groups they took,
> And we are very sorry that we can't print them in this book.
> But alas! none were printed, from the ones they took that night,
> For the teachers took the camera, do you think that that was right?
> Every one of those fair revelers a private lecture got,
> Surely 'twas a hardship that fell unto their lot.[111]

In 1906, "onion feasts" became the rage as invitations were passed out or word-of-mouth would pass around the time and place to snack on onions, rolls, butter, and salt for "all who felt the pangs of hunger."[112]

If feasts didn't provide enough food to qualm the collegiate stomachs at Irving between dining periods, then the students took to Mechanicsburg for much-needed sustenance. Since boarding students only had a two-block radius to travel unless chaperoned, Simpson's Grocery, which stood on the northwest corner of Main and Walnut Streets, was one of the only eating places around and thus saw a lot of Irving students. "I can remember Mrs. Simpson making ham and cheese, and I can remember the smell of the pickles. She'd always slice pickles to put into the sandwiches."[113] The student regulations mention Bobb's as an eatery students could also visit since it fell within the two-block radius (see Table 2.2).

Even with the large number of strict regulations, most students seemed satisfied with the school simply because of Dr. Campbell. "Where is the college president that takes such an interest in his own girls as our own Dr.?," asked *The Sketch Book* in 1895.[114] With lectures in Monday morning chapel to inspire students for the week ahead, sleighing in the winter, bicycling after supper on warm spring days, and telling stories during evenings off, Dr. Campbell entertained the students who admired him in return. Being well-liked, students had fond memories of him and

---

111. *Irvingiana '01*, 105.
112. *The Sketch Book*, Vol. VIII, No. 8, May 1906, 13.
113. Oral History, Betty Boffemmyer Stram '29, April 22, 1993.
114. "The Pleasures of an Irving Girl," *The Sketch Book*, Vol. I, No. 4, May 1895, 136.

had funny stories to tell about his humor.[115] One time Marion Strouse Scharf '18, sneaked downtown to the grocery store, bringing back a bag of groceries when she ran into Dr. Campbell at the edge of campus. He asked Marion to come over to him. Terrified, Marion did as he asked and approached Campbell, who only egged her on to try the coconut milk he had instead of scolding her for sneaking off campus as she thought would happen. Campbell did institute a strict rule system, but his sense of humor and general love of humanity made him likable and well-respected among the student body. According to living graduates, Dr. Campbell never treated his own children who attended Irving any better than the remainder of the student body since he considered all the students to be under his care. This probably accounts for his close relationship with so many of his students.

Though many liked Campbell, there did appear to be some students who showed some distress because of the multitude of rules. Marian Claire Fisher '27, frequently complained her senior year about Irving: "oh how happy I am to leave this stupid place [for Christmas],"[116] "Just 4 more weeks. How I hate this place,"[117] but when it came time to graduate, she shared the sentimental feelings that many Irving students showed: "Rev. Trowbridge gave a lovely farewell speech—[at] our very last chapel. Oh, how I hate to say goodbye."[118] Students were willing to abide by Campbell's rules, though they did try to relax them over time, especially in certain areas, though "Dr. Campbell's mind on dancing never change[d]."[119] A strict and tough disciplinarian, Campbell's personality and fun-loving nature created the family atmosphere he wanted and that the students cherished at Irving.

---

115. One interesting story about E. E. Campbell involves a little stray dog that was attached to Campbell and followed him around town. Jane Campbell Beard, '29 remembered the dog during her oral history interview on April 12, 1994: "my father had a little dog that would follow him around and go downtown with him . . . [Even] the street car would stop, and the dog would get on and ride down to the college and they would let the dog off there." The dog became so associated with Dr. Campbell that "[he] was walking down Main Street one day and he heard some woman opening her front door and saying, 'Get out of here Dr. Campbell!' It turned out she was talking to the dog! [She] [c]alled the dog Dr. Campbell too!" E. E. never adopted the dog and Jane believes that it was run over by a train on Main Street.

116. Fisher, Marian Claire, '27. Hymnal Annotation, December 16, 1926, 51.
117. Fisher, Marian Claire, '27. Hymnal Annotation, February 22, 1927, 351.
118. Fisher, Marian Claire, '27. Hymnal Annotation, May 30, 1927, 249.
119. "The Pleasures of an Irving Girl," *The Sketch Book*, Vol. I, No. 4, May 1895, 137.

The arrival of Dr. Campbell to Mechanicsburg helped to create a strong link between the town and the college, and thus the townspeople and the college students. "Everybody liked Dr. Campbell ... the townspeople had great respect for Dr. Campbell, for the girls. It was quite a loss [for the town] when the college closed."[120] "The Irving girls are much in evidence in our beautiful town and the glad hand of welcome is held out to them. They have brought a new life to the streets of the town and stores and shops will joyfully welcome them to their counters."[121] The town and students grew to have a close relationship over the years, with townspeople attending school functions in full force and students patronizing local stores. Brindle's Notions Store was very attached to the Irving girls: "they would sew buttons on for us, do a lot of things for the students that they [the students] couldn't do themselves ... we used to go in there and sit and talk."[122] "[T]he town just packed that chapel when they knew anything ... was going on at the college, they supported us 100%."[123] Attending Commencement services, May Day fetes, and music recitals, Irving offered a variety of entertainment for Mechanicsburg and the town showed their support in return.

Since townspeople and students cohabited well in Mechanicsburg, it is interesting to note the internal relationships among the students at the school. With sororities existing on campus from the late 1800s through the early 1900s, cliques developed on campus even with Irving's small population. With day students left out of the everyday fold, and five-day students missing the weekend social events, cliques very easily could have developed separating further those groups of students. In the late 1920s, the "Four Horsemen" formed on campus, acting as leaders of the student body. "They were kind of special. And they got away with things that the other girls possibly wouldn't."[124] What clubs the student joined, and what courses she enrolled in helped to form the group of girls that would form her clique. "We had groups of girls who flocked together, we had different, little groups of girls."[125] Though no other rumors of

---

120. Oral History, Mary Shope, '26, June 6, 1993.
121. *The Daily Journal*, Vol. II, No. 39, January 9, 1902.
122. Oral History, Marion Strouse Scharf, '18, May 18, 1993.
123. Oral History, Catherine Steck, '18, October 16, 1993.
124. Oral History, Marjorie Wise Mohler '27, February 1, 1995.
125. Oral History, Mary Lu Shaffer Heinze (1925–1927), May 12, 1993.

cliques survived, the volume of unique and small student clubs, their specific interests and special designation, and the multi-separation of the students by student-type, student-class, and student-interest, probably created cliques out of the 100–130 students attending.

Cliques, student clubs, and organized dances tended to be highlights on campus, but as student activities affected only the resident population, greater social events in the country had its effect on the students at Irving as well. As the War Between the States affected the alumnae from Marlatt's tenure, other major events in United States history affected the students of E. E. Campbell. World War I brought out a large amount of active cooperation from Irving College, as faculty and students participated in Liberty Bond sale parades, Red Cross parades, and saved war stamps. "The College is practically 100% in Baby Bonds or Thrift Stamps or Liberty Bonds, and very active in Red Cross work of a practical and helpful sort."[126] Support at Irving was as strong as at other schools as Mount Holyoke, Wellesley, and Vassar students staffed college farms as war work, and Smith alumnae sent a Red Cross relief unit to Europe.[127] The Irving College YWCA supported a French war orphan for two years during the war, the students subscribed and paid $500 to the war fund, and informational brochures circulated around campus asking "What are you going to do to help the boys?"[128] Though the students rallied around the troops in WWI, they did not become involved in the women's suffrage movement. The conservative Irving students did not appear interested in the liberal movement for women's rights or especially the right to vote. Few accounts survive exhibiting a strong feminist opinion on campus. Since most of the students tolerated the strict discipline under the pleasant Dr. Campbell, it eliminated the need to stage campus rallies. The occasional feminist works that do surface in *The Sketch Book* or in commencement essays are more concerned with equal education for men and women than suffrage or other liberal women's issues. Students concentrated more on the everyday campus life than national issues even from their first day of school.

---

126. Irving College Board of Trustees Minutes, June 4, 1918.
127. Horowitz, 286.
128. This Brochure contained informational clippings from papers on soldiers of World War I and editorial jokes about the Kaiser in Germany. Located in Nelle McCracken's Scrap Book, 1917–1918.

When a student arrived on Irving soil for the first time, she was greeted with the family atmosphere that remained throughout the rest of her stay. Usually "canvassed" or visited by Dr. Campbell during her decision process, the new student would become introduced to the president and the college ideals, while her parents would be assured that she would be well taken care of under Campbell's tutelage: "The aim at Irving is to preserve the homelike features so often ignored in 'boarding schools.' Every effort is made to inspire a greater love for parents and home, and to make the school a safe Christian home and a happy family, as well as a place to gain a thorough education."[129] Students often followed their sisters to Irving or heard about the school through word of mouth, college catalogs, and advertisements circulated through prospective households. Upon a student's first September arrival either the preceptress or a residing teacher from the student's hall floor would be there to greet the new student, and the newcomer would be escorted to her newly assigned room. The YWCA also greeted new students, having upperclasswomen available to help with baggage and direct the new students to the college office (on first floor of Irving Hall) to pick up their room keys. Some students sent their trunk ahead of time whereupon they resided in the college office until the students picked them up on moving day. Each student scheduled their classes with an assigned faculty advisor and the new student received notification to look out for the "for sale" signs around campus to pick up bargain books and furniture. School supplies could be purchased at the college office, though a few students purchased their books at secondhand bookstores or from other students. In general, the cost of books usually came out to $25 per year per student, although this certainly varied according to a student's concentration and course load. "[W]e purchased our own books, but they were mostly second-hand books from the girls who'd been there the years before, so that you could buy them inexpensively and then sell them when you left."[130]

After receiving their room assignments, the students moved in, met their roommates, and decorated their rooms. In the 1920s, students littered their rooms with magazine covers and numerous school pennants

---
129. Irving College Catalogue, 1893–1894, 14.
130. Oral History, Mary Lu Shaffer Heinz (1925–1927), May 12, 1993.

representing not only Irving, but nearby men's schools, where they would often visit for weekend football games.[131] Students hung framed pictures on the walls, brought many books, and tended to own Irving blankets, pillows, or paraphernalia showing their school spirit:

> We are trying to fix up our room. Charlotte has one pennant and I have two pictures. The result is handsome. We aren't allowed to use nails so we tried to put our tennis rackets above our beds, held by thumbtacks! Luckily for us, when they fell down we weren't in bed! Hers fell first and the jar [from] it made mine fall. We were both sitting here writing and you should have seen our expressions when it happened.[132]

The college furnished the young women with writing desks, dressers, beds, end tables and chairs, usually made of wood, while providing wallpaper, carpets, draperies, and shutters. Some students were fortunate enough to even have a balcony.

Once settled into their rooms, the college bell woke the students out of their cherished beds at 8:00 A.M. for breakfast followed by 15-minute chapel services, classes, and music practice throughout the remainder of the day. Students often suffered from "The Race Problem — How to dress and get to breakfast in five minutes."[133] But breakfast was not the only meal missed: "Some of the girls of Irving Hall evidently believe that sleep is a great beautifier. They have actually been known to sleep through the dinner hour."[134] Students even raised a riot when Elmer, who was the school caretaker in 1929, rang the breakfast bell ten minutes early, causing most of the students to rush or lose valuable sleep. Students generally had from three to six classes per day, including any practice periods in elocution and music that the student enrolled in (see Appendix B, table 3). With the dinner periods rounding out the day at 5:00 P.M., studying and practicing commenced until every student retired to their room by 9:45 P.M. in order to have their lights

---

131. Irving students often made day trips to especially see Dickinson and Gettysburg football games.
132. Diary entry from an unknown student, September 28, 1925.
133. *Irvingiana '03*, 122.
134. *Irvingiana '03*, 122.

out by 10:00 P.M. Such full schedules left students so little time for studying once meals, a morning chapel service, an afternoon walk, and any extracurricular activities were added to the daily routine. Students attended classes on Saturday mornings, but Mondays tended to have a lighter schedule early in Campbell's tenure. By 1924, Saturday classes became less common (though music classes and practice may have been scheduled on Saturdays), while Mondays entertained a heavier course load (see Appendix B, table 4). The schedule for the college preparatory students, who studied in easier and simpler subject classes than the college level work, was probably just as full and lengthy (see Appendix B, table 5). Specials, who acted as the Irving College continuing education students taking only classes they wanted and earning no specific degree, had a much more open schedule depending on what classes they decided to take (see Appendix B, table 6).

Class sizes ranged from eight to eighteen students with music classes being much smaller, therefore: "You got a lot of personal attention and instruction because the school was so small . . ."[135] Faculty knew the students well and the students benefited from such small classes: "There was about [Irving] an environment of spirit and culture and closeness. It was as much a big family as a school. The teachers had individual understanding of the students and the students knew the teachers personally."[136] When classes commenced, students gathered and waited for the teacher at the appropriate time, but questions arose as to how long students should wait if a professor failed to show up:

> At the hour of 12.15 [*sic*], October 28, six Seniors in cap and gown came into geology class. After waiting a few minutes a dreadful silence ensued, listening for the well known footsteps of the Prof. Suddenly an idea struck the class. In all the annals of Irving it had been the time honored custom to wait ten minutes for the delinquent Prof., and act not a second longer. The breathless silence continued. Watches were held in hand and each fraction of a second jubilantly noted as they passed. At last

---
135. Oral history of Mary Lu Shaffer Heinz (1925–1927), May 12, 1993.
136. Beers, Paul B., Unknown News clipping 1961.

the tenth minute had dragged itself away to join the innumerable army already passed into eternity. Six guilty Seniors stole silently up the back stairs to loaf and eat cake.[137]

[O]ne day at school [Miss Hemminger] didn't came [*sic*] to class . . . I didn't know all these rules, but of course the boarding students did. If we were in the class for ten minutes and the teacher didn't come, we were allowed to leave . . . Some of the girls kept watching, you know, to see what the time was. Actually, I think we stayed a little longer than ten minutes, but after that everybody went . . . After a while Miss Hemminger appeared and we all had to go back to class. She was angry. She was kind of cranky anyhow . . . We didn't know what was going to happen. But we knew [by] the way she talked, we were going to be punished . . . We never got punished . . . Dr. Trowbridge probably interfered and said "No you can't punish them, because that was the rule."[138]

Though a close-knit campus, students maintained age-old traditions of leaving class, knowing quite well that when and if the teacher showed up, he or she immediately knew the deserters.

With social clubs, dances, and food feasts luring students away from their studies, students had to find time to study for classes. Irving's library, which was probably inadequate for the student body, was not a great place to study. Betty Boffemmyer Stram '29, did her studying at the Harrisburg High School library because "[t]here were lots of music students, and the pianos were going, practicing all the time, so it was more or less noisy over there [at the Irving library]." The library had valuable reference materials: *The Encyclopedia Brittanica; the Century*, Webster, and Worcester Dictionaries; *The Dictionary of American Biography*; and Chamber's and Appleton's Encyclopedias, while the reading room had newspapers, journals, church papers, magazines, and other

---

137. *The Sketch Book*, Vol. VI, No. 1, November 1903, 6–7.
138. Oral History, Betty Boffemmyer Stram, '29, April 22, 1993. Betty walked to school with Rev. Trowbridge one morning and they discussed the situation; Trowbridge believed then that Betty and the other students did not do wrong by leaving the class.

college publications. Though described as having "the choicest literature and most wholesome reading," Irving's library seemed small compared to other schools and did not grow much under Campbell's tenure. Ege did add to the college library, increasing it from 1,000 volumes in 1870 to 3,000 volumes in 1874 and 5,000 in 1880 [see table 2.3], the highest number of volumes Irving ever achieved. With 2,000 volumes in 1873, Ege had a college library that reached the higher tier of the smaller and lesser-known female colleges; most of these colleges had five to six hundred volumes.[139] After the school's closing in 1883, Ege must have carted the school's 5,000 volumes with him, and since he officially owned the books and Irving, he could do with them as he pleased. He may even have sold them in order to pay some debt, leaving Kessler and Campbell to start from scratch with the library. In 1900, the library is listed as having 1,000 volumes, while Wellesley had 52,335, Vassar 38,000, Bryn Mawr 33,753, Radcliffe 17,000, Elmira 6,070, and Smith 7,500. It is interesting to note that for the first 25 years of Campbell's tenure, the library holdings did not increase significantly, despite Campbell's widespread growth through other areas of the school. It certainly appears that the school could afford 5,000 volumes (or at least 2,500) and it is interesting to consider why Campbell did not increase the number of books and publications. The library's size became a key issue in the closing of the school in 1929 despite several gifts of books from alumnae.

TABLE 2.3. IRVING COLLEGE'S LIBRARY HOLDINGS. The following is a listing of the number of volumes in the Irving College library for selected years as obtained through the *Commissioner's Reports to the U.S. Board of Education*, from 1868–1929.

Year	Number of Volumes	Year	Number of Volumes
1870	1,000	1894	1,000
1873	2,000	1895	800

---

139. According to the *Commissioner's Report to the U.S. Board of Education*, there were several colleges and seminaries among these smaller Division B schools (Vassar, Smith, Elmira, and others of the like were Division A) that had a large number of volumes. Oakland Female Institute in Norristown, Pennsylvania, had no state charter, but had 11,500 volumes. The Moravian Seminary for Young Ladies in Bethlehem had 4,700 volumes, though no students in a collegiate department.

1874	3,000	1896	1,000
1880	5,000	1900	1,000
1888	200	1902	1,200
1889	50	1903	1,000
1891	300	1913	1,100
1892	500	1915	1,000

Campbell did provide a library for students to study in (whether they used it or not) as students had to take advantage of what study time they could with their busy schedules, being in a classroom or at a meal for most of the day. The students got from class to class and from breakfast to dinner through the help of a bell system, which was very similar to what other schools of the time also had in place. Originally, the ends and beginnings of class periods were signified by a metal bell that hung in the cupola above Irving Hall. Campbell had an interior and most likely an electric bell system installed during his tenure for more modern and accurate timekeeping. After the bell and the cupola were removed from Irving Hall at the college's closing, the Campbell family donated the bell to the Washington Fire Co. in Mechanicsburg, who still owns the bell today. The bell acted as a signal for students to follow their rigid school schedules.

When the dining bell tolled, students entered the dining hall and took seats at the ten or so tables situated within. A faculty member sat at each of the student tables, monitored the behavior and manners of the students, and rotated responsibilities for leading the prayer to start the meal. Occasionally, if a faculty member was absent from the dining hall, she would ask a student to be at the head of the table and lead in the prayer. The faculty members rotated around the different tables (which were probably organized by the different floors or sections of the dormitories) in the course of a year, and only they or a senior were allowed to talk with the staff working. Most of the staff, from in-town Mechanicsburg, often served soup and chicken pot pie in enormous tureens for dinner, bringing one for each table, or serving fresh strawberries and whipped cream for occasional breakfasts.[140] The Campbell family resided at their own table in the dining room where they ate meals right along with the students. Meals were not included in the prices for day students, so they either ate in town (Simpson's Grocery being the closest eatery in the 1920s) or brought pack lunches to eat in the "day student room," which was the first-floor parlor in Irving Hall to the right of the entrance.

Local merchants delivered food for the Dining Hall to Irving on a daily basis depending on what was needed for that day or week. Milk came most days early in the afternoon from Mr. Weber, while Simpson's and other local grocers delivered the additional needed foods. About every month Irving spent $5.00 for 100 lbs. of sugar, $75.00 for groceries, $40.00 for meat, $5.00 for Coal Oil, and anywhere from $65.00–$85.00 for anthracite or bituminous coal (depending on what was available) to heat the school.[141] In 1894, Campbell spent $30.59 on milk, $30.60 on coffee, $20.50 on gas, $107.79 for meat, and $85.00 for a new gas range. The large amount of sugar suggests a good deal of baking at Irving for students' meals and events, while milk appears to have been the staple drink for the students and coffee for the faculty. Ice cream was certainly the hot commodity among Irving students, especially with an ice cream manufacturer in town. Rakestraw's ran a company store at the southern end of town, but since students were not allowed past the two-block radius of campus without faculty supervision, most students sneaked to the ice cream parlor during organized walks in the afternoon or at any opportune time. A special treat was when deliveries of Rakestraw's Ice Cream showed up on campus (generally on Monday and Wednesday), coming in metal containers packed in ice inside a wooden bucket.

Chapel services, which would go on directly after breakfast, were a method of getting the entire student body together for announcements, prayer, and starting the day. Chapel resembled a Lutheran service and was led by one of the ministerial faculty or sometimes by Dr. Campbell. Forced out of their warm beds probably far earlier than each wanted, the students often stayed awake in chapel if only to converse back and forth through their hymnals. Since the students had to maintain a quiet and proper demeanor during the service, students would communicate with

---

140. In Marian Claire Fisher's annotations in her hymnal, she mentions having fresh strawberries and whipped cream for breakfast in 1925 while sitting at Miss Hade's table.
141. Irving College Account Book, 1891.

each other by writing notes in each other's hymnals and then switching them when no teacher was looking. Marian Claire Fisher '27, kept many notations regarding parties, weekend plans, and any letters from boys within her hymnal, which contained several writings each week for the four years she attended Irving. Since each student received their own hymnal for singing during chapel services, many students gossiped during chapel using this method.

Sometimes as a part of chapel, and often after, students would sing Irving songs. Whether the singing included the alma mater or other such student favorites as "Dear Old Irving," "Irving Must Shine," or "Rah for the Gold and the Blue," they raised student spirit at class day, during receptions, at parties, and at Irving sporting events (see table 2.4). The alma mater for Irving (see table 2.5) was written by an Irving student, Lenore Embick Flower, '04, apparently during her senior year at the college. Before Embick, the school appears not to have incorporated an official alma mater, though other frequently sung songs may have unofficially acted as such.

TABLE 2.4. IRVING SONGS, 1923. The following songs were taken from the *Student's Handbook* of the Irving YWCA, 1923, pages 14–17.

DEAR OLD IRVING
Here's to Irving, Dear old Irving—
You're the one that's got the rep;
You're the one that's got the pep.
Here's to Irving, dear old Irving,
And the others find it hard to keep in step.

IRVING MUST SHINE
Irving must shine tonight
Irving must shine; [repeated twice]
When the sun goes down and the moon comes up,
Irving must shine.

O ME! O MY!
O me! O my!
We'll get there by and by;
If anybody loves old Irving,
It's I, I, I, I, I.

WE'VE GOT PEP
They say that our Irving, it ain't got no pep;
It's got pep in every step [repeated twice]
[repeat]

[UNTITLED]
Irving girls, Irving girls,
Irving girls are we,
Always singing merrily,
Irving dear to thee.

Oh, we've got pep;
we've got pep;
We've got knowledge too,
And we'll always give the honor,
Irving dear to you.

A COLLEGE GIRL
I want to be a college girl,
Mm, and a little bit more.
I want to be an Irving girl,
Mm, and a little bit more.
I want to be a Y. W. girl,
Mm, then I'll ask no more,
For I've got all that's coming to me—
Mm, and a little bit-mm,
And a little bit, mm, and a little bit more.

RAH FOR THE GOLD AND THE BLUE
Rah! Rah! Rah! Rah!
Rah! for the gold and the blue!
[repeat]

TABLE 2.5. IRVING COLLEGE'S ALMA MATER. Written by Lenore Embick Flower, Class of 1904.

IRVING COLLEGE ALMA MATER (to the tune of "Maryland, My Maryland")	
Dear Alma Mater! 'tis to thee We raise our songs of loyalty. Our steadfast hearts shall ever be Thy bulwark of security.	Oh, Alma Mater tried and true, Our hearts turn ever back to you. May years increasing to you bring More honors than we e'er could sing.
Dear Mother Irving! thee we love, Thy pennant proudly hold above. Thy daughters ever faithful are Though scattered wide in lands afar.	Oh blessed ties thus formed by thee Of friendship and sincerity! Thy daughters all revere thy name And seek to add to thy just fame.
Sacred is each ivied wall, Each aged tree and classic hall, With memories mingled sad and gay Of school time grand or festal day.	Then here's to thee, Old Irving dear, The mother whom we all revere While thou shalt live, till time shall end, Thy daughters will thy name defend.

Though the schedule for students was rather rigid, many found time to horse around during their free time. "A real fun time . . . was getting together each evening after dinner for an hour in the chapel, when we danced with each other. Good piano music was provided by one of the girls, a music major, who could play a tune called for by ear."[142] As the train traveled through downtown Mechanicsburg, "[r]ight at the side of the school they crossed over the highway, and blew the whistle and we used to let off steam at the top of our voices when the whistle blew."[143] Though the administration looked down on card-playing, games like pinochle and checkers were a way to spend free time. Flag battles between classes with their respective flags occurred at several points in Irving's history, with one year's battle resulting in the changing and swiping of others' class flags on a flagpole on Irving Hall's roof. One prank developed into a repeated ritual:

> There was a sign near the top of the main building stating that the college had been "Founded by Solomon P. Gorgas." We

---
142. Oral History, Catherine Steck (1915–1918), October 16, 1993.
143. Oral History, Mary Lu Shaffer Heinz (1925–1927), May 12, 1993.

had gone up to the third floor to get some props for a play and strangely enough had some plaster of paris with us. Inasmuch as I was the smallest among the girls, they held me out of a window by my heels and I covered "P. Gorgas" with the plaster of paris. This the sign read, "Founded by Solomon."[144]

This prank evolved over time as one time the students also covered up the "Fe" on the sign to read: "Irving male College, Founded by Solomon."

Though students planned pranks, attended classes, and studied together, Irving students established their own unique existence through their class year. Fierce competition existed between first-year students and the sophomores, as each usually teamed up with the juniors and seniors respectively, bragging about their winning basketball team, stellar grades, or victory in some school contest. Competition often appeared rather humorously in school publications, with one class poking fun at another. In *Irvingiana '07*, the junior class predicted the professions of graduating seniors, who were thought to be "washing dishes," the "leading lady in a 10¢ show," "keep[ing] house for some one's brother in New York," and even a "YWCA secretary in Honolulu." Each class had its own elected officers (president, vice-president, secretary, treasurer) which included a class historian to write class achievements and stories for *The Sketch Book* or the *Irvingiana*, and a class poet to write the class poem. Class flags, class colors, class flowers, class mottoes, and even class constitutions all supplemented those of the college, to add pride and prestige to one's own class. Some classes even had their own yells, though the Irving yell was used a great deal too:

Rickety, rackety, Sis, boom, bah! Irving, Irving!
Rah, rah, rah![145]

Billa-billoo, billa-billee,
Ziga-marag, ziga-maree, Who are you? Who are we?
Irving, Irving,
I. C.[146]

---

144. News Clipping, Hagee, Dorothy. "Days at the Morn," August 19, 1967.
145. *Irvingiana '03*, 11.
146. *Irvingiana '03*, 11.

Most of these activities from *The Sketch Book* to Halloween parties essentially engulfed the extracurricular life of Irving's boarding students. Often times, the other students who attended Irving—day students and specials—were not a part of these events since their time on campus could be rather limited. Day students came from the surrounding area taking the train to Irving for the day, not staying in the dormitories and not eating in the dining hall. These commuters suffered from a lack of Irving exposure and were often not included in social activities because they would go home once their classes ended. "It was not a good arrangement for the day students . . . I think we were ignored a great deal. I don't think we knew a lot of the things that were going on, it was never explained [made apparent] to us."[147] As day students, "you missed a great deal . . . because things would go on after dinner in the evening . . ." though the commuters had opportunities to use the athletic facilities and were required to attend chapel in the morning.[148] Being largely separated from campus life, some day students even felt alienated from Dr. Campbell: "he would talk with you if you got right up to him . . . [but] he never went out of his way, as far as I know, to bother with the girls. He may have with the girls that lived there, but as far as the day students, . . . I don't think he did."[149] Day students hung out in the first-floor parlor of Columbian Hall during their off-time, which had an inconvenient bathroom located on the second floor at the opposite end of the building. Some of the day students felt ostracized by the boarding students, though they agreed it was not intentional. Some day students did get involved with different activities, though it appeared that the boarding students tended to be the presidents of the organizations, the editors of the publications, and the lead roles in the presentations. Acting much like the commuters of modern-day colleges, the day students would have little time during busy school days to socialize with anyone but other commuters, some of which even walked home for lunch.

There were five-day students who did stay overnight, but only through the five days of classes, traveling home each weekend. This five-day approach apparently arrived late in Irving's existence, although with

---

147. Oral History, Ruth Hoy Diffenderfer, '26, June 9, 1993.
148. Oral History, Ruth Hoy Diffenderfer, '26, June 9, 1993.
149. Oral History, Ruth Hoy Diffenderfer, '26, June 9, 1993.

the college's open approach to admitting all sorts of women, it may have been a process that had been in place for some time. After 1914, students who came to Irving for five days paid a reduced rate and left their dorm rooms empty on the weekends. Even with more exposure to the other boarding students, these five-day students also felt estranged since the majority of school events occurred Friday night through Sunday, and the rigorous student schedule left little time for socializing during weekday evenings.

Day students had more freedom than the boarders did since they could walk to school and leave once class was over, therefore enabling them to walk where they wanted and not answering to Dr. Campbell. Specials on the other hand were a unique brand of student that sometimes took one class or a group of classes rather than falling into a hard course structure. "Who would not be a special? It is like going into a café. You look at the *menu*; you really do not care for anything, not even one of the French *entrées*. You tell the waiter you want a special order. He brings it to you and you enjoy it, all but the price. We have nothing to do with the making of that."[150] Even though students labeled as specials chose particular studies that filled their needs, like the boarding students they lived in the dormitories and participated in school events, though without a rigid schedule to burden them. With a flexible choice of courses, specials had an open schedule for taking them over time: "Now an honorable Senior leaves for good, forever, but the special, like the cat, comes back." [see Appendix B, table 6][151] Women who prepared for teaching could, with Kessler's advice in 1890, "select such studies from the regular course as will thoroughly equip them for this profession; or, by a judicious selection of studies prepare themselves for any special line of work."[152] With Kessler's help, the future for some teachers and many domestic science and secretarial students was established, since students could come in, take classes in those areas, and leave for a job.

Since they really did not fit into one class, specials had their own class flag, color, flower, and yell, elected their own student officers, and

---

150. "Why I am a Special," *The Sketch Book*, Vol. I, No. 2, March 1895, 72.
151. "Why I am a Special," *The Sketch Book*, Vol. I, No. 2, March 1895, 73.
152. Irving College Catalog, 1890–91, 8.

originated from different parts of the Eastern U.S. like the regular course girls. Specials sometimes sponsored their own activities, such as in 1923 when they promoted a picnic at Boiling Springs for the second-year girls, a hare-hound chase to Silver Springs, and a St. Patrick's Day dance.[153] Specials, as a group, tended not to organize these social activities as often as other student groups, as a comment after a February 1904 reception notes: "Not for years have the 'Specials' taken any prominent social part in the college world as a class. The evening was very delightfully spent . . ."[154] Though the specials developed their own identifiable clan, their variability changed from year to year, making the specials in certain years small enough in numbers that receptions and parties probably were not a viable or necessary option [see Appendix B, table 8].

Because Irving was a small school, Irving students were a tight bunch, and circulated a class letter from student to student over the summer to find out about everyone, with each student writing something of general interest. This closeness grew into a strong Alumnae Association and several Irving clubs across Pennsylvania. The Alumni Association started in 1879, had 37 students paying dues 20 years later, and rose to 169 by 1920 (see table 2.6). The Association held an annual meeting in June which often featured entertainment by graduates and awards to current students for essays or grade achievement. Several alumnae clubs existed for Irving in addition to the Alumnae Association, which only included graduates. The Pittsburgh Irving College Club (PICC) began in 1914 and held monthly gatherings of former students from around the Pittsburgh area. Other regional clubs formed sponsoring luncheons and receptions in the central Pennsylvania area, in Philadelphia, Altoona, and one nearly started in York. As the school closed, interest in the school waned, and graduates slowly passed away, until by the 1960s the clubs began to dissipate, and the Alumnae Association eventually began admitting nongraduates. The Reunion Club, organized in 1940, met since 1944 at the Allenberry Playhouse in Boiling Springs with about ten members still attending each year into the 1990s. The Reunion Club

---

153. The hare-hound race pitted two groups against each other to race to Silver Springs (depending where exactly, it was probably 2–5 miles) with the hares starting first and the hounds second trying to catch them. On this day, the hares arrived at the point first where bacon and "doggies" were cooking.

154. *The Sketch Book*, Vol. VI, No. 4, February 1904, 6.

and Alumnae Association show the great interest of the graduates in the school (see table 2.7) with 83% of the graduates of the years 1895–1929 being involved in the school at the alumnae level.

The alumnae offered different gifts and scholarships to the school over time beginning with a $100 scholarship to an Irving student in 1923. The scholarship was suspended over the Great Depression but evolved into a scholarship for a senior graduate of Mechanicsburg High School.[155] The Association awarded a bronze tablet in 1920 to three alumnae for their recognition of service during WW I, donated 450 volumes of books worth $300 on Washington Irving's birthday in 1929, and another 1,873 volumes and $100 to purchase "technical research books" just two months before the school closed.

Table 2.6. MEMBERS OF THE IRVING COLLEGE ALUMNAE ASSOCIATION. This table is a measure of how many alumnae paid dues during each year to the Alumnae Association as recorded in the Association's account books. Though it seems quite possible that the Association had higher numbers in certain years, the account book lists only those former students who paid dues in those particular years.

Year	Number of Members	Year	Number of Members
1891	16	1912	96
1892	20	1913	99
1893	24	1914	94
1894	30	1915	95
1895	35	1916	148
1896	42	1917	113
1897	47	1918	116
1898	49	1919	135
1899	37	1920	169
1900	38	1921	135

---

155. Decided at a Reunion Club meeting in 1965, the scholarship was originally $125 which was first awarded to senior Peggy Nailor in 1967.

1901	7[156]	1922	122
1902	2	1923	144
1903	NA	1924	173
1904	NA	1925	160
1905	69	1926	155
1906	84	1927	166
1907	63	1928	156
1908	56	1929	135
1909	91	1930	17
1910	78	1931	78
1911	95	1932	53

TABLE 2.7. IRVING COLLEGE REUNION CLUB MEMBERS BY CLASS. The following table outlines how many of the graduates from each year were members of the Alumnae Association/Reunion Club from 1859-1929 as compared with the number of students who graduated from Irving that year. This material was taken from the listing of graduates given in the annual college catalogs, and from the Association's account books.

Class Year	Number of Graduate Members	Number of Graduates	Class Year	Number of Graduate Members	Number of Graduates
1859	4	14	1898	18	18
1860	5	17	1899	15	17
1861	3	10	1900	14	15
1862	3	8	1901	13	16
1863	NA	6	1902	21	24
1864	2	10	1903	13	16
1865	2	10	1904	13	13
1866	4	7	1905	15	15
1867	5	9	1906	14	17

---

156. The membership dues paid in 1901 and 1902 show only 7 and 2 people respectively which probably are far too small. Since both 1903 and 1904 have no listings, the information for these four years could have been recorded in another account book or just not recorded.

Year			Year		
1868	1	5	1907	17	19
1869	1	2	1908	16	17
1870	2	6	1909	19	21
1871	8	3	1910	18	23
1872	NA	6	1911	12	14
1873	4	6	1912	12	16
1874	3	5	1913	18	20
1875	2	3	1914	14	17
1876	3	4	1915	16	17
1877	4	4	1916	21	21
1878	5	6	1917	29	30
1879	4	4	1918	29	31
1880	1	5	1919	14	18
1881	4	6	1920	22	23
1882	2	3	1921	19	21
1890	2	2	1922	35	35
1891	4	4	1923	20	24
1892	6	6	1924	22	22
1893	6	6	1925	14	19
1894	4	5	1926	37	37
1895	5	6	1927	21	22
1896	9	10	1928	18	20
1897	12	13	1929	18	19
			Totals	717	855[157]

Though most Irving students went on to become teachers and a few organists, piano teachers, and clerks, a few graduates made a measure of fame and notoriety. Jane Deeter Rippin '02, went on to become the head of the Girls Scouts of America, traveling to Europe to meet with

---

157. Though the number of graduates listed in this chart equate to more than 855, there were repeating graduates in the college catalogue listings since many students graduate from several courses in consecutive years. Taking this into account, there are a total of 855 persons who graduated from Irving College.

similar organizations across the ocean. Jane also pioneered Philadelphia probation work through the Steighton Farms charity and at the Court of Domestic Relations. Ida G. Kast '92, became the first woman to practice law in Cumberland County, being admitted to the bar in 1896. Though originally not allowed to become a lawyer, she petitioned "The Board of examiners for Law Students" to allow her to take a preliminary test before being registered as a law student and when this was turned down, she filed another petition. With the local press behind her, on March 15, 1894, the appeals court ruled in her favor stating, "as the Supreme Court of our State has admitted a Lady to its Bar we are not disposed to refuse the prayer of this applicant."[158] In 1900, she was admitted to practice before the Pennsylvania Supreme Court in Harrisburg. Mary Baylor Havely '29, graduated in an accelerated course in home economics (three years instead of four) and later became the head dietician at Hahnemann University Hospital in Philadelphia, Elizabeth Zug '28, became an exceptional concert pianist, and Jean Dodge Keet '25, (the 1925 May Queen) wrote for *The Harrisburg Evening News* as the social page editor.

Students planning on attending Irving faced tuition that was not as exorbitant as other schools, though it did rise periodically. Beginning at $40 for tuition in the Collegiate Department per term (room and board were $120 extra) in Marlatt's tenure, by the closing of Irving's doors, tuition stood at $150 per year for the Academic Course (while room and board were $425) [see table 2.8]. Irving fared well in competition with other schools' tuition costs. In 1857, tuition at Mount Holyoke was $80 and it rose to $125 by the Civil War, while Irving's costs were $60 through 1867. Wellesley charged students $300 in 1881, and about that time Radcliffe instruction cost $400, while Irving ranged from $250–320 around 1870 (those figures probably including room and board). In 1905, Smith charged $100 for its student tuition, the University of Michigan $30, and Irving about $50. Barnard College in New York City charged $150 in 1914, Cornell, who had then opened to women, charged $150 in 1917, while Irving probably cost between $50–100, though student costs in college catalogues included one flat

---

158. Letter from Reunion Club to its members, August 20, 1983.

price. Around the time of Irving's closing, tuition was at $150, while Sarah Lawrence College in Bronxville, New York charged about $1,600, and Bennington College in Vermont charged a similar $1,675. Though initially students could pay for only one term at a time, during the Ege administration, students had to put up the tuition and board money for the entire year at the outset. Tuition costs were often included with room and board costs in college catalogues and this price often covered the fuel costs, clothes washing, class elocution, steam heat, physical culture, and by the 1870s, modern foreign language. Irving tuition was at a reduced rate for minister's daughters (free by 1895) and for sisters of current students, who received a discount.

Costs other than tuition also had to be covered by the student. Though schoolbooks and stationery were included with tuition prices in Ege's tenure, Campbell-era students purchased their books at city retail prices at the college office, though it was possible to receive used copies of texts from older students. "Graduation costs" were introduced in 1861, probably to cover caps, gowns, and printing diplomas. A $2 medical services cost appeared in 1867 and a $1 offering was recommended for a student's seat in the church of their choice (attendance for students was mandatory). Any meals sent to a student's room, any extra laundry washed, private elocution classes (as opposed to the public class), and rooming in the dorm over the Easter and Christmas holidays all involved extra fees. Music and drawing classes meant extra costs until music was incorporated as its own specialty course in 1903. At this time, the music course was listed at the same tuition price as the regular curriculum, without as strong of an emphasis on the classics and college courses (an art course also was developed along the same lines). By the 1920s, courses in elocution, art, violin, secretaryship, and domestic science were offered and regular college course students could take these for an extra fee. Music students had their own fees to handle in addition to the course tuition, paying not only for the use of their instruments, but also for additional practice time, harmony and theory classes, and if so chosen, the benefit of studying under the Music Director (as opposed to his or her assistants).

Student Life, 1856-1929

TABLE 2.8. COSTS AT IRVING, 1857-1929. Taken from the college catalogues, college prices are listed for a variety of college offerings from the school's second year until its closing. Due to the lack of a comprehensive collection of catalogues, some years are absent. In order to save space only years where prices changed are included, therefore, years are in sequence but experience gaps. A double asterisk [**] indicates that the particular price is included in the Room/Board price. All prices listed correspond to an entire school year. The 1872-1873 and 1878-1879 school years were obtained through: U.S. Commissioner of Education. *Report to the Board of Education*, Washington, D.C.: U.S. Government Printing Office, 1873, 660 [1879, 524]. A section symbol [§] in the table indicates an approximation.

Year	Tuition	Room/Board	Instrumental Music[159]	Modern Language	Vocal Music[160]
1857-1858	$ 40	$ 120	$ 40	$ 20	$ 4
1861-1862	50[161]	120	40	20	10
1867-1868	**	250	50	**	10
1869-1870	**	250	50	**	10
1871-1872	**	300[162]	50	**	25
1872-1873	80[163]	220	50§	**	30§
1877-1878	80	270	50§	**	35§
1888-1889	50**[164]	250[165]	50	**	40
1889-1890	**	225	50[166]	**	50
1895-1896	50	175	50	**	50
1900-1901	**	250	50[167]	**	50

159. Piano appears the most frequent in college catalogues, so its price is used for this particular table though mandolin, guitar, organ, and other instruments were offered at different times.
160. Private lessons for vocal music began in 1867–1868 and cost $10 in that year. In 1869–1870 it rose to $20, and in 1871–1872, to $25. From 1888 on the private lesson price for vocal music is listed in the chart, as no apparent non-private lesson is listed.
161. Includes Stationery and Penmanship.
162. Includes schoolbooks and stationery in addition to tuition.
163. Prep students paid a $50 tuition in 1872–1873 and 1877–1878.
164. Tuition for non-primary day students is $50 per year, though this cost is included in the room\board price for boarding students. The number is included here for reference.
165. Includes board, washing, a furnished room, fuel, light, tuition, Latin, French, German, and Freehand Drawing.
166. A $10 fee for use of pianos begins to be charged in addition to the $50 course fee in 1889–1890.
167. Beginning in 1900–1901 the student is charged $3.50 for each practice periods of 45 minutes for the year. The $10 instrument rental fee is now either incorporated in the room/board price or done away with altogether.

1901-1902	50[168]	200[169]	50[170]	**	50
1903-1904	**	275	**[171]	**	**
1906-1907	**	300	**	**	**
1908-1909	50	250	50	**	50
1910-1911	50	250	60[172]	**	50
1913-1914	**	325[173]	350[174] 375	**	60
1917-1918	**	400[175]	425[176] 450	**	425[177]
1918-1919	**	400	450[178]	**	450
1919-1920	**	450	500	**	500
1925-1926	150[179]	400	150[180]	**	150[180]
1926-1927[181]	150	425	150[182]	**	150

---

168. Includes French and German languages.

169. Includes a room furnished and attended, steam heat, electric light, laundry, physical culture (physical education), class elocution, use of the library and other privileges. A $5 charge is added to those students who remain in the dorm rooms over the Christmas and Easter holidays.

170. There is a $7.00 charge for the use of pianos with any additional practices beyond the normal allotment costing another $7.00.

171. Students taking the music or vocal music courses are still paying the $50 fee put in place before since it is now incorporated in the room/board price. However, should the student wish to take the academic course in addition to music, an additional $25 is charged. In 1905–1906 this price is raised to $50, while the price remains at $50 for 1906–1907.

172. Piano lessons are now being taught by the music director, therefore the higher price for piano than vocal music.

173. The boarding student is charged $325 whether they enroll in the Collegiate (Academic) Course, the Elocution Course, the Art Course, or the Violin Course.

174. The instrumental music price listed is now independent of the room/board price, as this column of the table includes the entire room/board and music course price until 1925. $350 is the price for preparatory and freshmen music students, $375 is for sophomore, junior and senior music students.

175. In addition to the College, Elocution, Art and Violin Courses, the Secretarial, China Decoration, and Public-School Music courses are added costing a boarding student $400 each.

176. $425 is for prep and first-year students, $450 for sophomores, junior and seniors.

177. Vocal Music is now independent in the table from the room/board column. Students who take the Vocal Music course now pay $425 for room, board, and the course while academic boarding students who do not take music pay $400.

178. Regardless of which area of music the student takes, or the class of the student, she is charged $450 for room, board, and the course.

179. $150 is the tuition price for the regular Collegiate Course, or the Private Elocution, Home Economics, or Secretarial Courses.

180. Music and Vocal Music are once again charged separately from the room/board price. $150 allows the student to take one of the following courses: Piano Forte, Pipe Organ, Violin, or Voice Culture (Vocal Music).

181. The last two years of Irving's existence also have these same tuition and board prices.

182. This price enables the student to work under the assistants to the Music Dean, though an $175 tuition fee can be paid instead to study directly with the Music Dean.

Unlike today, Irving students of the nineteenth and early twentieth centuries could not expect scholarship money to help pay tuition. However, in 1920, certain alumnae instituted a scholarship program to help incoming or current students, giving four different students $100 each. The scholarship money, which came from the Alumnae Association, the Pittsburgh Irving Club, the York Irving Club, and individual donors acted as an interest-free loan instead of grant money at the student's disposal. "In each case $100.00 is advanced to a deserving student, for the year, and later when she earns her own money, she is expected to return the amount, and then this sum returns to help other students."[183] How long this "scholarship" lasted or whether any student ever paid back the money provided is unknown, but it is the only mention of any financial aid for students. No living graduate in the 1990s knew of any available scholarships or loans.

---

183. Irving College Board of Trustees Minutes, June 1, 1920.

An 1876 view of Irving College.

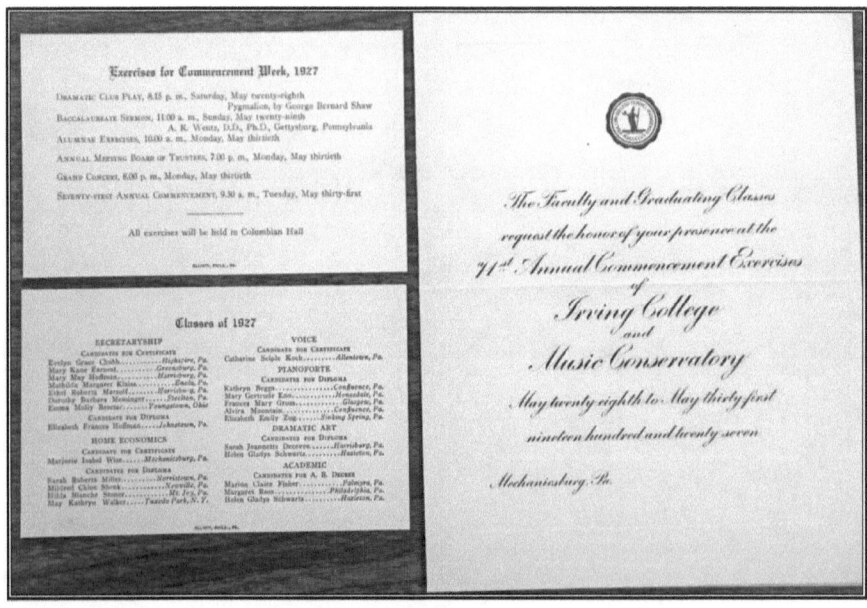

A commencement announcement and invitation for Irving College in 1927.

Cover of the sheet music for the song "Silver Spring," which features an engraving of Irving College. Though the song was not specifically about the college, the publisher used an engraving of Irving Hall as its main image.

General Robert Charles Anderson, the general in charge of the militia stationed at Fort Sumpter when it was fired upon to start the Civil War. Anderson had a unique visit with multiple Irving students on a Cumberland Valley Railroad train in 1861, months after defending the fort from Confederate armies.

The Sketch Book, the literacy magazine of students at Irving College. Named after one of Washington Irving's most famous works, the student publication began in 1895 and was published intermittently until the college closed in 1929.

Student Life, 1856-1929

The Eta Nu sorority at Irving College in 1912. Originally titled the Gorgas Literary Society, Eta Nu was one of Irving College's longest lasting sororities, though had a literary focus and even held mock elections.

An Irving College basketball team, ca. 1920s. Students at Irving largely did not play collegiately versus other schools (since the college lacked in competitive athletic facilities), but sports such as tennis and basketball were popular among students.

Class Day festivities at Irving College, ca. 1920s. Activities varied from year to year for the event with classes often having their own song, cheers and colors, but some Class Day events featured plays where students portrayed members of the faculty or involved ceremonial plantings on the campus.

Cast members of a play at Irving College, ca. 1920s. Students were involved in sorts of extracurricular activities from music concerts, holiday events, dances and even dramatic plays.

An Irving student pretending to blow a trumpet for May Day festivities at the College. The pageantry of the annual May Day event involved the crowning of a May Queen, dancing around the May pole and dramatic stories that usually centered around the return of spring.

Irving students visiting Mount Vernon in Virginia, ca. 1910s. Irving students often traversed off campus for football games at neighboring men's colleges, to perform concerts at Mechanicsburg churches or even to visit places such as Harper's Ferry, Gettysburg or Mount Vernon.

Irving students, ca. 1910s. Women from various states and even other countries came to attend college at Irving. Though most students boarded on campus, others were day students from in town who walked to the college from their homes and 'specials' had a modified curriculum that suited their need whether even if it was only one class.

Student Life, 1856-1929 165

Dr. E.E. Campbell, President of Irving College from 1891–1917, 1918–1926. Campbell enforced a strict discipline among students at the college and the "policy of the school as to discipline is to appeal to the noble quality of the girls and to trust to their honor instead of continuously being on the watch."

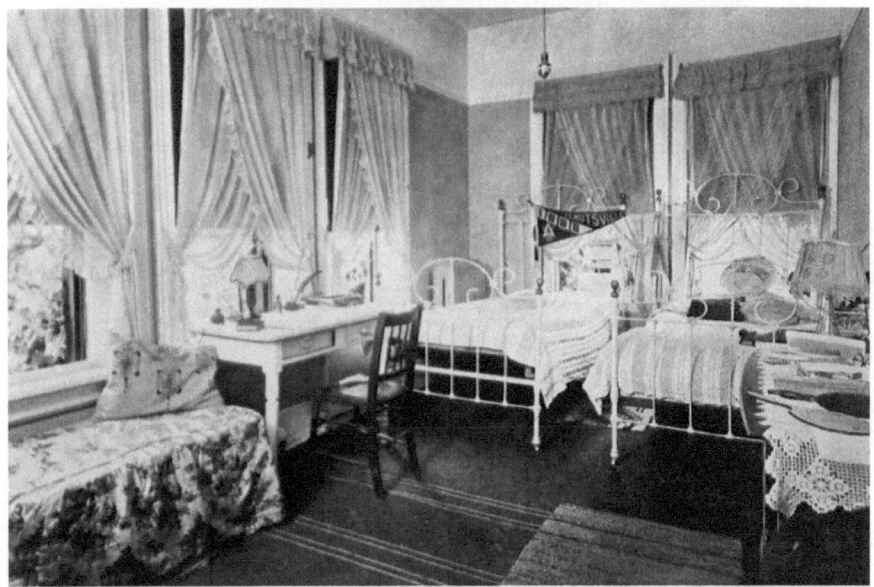

A typical student room at Irving College. Students had a floor monitress among their student body that followed up on chapel attendance, lights out and other disciplinary actions to ensure students stuck to their studies.

Seems Like Old Times

Among those gathering for the Irving College Reunion Club's recent get-together at Allenberry were, in front row, Mabel Bottomley of Danville, left, and Eva Sprenkle Laver of Camp Hill, both members of the Class of 1917. Behind them are Nellie Ray Burchfield of Wilmington, Del., left, Class of 1922; and Matilda Klaiss of Harrisburg, president of the club.

Several Irving alumnae gathering for a reunion in 1982. Various Irving clubs started around the state and former students held reunions long after the college closed. Many former students joined the alumnae organizations and also tried to restart the college after it closed.

CHAPTER THREE

COURSE CURRICULUM, 1856–1929

> Among the many excellencies of Irving there is none to which she points with greater pride than her atmosphere of honest hard work . . .
>
> —*Greater America Magazine*, 1899[1]

CURRICULUM IN IRVING'S EARLY DAYS, 1856–1883

Curriculum at many of the first women's colleges stood far below standards for men's schools. Though the institutions often called themselves colleges, they were only so in name; their curriculum tended to be less rigorous than even women's seminaries. Classes in Latin, Greek, and the sciences—the foundation of men's colleges in the nineteenth and early twentieth centuries—were often absent from women's colleges, or minimally offered. In the first fifty years of women's higher education, most women's colleges required some Latin, Greek, English literature, composition, and grammar, in addition to algebra, geometry, history, and geography, but the schools offered them on a lesser scale than did men's colleges. The Georgia Female College, the first so-named women's college founded, required only reading, writing, English grammar, and

---

1. *Greater America*, 3.

arithmetic for entrance in 1842, requirements far below those of most female seminaries of the time. Oxford Female College required no Latin or Greek in 1855, but they made up for it with a very good classical curriculum which nonetheless was below that of men's colleges of the time. Ohio Wesleyan Female College required proficiency in reading, arithmetic, geography, grammar, physiology, and penmanship for admission in 1853, and Elmira College, having the strongest entrance requirements of the time, required knowledge of analysis, arithmetic, Roman and Greek antiquities, English grammar, algebra, geography, rhetoric, Latin grammar, natural philosophy, criticism, the *Aeneid*, physiology, anatomy, bookkeeping, hygiene, knowledge of the Bible, and zoology in 1855.

When Irving opened in 1856, its entrance requirements were not very strong in relation to the so-called women's colleges of the time, but the requirements for its A.B. degree were on par with other schools [see table 3.1]. Though Vassar had the strongest classical curriculum requiring *Ajax, Agamemnon, The Iliad,* and *Phaedon* in addition to grammar and histories which most schools neglected to offer, Irving's implementation of the writings of Cicero, Caesar, and Virgil appeared at other schools listed [in table 3.1]. As the nineteenth century progressed, colleges added additional classes in Latin or higher levels to bring their curriculum up to date with first-rate colleges like Vassar.

TABLE 3.1. CURRICULUM AT IRVING AND OTHER WOMEN'S COLLEGES, 1850S AND 1860S. The following table shows the entrance requirements and course curriculum of Irving and other women's colleges of the 1850s. The study of the classics is considered as the most important requirement for college entrance and degrees, therefore the majority of the schools in this table are only signified by their number of requirements in Greek and Latin for the A. B. degree. The date after the college name refers to the year that the information pertains to. The information on Irving was taken mainly from the college catalogues available from the first few years at Irving, while the remaining schools were taken from: Woody, Thomas. *A History of Women's Education in the United States*, in two volumes. Lancaster, Pennsylvania: The Science Press (1929), 154-183.

College	Entrance Requirements	Curriculum for Graduation in College Tract
Irving College (1857)	None: students admitted at any age and educational level.	algebra, analysis, arithmetic, Caesar, Cicero, English grammar, geography, Greek grammar, Greek reader, Greek testament,[2] history, Latin grammar, Latin reader, penmanship. reading, Sallust, spelling, Xenophon's *Anabasis*, Virgil
Elmira College, Elmira, New York (1855)	algebra, the Aeneid, analysis, anatomy, arithmetic, the Bible, bookkeeping, criticism, English grammar, geography, Greek antiquities, hygiene, Latin grammar, natural philosophy, physiology, rhetoric, Roman antiquities, zoology	Greek composition, Greek exercises, Greek grammar, Greek testament, Tacitus's *Agricola*, Tacitus's *Germania*, et. al.

---

2. Two modern languages can be substituted for Greek.

Lindenwood College, St. Charles, Missouri (1863)	NA	the Bible, Caesar, Cicero, Greek grammar, Greek reader, history, Homer, math, modern language, Ovid, science, Tacitus, Virgil
Mary Sharp College, Winchester, Tennessee (1851)	NA	Cicero, Greek grammar, Horace, Latin grammar, testament, Virgil
Maine Wesleyan Seminary, Kents Hill, Maine (1861)	NA	de Officiis, de Amicitia, de Senectute, Horace, Latin composition, Latin exercises, Latin prosody, Livy, Plautus, Tacitus's Germania, Tacitus's Histories[3]
Ohio Wesleyan Female College, Delaware, Ohio (1853)	arithmetic, geography, grammar, penmanship, physiology, reading	The Anabasis, Cicero's Orations, geography, Greek testament, history, Livy, math, Nepos, philosophy, science, Strong's Harmony, Virgil[4]
Oxford Female College, Oxford, Ohio (1855)	no Latin or Greek	Caesar, Greek grammar, Greek reader, Latin grammar, Latin reader, testament, Virgil, et. al.
Vassar College, Poughkeepsie, New York (1865)	Caesar (two Commentaries), Cicero (two orations), French, Latin grammar, Latin prose, Latin syntax[5]	Agamemnon, Ajax, Cicero, Greek grammar, Greek historians, Greek prose, Greek syntax, Horace, the Iliad (six books), Livy, Plato's Phaedon (in Greek), Tacitus

Though some women's colleges, like Vassar, opened with stringent admission requirements that few young women could fill (forcing the college to lower their entrance requirements or provide preparatory departments), Irving provided for those students at the outset. In 1864, "The Preparatory

---
3. Modern Language could be substituted for Greek.
4. Here also, Modern Language could be substituted for Greek.
5. Surprisingly enough, though Vassar's requirements were stringent, it did not require any Greek.

Department was declared self-sustaining and increasing in interest,"[6] as many of the incoming women took preparatory classes to fulfill entrance requirements or went to Irving in place of their local high school. Students were admitted at all ages and at "any stage of improvement" into either the Preparatory Department to form the "basis of a thorough English education,"[7] or the Collegiate Department which emphasized classical, polite, and Christian education. The Prep Department divided into three classes: juvenile, second preparatory, and first preparatory, while the Collegiate Department had the traditional sophomore, junior, and senior divisions. With girls aged eight through twelve being admitted to Irving at reduced rates in 1863, the campus was full of women of varying educational levels throughout Marlatt's and Ege's terms.

Other women's colleges admitted younger women to their campuses, though not nearly so young as Irving did. In the 1830s, the Georgia Female College admission age was twelve, though most female seminaries varied in their minimum age for admission from between twelve and sixteen years of age.[8] Sunderland College, which was originally Montgomery Female Seminary in Pennsylvania, had an entrance age of thirteen to fourteen. In 1853, Vassar admitted girls at fifteen, while the best college of the 1850s, Auburn University (later Elmira College), only admitted women at least sixteen years old in 1852.[9]

Regardless of the ages which Marlatt allowed at Irving, the students still had to meet the curriculum requirements established by the school. Marlatt based his student coursework on suggested requirements from the Convention of Female Colleges held in Cincinnati on May 4–5, 1853. The conference put together guidelines for classical and collegiate courses in women's colleges as a reference point for new and existing colleges in this dawning age of the educated woman.[10] Marlatt incorporated the A.B. [*Artium Baccalaurea*] and M.E.L. [Mistress of the English Literature] degrees, which students first graduated with in 1860 and 1858 respectively.

---

6. Irving College Board of Trustees Minutes, June 28, 1864.
7. Irving College Catalogue, 1857–1858, 12.
8. Woody, 164.
9. Woody, 179.
10. For purposes of this study, courses refer to the curriculum required for graduation and not an individual class (meaning that here a student may have taken one class called Latin III, which is a part of a four-year Classical Course).

The A.B., the stronger of the two degrees, required four years to earn and consisted of study in the ancient languages, English, geography, algebra, arithmetic, American and English history, and penmanship [see table 3.1]. The emphasis on Latin and Greek for the A.B., with grammar and various readings from Caesar to Cicero, made the A.B. more challenging than the M.E.L. and was more on par with men's collegiate degrees. The Mistress of English Literature allowed a women student to take the following classes for a minimum of two years: algebra, rhetoric, natural philosophy, physiology, botany, bookkeeping, general history, English grammar, trigonometry, astronomy, higher arithmetic, geometry, logic, political economy, chemistry, geology, mental philosophy, moral philosophy, evidences of Christianity, and criticism. Both A.B. and M.E.L. students registered for the above classes; and many took French, German, music, and art often for additional costs. Each student class had their own prescribed curriculum and a wide variety of offerings, considering that there were but 5–10 faculty members present during a normal school year [see table 3.2]. Though certainly not the best or hardest school for women, Irving offered a variety of classes to its diverse student body.

TABLE 3.2. **CLASS SELECTION AT IRVING COLLEGE, 1867-1868.** As prescribed by the Cincinnati convention of 1853, the following is a list of available classes for students of each class. No freshman class is listed, as first year students were considered part of the Preparatory Department. The following information is derived from the Irving College Catalogue, 1867-1868, 10.

Class at Irving	Classes Available for Registration
Sophomore	Latin Grammar, Physiology, Science of Common Things, English History, English Grammar, Composition, Drawing, French (Fasquelle's), Geography, U.S. History, Arithmetic, Elocution, Penmanship
Junior	Latin (Grammar, Caesar), Physical Geography, Philosophy, Astronomy, Ancient History, Algebra, English Grammar, Composition, Drawing, Penmanship, French (Fasquelle's, Telemaque's) Natural History, Rhetoric, Geometry, Elocution

Senior	Latin (Cicero, Virgil, Horace), Mental Philosophy, Chemistry, Algebra, Trigonometry, Composition, Drawing, French (Racine, Molliere), French Composition and Conversation, Moral Science, Geometry, Elocution, Penmanship

Marlatt's students studied their classes in penmanship, algebra, Latin, and history during a ten-month collegiate year that lasted from September to June. Irving's first term began the first Wednesday in September and lasted until the final week of January, while the Spring Term ran from February until the last Wednesday in June. Students only vacationed in July and August, obtaining no spring break between terms. They were able to relax for one week at Christmas and had some time off at Good Friday and Easter.

While the Preparatory Department theoretically lowered the college's entry standards, it is not necessarily correct to assume that the women at the collegiate level received easy treatment. By using the daily and weekly newspapers that resided in the Irvington Society reading room, the students were encouraged to read about the important events of the day and be familiar with the "history of their own times."[11] To ensure that the young women kept up with this reading, daily examinations were given to the students covering the events that occurred the previous day. Teachers exercised students daily in penmanship and vocal music, while requiring essays every Monday morning, which they critiqued and returned. The Irving classroom stressed that students learn the subject material as opposed to any single author's view, and therefore used textbooks as a guide, relying on oral learning and recitation. In the 1870s, the student monitors remarked about the weekly Saturday compositions: "Our little band seems more quiet and thoughtful this morning, I attribute the cause to this being composition Saturday."[12] "From all appearances now, the composition box next week will be filled with literary productions of no inferior order."[13] Marlatt and his faculty instituted monthly class reviews where each frightened student sat in front of the entire faculty

---

11. Irving College Catalogue, 1857–58, 18.
12. Monitress' Journal, October 19, 1872.
13. Monitress' Journal, March 8, 1873.

telling what she had learned in the previous month. These were the greatest of "bug-bears" to the student body.[14] Students read Cicero, Caesar, Virgil, and Sallust in Latin classes, Homer and Xenophon in Greek, and Longfellow, Whittier, Bryant, Dickens, Thackeray, and a host of others in English class.[15]

Class examinations commenced on the last Friday of every month covering the subject material studied in that particular time. The senior class took examinations for degrees the second Monday before Commencement, which included the entire course of study. Underclasswomen crammed for exams on the first Monday before Commencement, concerning all the material they had learned that year:

> For the public examination there is no especial preparation allowed by the faculty. The student goes on in the even tenor of her way with her studies, up to the very day of examination, not knowidg [sic] on what branches of study, or on what particular part of any branch of study, she is to be examined, so that the parent or guardian who may be present has a fair opportunity of ascertaining whether the student thoroughly understands the branches she may be pursuing.[16]

Though the school's curriculum was not equal to the men's colleges of the time, the examination process surely must have been a strain on these innovative women, testing the opportunities of education in Central Pennsylvania.

All this hard work paid off not only with excellent report cards, but with significant honors which the school awarded in certain areas. A Classical Honor was bestowed on the student most proficient in language; a Mathematical Honor, a Musical Honor, and a Deportment Honor (for excellent behavior) were also awarded. Students received their awards during the Commencement, though they were warned that "[n]o Honor

---

14. Kennedy, Mary E., '61. "Reminiscences of Class of '61," *The Sketch Book*, Vol. I, No. 4, May 1895, 141.

15. Irving students also read Prescott, Hawthorne, Irving, Wordsworth, Scott, Cooper, Goldsmith, Pope, Addison, Bunyan, Milton, Shakespeare, Spenser, and Chaucer in English classes.

16. *The Weekly Gazette*, January 14, 1857.

will be assigned to any student, although proficient, whose deportment has not been exemplary."[17] Within a few years, Ege added his own honor for *Belle Lettres*, for the student most proficient in writing, replacing the Mathematical Honor at Commencement.

Ege made few modifications to Marlatt's system of education, maintaining the system in place. One major change that he added came in 1869: "In view of the fluctuation of pupils often leaving in the middle of the school year, the President desired the Sanction of the Board, in the adoption of the <u>One Term System</u> and insisting thereby on receiving pupils only for the full School [*sic*] year, with prompt payment, in advance."[18] The board accepted the plan, which brought students to school in September and aside from breaks, ended their term in late June. It is interesting to note that Ege seemed to have a problem with students leaving mid-term and, due to the financial stress facing the college at this point, it was probably necessary to institute such an advanced-payment system in order to ensure not only that the students would stay, but also that they *would* pay for an entire year. Ege apparently increased the difficulty of Irving's curriculum, graduating a class of only two students in 1869: "in view of an addition of one year to the Course of Study, and hence only the Two Young Ladies named [Mattie Yarnall and Flora L. Best], could measure up to the standard."[19]

As mentioned in Chapter One, Ege stressed the success of Irving and dismissed apparent hardships, despite a decline in students and graduates from the 1860s. Ege also made big claims about the students' coursework: "Our course is also in direct line with Vassar, Wellesley and Smith Colleges, and prepares pupils who desire it, for their examinations, or for the Harvard examinations for women."[20] This was at best a little far-fetched and urbanely hyperbolic; Ege knew that Irving's entrance requirements and course curriculum remained far below those of Vassar or Wellesley, though the rigor of their coursework had similarities. Vassar set up nine schools within its college. Each student passed from one school to the next, receiving a B.A. degree when she earned five certificates. Vassar and Smith developed college curriculums for women that mirrored those

---

17. Irving College Catalogue, 1857–1858, 19.
18. Irving College Board of Trustees Minutes, June 22, 1869.
19. Irving College Board of Trustees Board Minutes, June 22, 1869.
20. Irving College Brochure, circa 1875.

of men, and by the 1880 Report of the U.S. Commissioner of Education, both colleges and Wellesley achieved placement in the Division A category for colleges, while Irving appeared in Division B for lesser schools and seminaries. Ege probably adapted the catalogue statement as an advertising ploy to attract students, as Irving's college courses were strong, but these other schools blazed the trail further for equality in higher education.

EDUCATIONAL EXPANSION, KESSLER, CAMPBELL, AND IRVING, 1888–1929

> The advantages of instruction offered at Irving are unsurpassed, it is believed *by any* Christian schools in *this country*.
> –*Greater America*, 1899[21]

Though Irving stood behind the big-name women's colleges like Vassar and Wellesley, E. E. Campbell tried his best to upgrade the school, though he maintained some of the ideas put forth by Marlatt originally. He continued the A.B. and M.E.L. degrees after his purchase of Irving, the latter degree extended to four years and eventually phased out by Campbell to add more weight to the school's reputation. Campbell expanded these degrees, offering a Latin-Scientific Course leading to a B.S. and a music course leading to a Bachelor of Music by 1899, and secretarial and domestic science certificates by the 1910s. The Faculty Committee aided Campbell in restructuring Irving's curriculum in the summer before the 1906–1907 school year, abolishing the M.E.L. degree for any incoming students and adopting a diploma in elocution and a certificate in the Commercial Department (secretarial). "It gives a little more flexibility, and gives more opportunity for better work."[22] The A.B. at Irving required 158 points (or credits) of study with concentrations in Latin, languages, math, and other traditional subjects [see table 3.3]. Similar to Marlatt and Ege, Campbell required his seniors of 1895 to

---

21. *Greater America*, 1.
22. Campbell, E. E. Presidential Report to the Irving College Board of Trustees. Contained within the board of trustees Minutes, June 4, 1907.

pass written exams in all their studies, achieving a 75 percent or higher on each, and in 1899 inflicted an 85 percent minimum passing grade on final exams for students to move from one class to the next. Though Campbell increased the prestige of the school by increasing the difficulty for the students, "a very small per cent of the student body fail to attain the desired grade, showing the stimulating effect of the system."[23] Though Ege shortened Marlatt's original school year from forty-four to forty weeks, E. E. shortened it to thirty-four weeks, dividing the school year into four terms of about eight and a half weeks to fit his plan for increasing the standards of the school. "[T]he curriculum is being raised as fast as circumstances will permit . . ." in 1900,[24] while "[t]he various courses of instruction have been raised from year to year so that our Sophomore Class at present time [1906] is doing more advanced work than our Senior Class did ten years ago."[25] Campbell maintained the constant writing that Marlatt and Ege imposed on students, requiring chapel essays for seniors ranging from "Keats, the Poet" to "Esperanto" and "The Webster and Hayne Debate."[26] Since Campbell incorporated at least 218 hours of pedagogical work in Irving's course, the State exempted Irving graduates from taking any examinations for teaching certificates in Pennsylvania, which required only 200 hours for certification.

Campbell continued to reshape Irving's degrees as the need arose and as new classes were added to the catalogue. In 1912, students could enroll for a fifth-year class in Latin, and a sixth or seventh if they studied at Irving past their four-year degree. B.S. candidates, on the other hand, had virtually no Latin requirement (only one class required), as they concentrated on chemistry, geometry, astronomy, and algebra. By 1913, students were required to declare two major subjects of study, or to maintain study for six consecutive class hours in one subject. With Campbell's upgrading, Irving increased its standards to levels higher than ever in its history; students that took classes and applied for admission faced an even tougher challenge.

---

23. *Greater America*, 3.
24. Irving College Board of Trustees Minutes, June 4, 1900.
25. Campbell, E. E. Presidential Report to the Irving College Board of Trustees. Contained within the board of trustee's minutes, June 5, 1906.
26. *The Sketch Book*, Vol. VIII, No. 14, May 1907, 15.

TABLE 3.3. REQUIREMENTS FOR COMPLETION OF THE A.B. DEGREE AT IRVING COLLEGE, 1906-1907. Taken from the Irving College Catalogue, 1906-1907, 11, the following is a list of classes students needed to take if they were enrolled in the college course for the A. B. degree.

Requirements for A. B.:	Years	Requirements for B. S.:	Years
Language: Latin	4	Language: Latin	4
and Greek	4	Modern Language	4
or: Latin	4	History	4
and Modern Lang. I	4	English	4
History	3	Elocution	2
English	4	Evidences of Christianity	
Elocution	2	Biblical History	
Evidences of Christianity		Math-Algebra and Geometry	
Biblical History			
Math-Algebra and Geometry			
Science-Chemistry			

Students faced an application process and admission requirements that enabled Campbell to monitor the students coming into his school. Young women used academy, college, or high school certificates and examination for admission in the 1890s, in order to present "testimonials of good moral character," and demonstrate "scholastic pedigree in detail."[27] Applicants received acceptance even if they did not measure up to the college course, being admitted to the Preparatory Department continued from Marlatt times.[28] Applicants needed to sustain a 75 percent in the following subjects in order to enroll as a first-year academic student in the classical course: U.S. history, arithmetic to percentage, physiology, composition, geography, English grammar, English analysis, and spelling. One student, Miss Anna E. Reen '91, graduated from a high school in Newport, Pennsylvania and surprisingly "entered the Junior Class in 1889" because of her previous coursework.[29] Irving still

27. Irving College Board of Trustees Minutes, June 3, 1924.
28. "Irving College for Young Women," *The Sketch Book*, Vol. I, No. 4, May 1895, 162.
29. Irving College Board of Trustees Minutes, June 9, 1891.

accepted students at all stages of educational achievement. Supplementing a school's certificate was a recommendation from the superintendent of a student's former school, a recommendation from her family physician, and a recommendation from her pastor. Campbell carefully scrutinized all applicants to Irving. Students took entrance exams only if absolutely necessary by 1899: "Students who are able to satisfy the faculty concerning the work done and to name the authors of text books studied will be saved the annoyance of entrance examination," though it appears that Campbell required it otherwise.[30]

Some of the required readings for the incoming student in 1900 suggested by The Association of Colleges and Preparatory Schools in the Middle States included John Dryden's *Palamon* and *Arcite*, Alexander Pope's translation of *The Iliad* (books I, VI, XXII, and XXIV), Sir Roger de Coverly's Papers in *The Spectator*, Oliver Goldsmith's *Vicar of Wakefield*, Sir Walter Scott's *Ivanhoe*, Thomas De Quincey's *Flight of a Tartar Tribe*, James F. Cooper's *Last of the Mohicans*, Alfred L. Tennyson's *Princess*, and James Russell Lowell's *Vision of Sir Launfal*.[31] Some students achieved these requirements and were even awarded advanced credits in most classes that a student may have taken in high school or another college.[32]

By 1921, incoming students whose previous work reached a level less than satisfactory encountered new obstacles to overcome upon entrance. These students and current students who performed unsatisfactorily in classes were "conditioned" in the subject(s) with which they struggled. New students were allowed one year to make up these deficiencies and maintain their pace with their classmates who faced no such restrictions upon admission. The college removed this condition when the student completed an assigned amount of supplementary work according to the teacher's instructions. If the condition still remained by the end of the time limit required by the teacher, the class was marked as a failure. Any

---

30. Irving College Catalogue, 1899–1900, 18.
31. In 1901, George Eliot's *Silas Marner*, Shakespeare's *The Merchant of Venice*, and Samuel T. Coleridge's *The Rime of the Ancient Mariner* were added to several of the literature readings required in 1900 [Alexander Pope, Roger de Coverly, Oliver Goldsmith, Sir Walter Scott, James F. Cooper, and Alfred L. Tennyson].
32. In a 1926–1927 transcript nearly every class available at Irving could have been advanced credit for an incoming student, making for a very flexible transfer and admission for those students so long as the courses they took previously, Irving offered.

student holding more than three conditions lost her classification, slipping down one class until she made up the work.

For those students who did not measure up to the college course, there was the two-year Preparatory Department, instituted from the early days of Irving. Designed to prepare young women for the college course and to aid in weaker subject areas, students enrolled in the prep classes for as long as needed; some students took one year of prep classes, others had their four years of high school at Irving. While college course students studied French, astronomy, botany, and algebra, preparatory students worked their way through general science, English grammar, advanced arithmetic, U.S. history, geography, and beginner Latin in order to establish a good background for college studies.

The application for admission was not the lengthy paperwork that students fill out for college entrance today [see table 3.4]. Students paid a $10 entrance fee by the 1920s, though it is unknown whether an application fee appeared prior. Should a student decide not to attend at the last minute and "[i]f notice of withdrawal is received at the college before[,] the fee will be refunded. In all other cases it is forfeited to the college."[33] Boarding students secured a room for the school year with an additional $10 security deposit that added to the student's account upon their arrival. The form, which the applicant's parents filled out, asked for the essential information such as address, birth date, schools attended, type of study desired, the condition of health, and the denominational church of the applicant. Campbell's keen interest in examining the educational as well as medical and religious backgrounds of the students enabled him to create a healthy campus and a religious student body for Irving.

---

33. Irving College Application, circa 1920s.

TABLE 3.4. IRVING COLLEGE APPLICATION CIRCA 1920S.

Application for Admission to Irving College and Music Conservatory Mechanicsburg, Pennsylvania
_____ 192___
I hereby apply for the enrollment of my _____ Miss_____ as a boarding student at IRVING COLLEGE AND MUSIC CONSERVATORY, Mechanicsburg, Pa., for the session beginning_____ and ending_____
I enclose herewith ten dollars to secure the reservation of a room. I have read the conditions governing the acceptance of application and payment of obligation to the College as given in the current annual catalogue and agree to abide by them as if the same were written herein.
_____ Parent or Guardian
1 Address of Parent or Guardian_____ 2 Full Name of Applicant_____ 3 Year_____Month_____and Day_____of Birth 4 Name of School last attended_____ 5 Course of Study desired_____ 6 Condition of Health_____ 7 Are you a member of a Church_____ 8 If so, of what denomination_____

Rules governed student registration of classes. A student could drop classes or withdraw from a class, so long as the form she filled out had presidential approval. But by 1913, any student assigned to a class could not discontinue the class after thirty days. No student could enroll for more than twenty-three periods or less than eighteen periods per week in her schedule, nor could she postpone a required study, take a study ahead of her class, or change her election of study without special permission.[34] Credit for Greek, French, or German was not given until the student completed two years in the language elected, and two different beginning classes of a modern language could not be studied in the same year. After the assignment of classes, if less than four students belonged to an elective class, it dropped from the schedules unless the enrolled students made special arrangements.

---

34. The number of periods taken by a student changed into the 1900s, though these restrictions are taken from the 1906–1907 college catalogue. In 1908–1909, students could take up to 24 periods, but no less than 18.

As mentioned in the previous chapter, Campbell divided the college into different courses depending on the students' interests, with most young women enrolling in the regular college course or the music conservatory. Students could take home economics by 1914, a secretarial course by 1900, and art courses, though sporadically, throughout Campbell's tenure. The administration permitted student enrollment in multiple tracts, and many of the students completed the college course in addition to another, often graduating with several degrees over several years. However, the college did not permit students to finish these tracts all at once: "Students desiring to do extensive work in Music, Art or Expression, with a view to graduation in these subjects, will not be allowed to take the full number of hours in any one year of the Classical Course."[35]

Students attended the one-hour classes anywhere from one to four times a week depending on the subject and its importance to their course. Elocution, which students attended every term in their college career for attitude refinement and proper manners, met only once per week; intensive studies in Latin or French required student attendance four times a week and lasted the entire four terms of a student's year.[36] Other classes like geometry or art history lasted half of the year, while classes in trigonometry and Evidences of Christianity lasted only one term (one quarter of the year). Credits earned for classes depended on class difficulty and the number of class periods per week. A difficult class such as Latin (offered four periods/week for thirty-four weeks) earned a student eight credits, while a seemingly easier class such as Elocution (offered two periods/week for thirty-four weeks) was worth only 4 credits [see Appendix B, table 7]. By 1904, Campbell reduced period lengths to 45 minutes, with piano lessons at 30 minutes per period, though later records show classes lengthened to 60-minute periods and the school year increased to 36 weeks. Campbell experimented with different arrangements in order to run his college efficiently and maintain the effective course load for students.

The classes available at Irving grew greatly over time, as Campbell wanted to afford his students a wide variety of opportunities. As a result,

---

35. Irving College Catalogue, 1913–1914, 22.
36. Elocution is also referred to as "Private Expression" in some college catalogues.

Irving's classes grew each year under Campbell's leadership. 1895 saw the introduction of domestic science classes in plain sewing and basketry,[37] in addition to Spanish since "[o]ur nearness to our South American neighbors and to our Mexican disturbers more than suggest the practical importance that this language will exercise in the next few years."[38] German, a mainstay in the language curriculum since Marlatt times and always an added benefit in rural, German Pennsylvania, disappeared from class schedules in 1918 when stricken unanimously by the board of trustees for the remainder of WWI.[39] Psychology, civil government, and calisthenics appeared in class listings for 1897, sociology for 1899, secretarial classes in stenography, bookkeeping, and typewriting for 1902, public finance for 1903, pedagogy for 1912, development of drama for 1913, and cooking and advanced sewing classes first appeared in 1915. Campbell witnessed important changes with women in 1914 and offered a:

> new course—one not offered in any institution to my knowledge—[which] will be given next year in Parliamentary Law. This seems to be woman's day. Whether we be pro or anti suffrage, the fact remains that woman now is called upon very frequently to preside over and conduct women's clubs, civic clubs, social and religious organizations.[40]

Campbell added shorthand and commercial correspondence in 1916 due to the ever-growing student interest in secretarial classes and added bacteriology and dietetics in the same year for the growing Domestic Science Department. Additional classes in social psychology, household accounting, laundering, journalism, business writing, theatre make-up and costuming, pantomime, Italian, and political science showed up on student schedules right up until Irving's last year. Even Marlatt offered art classes as early as 1857 (if not from the start), but a full course appeared

---

37. Though domestic science classes appeared as early as 1895, the course for domestic science was not established until 1914.
38. Irving College Board of Trustees Minutes, June 1, 1895.
39. Irving College Board of Trustees Minutes, June 4, 1918.
40. Campbell, E. E. Presidential Report to the Board of Trustees, Contained within Irving College Board of Trustees Minutes, June 2, 1914.

in 1920, as students created in pen, pencil, chalk, charcoal, watercolors, and oils for class.

The religious Campbell offered Bible classes at Irving, maintaining the classes that had been available years earlier. During his tenure, several ministers taught Irving classes in Bible history or moral science, covering the educational importance of the Bible, the Bible as literature, the compilation and construction of the Bible, and its inspiration. Rev. H. N. Fegley's class in Biblical history (c. 1893–1910) covered those topics:

> This course in Biblical History is designed to supply an introduction to the History and Literature of the Bible, as preparatory to the study of Christian Evidences [another class at Irving]. By this means it is believed that there will be secured a broader and more profound knowledge of the facts of the Bible, as well as a sound faith in its mission.[41]

The class required students to keep a notebook to record the "principles of each subject, concisely stated" using the notebook to review and keep "himself [herself] thoroughly familiar [with the material]."[42] Teaching from a "messenger of God" standpoint, Fegley interpreted the Bible in a liberal way in relation to the new education of women: "The second person created was a woman, to be the companion and helpmeet [sic] of man, taken not from his head to rule over him, nor from his feet to be trodden on by him, but from his side to be his equal."[43] Therefore, students received the religious background their parents and Dr. Campbell required, while feeling supported in their education by the church.

In order to provide exercise for his students, Campbell required daily afternoon walks, and introduced physical culture, or physical education, at Irving. Students participated in drill-type exercises such as free hand movements, the use of wands, poles, and dumb-bells, and working on rings. Before instituting afternoon walks, Campbell mandated military drill for thirty minutes every day involving marching and manual of

---

41. Fegley, H. N. "Lectures on Biblical History," 1893, revised 1910, 1.
42. Fegley, 1.
43. Fegley, 1.

arms similar to those of the gym classes: "This half hour of rigid military discipline forms and cultivates habits of concentrated attention, prompt obedience and an erect and graceful carriage not otherwise attainable."[44] The drill teams divided into four platoons, each headed by lieutenants "selected for their proficiency," who all answered to commands of a teacher who had three years' worth of experience as an officer in the national guard.[45] Students drilled outside in the wide open spaces beside Columbian Hall unless inclement weather forced them inside. By 1929, physical culture included folk dancing for the students, requiring them to dance jigs of Ireland, Scotland, or Germany in order "to develop a sense of grace and rhythm in the student."[46] Drill and "free hand movements" dissipated with the entrance of sports for physical culture by the 1910s, with students dressing in long black serge bloomers, long stockings, and white middy blouses with neatly folded black silk ties (but no sneakers until late in Irving's history) for tennis, field hockey, and basketball. However, the emphasis on physical culture greatly diminished by the 1920s, when afternoon walks became the standard exercise, But, most students still tended to be involved in extracurricular sports.

Campbell's growth in the number of classes in large part resulted from the need of having Secretarial and Home Economics Departments by 1895. As students filled these specialty classes, additional and more specific classes from cooking and sewing to shorthand and typing were added. Secretarial or business faculty, as they were referred to in the early 1900s, arrived at Irving at the end of the nineteenth century as the opportunities in secretarial work began to present themselves to women:

> The business men of today are clamoring for efficient, reliable, resourceful and competent stenographers and secretaries. They want a girl who knows how and when a thing is to be done; one who can take dictation and then properly place a neatly and accurately transcribed letter upon the desk . . . The busy man of today needs a secretary who will relieve him of all detail, whether

---

44. Irving College Catalogue, 1893–1894, 31.
45. *The Sketch Book*, February 1895, 34.
46. Irving College Catalogue, 1928–1929, 29.

in answering letters, receiving callers, planning his trips or capably assuming charge of his affairs while he is out of the city.[47]

Students studied classes in stenography, bookkeeping, and typewriting in 1895, but with the ever-growing popularity in the subject, classes were added nearly every year in public finance, shorthand, commercial correspondence, commercial law, office training, and secretary training.

Domestic Science (later called Home Economics) arrived at Irving in 1895 with the announcement of a Domestic Science Department (headed by Miss Lena M. Booker) with basketry and plain sewing classes, but really gained steam in 1914, with a two-year course leading to a diploma. The program could not compare with other home economics programs across the state as 15 colleges (including 2 women's schools, Beaver College and Cedar Crest College) provided four-year programs in domestic science by 1928. Irving's course dealt with the working knowledge of household processes (especially those with food), the general principles of cookery in lab experiments, general chemistry and household chemistry, the threading of common stitches, the use and care of the sewing machine, and simple and complex weaves in basketry. By creating a science out of the household work women slaved at for centuries, women students flocked into the new curriculum despite Campbell's strong feelings about educating women in the classical courses instead. Students studying cooking and sewing concentrated on cooking techniques, the study of recipes, planning the cost and preparation of meals, methods of garnishing, the relative value and digestibility of foods, hand sewing, repair work, needlework, fancy stitches, hemstitching, and embroidery. The domestic science student's final exams consisted of preparing meals for the students, acting as the hostesses who kept up conversation at the dinner party, and serving the food properly. Despite the tasty dishes, every student had "visions of slipping something hot and creamy down some one's back, but it doesn't really happen."[48] Many times, the domestic science students would prepare faculty luncheons for a grade, serve teas for socializing, sew up to 140 dresses for school exhibitions, and even

---

47. Irving College Catalogue, 1928–1929, 59.
48. *The Sketch Book*, 1923, 40.

hold fashion shows with students modeling the street costumes, evening dresses, sport dresses, and negligees they created.[49]

Though secretary and home economics tracks offered students preparation for the job market once outside of school, Irving students also exercised the opportunity to enroll in an elocution course, studying the ways and manners of a proper lady. Though not readily applicable to any post-graduation job but teaching, elocution students studied a four-year course learning voice culture, elementary gestures, articulation, and inflection in their first year, and mastered rendering, recitation, dramatic attitudes, and extemporaneous speaking by their senior years.[50] Often reading Shakespeare, students had to analyze the expression of emotion, debate, dialectics, and study Delsarte's philosophy of expression. Therefore, the course involved more than just learning mannerisms and how to speak in front of an audience. Contests in elocution were held every year with the best of those students competing in the final contest during commencement week. One such contest involved Pennsylvania Governor Daniel H. Hastings, who honored Irving with his presence as a judge at an oratorical contest in 1897. *Greater America* magazine claimed that most colleges overlooked elocution as a course of study, and that Irving provided a service to its students by offering training in public delivery and oratory, now a required class for students at some state colleges in Pennsylvania. Shakespeare's writings tended to be popular in elocution classes, and students recited the words and used their dramatic skill for plays such as *The Merchant of Venice:* "Well, that time has now come, and at almost any hour you can hear either Antonio or Shylock yelling some places in the buildings," wrote one student in *The Sketch Book*.[51] Students who took the elocution course studied in classes with other students but had the option of paying more for private elocution classes, which by the 1920s were taught at Argyle.

Despite the job opportunities available through the secretarial and home economics courses, a majority of Irving's students went into school teaching aided by the public-school program Campbell put in place

---

49. *The Sketch Book*, April 1927, 24.
50. Irving College Catalogue, 1891–1892, 30.
51. *The Sketch Book*, Vol. VI, No. 7, May 1904, 7.

for such students. Referred to as "education" classes by Irving's closing, the public-school program taught teaching methods, held observation classes, and involved psychology and physiology in order to prepare the student for public school teaching. Many of these students centered their teaching on music and visited schools in the area from Harrisburg to Steelton to see the music work performed there. Students benefited in 1922 from two weeks of lectures by Dr. Dann, the State Supervisor of Schools, who talked on "Methods of Teaching Music in the Public Schools."[52] The course requirements did not far exceed those for the regular college tract, and the earlier students also obtained teaching positions with the A.B. degree Irving offered, but classes in teaching methods were added by 1929 as the growing need for specialization within the subject area became apparent. Regardless of whether the students took the classes in education or not, the A.B. degree did not specify whether the student received training in education areas, therefore, most Irving graduates taught with or without the specified training. Irving maintained strict classes and the faculty graded students for their preparation in class. Several exams have survived showing the vagueness of the questioning and the need for strong clarification in the answers. One logic exam from 1897 had students describing the different departments of knowledge, defining idea, notion, and thought, and explaining why fallacies must be considered in logic. A psychology exam from the same year asked where human individuality and psychology reveal themselves and asked for students to locate "the feelings of hunger in the infant, pains, fatigue, longing for health, parental affection, covetousness, avarice, kindness, patriotism, love of wisdom and of the truth, envy, anger, joy in prospect, hope, pride, loathing, satiety, longing for shade, weakness, migration of birds, and dissocial feelings."[53] One theme paper dating to 1912 required students to trace the development of Great Britain, which could not have been a small order; excellent summation skills therefore would have been required. Botany classes directed students to obtain 50 specimens for class, first-year students in English class read *The Ancient Mariner, Idylls of the King,* and *The Passing of Arthur,* and the chemistry classes traveled

---

52. *The Sketch Book,* 1922, 40.
53. *The Sketch Book,* June 1897, 164.

to a nearby gas house to determine how artificial gas was made. Though the exams and even the subjects appear vague and difficult, they probably were not any more challenging than those at other women's or coeducational colleges across the Northeast.

The college faculty maintained the strict Irving atmosphere by grading stringently on the wide variety of classes students took. "The Minimum [*sic*] grade, signifying sustained is 75[;] Good, 80 to 90; Very Good[,] 90 to 95; Distinguished[,] 95 to 100. When a study is completed[,] the student is examined thereon and the grade is entered."[54] This grading system evolved into letter grades by 1900 with A=Distinguished, B=Very Good, C=85–90, D=80–85, E=sustained and F=anything lower than 75. Essentially, the final exams given at the end of each term or year signified the student grades, though it is not clear whether any additional assignments, quizzes, or participation throughout the year may have figured into that total. Term reports listed grades for every class taken that term, the attendance record, church attendance, chapel attendance, excused and unexcused absences, the punctuality of the student, table etiquette, deportment, and neatness. Though most students passed through the classes satisfactorily, a few incidents a year surely drove teachers crazy:

> Josephine Barr stayed away from her Grammar [*sic*] final because she didn't want to take any. I was told she wasn't interested in credits. She can be given no grade until she passes an examination. I do not plan to give her one in the fall.
> —Gail Hemminger, Grammar Teacher 1928[55]

With final exams consisting of the majority (if not the total) of grades, students certainly felt the pressures to study and pass, though Josephine Barr appeared to be the exception.

Students earned grades for their behavior, as a grade for deportment appeared on student report cards, which was counted into the final grade. "A very few black marks, as we found out, materially altered the neat 100 that was supposed to stand in the deportment column, so we were careful

---

54. Irving College Term Report, December 1, 1897.
55. Irving College student term report, 1927–1928.

of our actions."⁵⁶ The behavior of students in class, the cleanliness of their rooms, and their punctuality to scheduled periods all played a part in the deportment grade, which must have been graded by a student's individual class teachers as well as the faculty member residing on her floor. Teachers issued demerits for everything from interrupting class, visiting during church hour, feasts after ten o'clock, to letter writing during study hour. Everyone from class teachers to Dr. Campbell himself issued demerits to students, which were usually no more than 3–5 for each offense of talking or disturbing class. Occasional 5–10 demerits were awarded for impudence to teacher, defiance of a teacher, climbing in locked rooms, and even sleeping with another student (which broke the lights out rule). In one incident, several students received 25–30 demerits for participating in a feast when they should have been on their best behavior with all the faculty away in Columbian Hall, probably for a faculty reception.

The strict discipline and increasingly difficult curriculum Campbell continued at Irving paid off with heralds and recognition when states evaluated the job of E. E. and his faculty. Campbell corresponded often with Pennsylvania's state educational board, but in addition received queries from other states asking about his graduate's qualifications, particularly in teaching:

> In the early fall the state Superintendent of Public Instruction of New Jersey telegraphed me [E. E.] to know whether we would receive a representative from his department. I replied that we would be pleased to do so. The next day the gentleman called representing the State Superintendent. He said he had been sent to learn more about our institution. Four of our graduates he said, were teaching in his state, and had applied for state recognition on our diploma. He said they never granted this without first making investigation, and he had come for that purpose. After a three hours' visit and inspection and examination he left. Before leaving I told him we were ready to stand or fall on the record our graduates made, and if those in his state were not giving a good account of themselves we would

---

56. "The Junior Class," *The Sketch Book*, Vol. I, No. 4, May 1895, 129.

not ask for recognition from his state. He hesitated and then replied. "It is because they have given such a good account of themselves that I am sent here." On leaving he said he was much pleased with his visit, and would report favorably on Irving. Our graduates now are recognized not only in the state of New Jersey, but also in New York state. For the Colleges registered by one of these states is at the same time registered by the other. This is a recognition of the good work done at Irving, that is most highly gratifying to all her friends [sic].[57]

The College and University Council of the state [of Pennsylvania], through Dr. N. C. Schaeffer, State Superintendent, notified me that under the new school code "Irving" would continue to be recognized as worthy of state recognition formerly accorded, and that now our graduates would be given their certificates without examination, and after three years teaching they would be given their Permanent State Certificates.[58]

This college has felt the continued and growing need for smaller colleges, so yearly limits its enrolment [sic], and combines the life of a small college with the instruction of a university, in so far as is possible. All classes are kept small, and intensive work is done by each student. For this reason, its graduates are making excellent teachers in our various high schools and institutions of higher learning.[59]

Through hard work and dedication, Campbell's graduates, most of whom went on to teach, became mentors for other young women to attend Irving, realizing that neighboring states recognized its degrees and accomplished work. Some debate arose in 1918 over its "unlimited charter," and whether it complied with recently set Pennsylvania state standards:

---

57. Irving College Board of Trustees Minutes, June 4, 1907.
58. Irving College Board of Trustees Minutes, June 4, 1912.
59. *Pennsylvania School Journal, Educational Review,* Vol. LXXVII, No. 3A, 26–27.

> As I understand it, the college had under its charter the right to confer degrees, and nothing has been done by the legislature to alter that right, and the excellent record of the college seemed to me to justify its encouragement.
>
> As to the College and University Council, they recognized Irving College [sic] in 1912 as to its graduates being competent to teach in the public schools, and I have no reason to think that they are not as well trained now as they were then. I believe they are, but that is, of course, a matter for the College and University Council to take up.
>
> —Henry S. Drinker, President of Lehigh University[60]

Campbell kept in constant touch with the office of the Attorney General of Pennsylvania, as did Henry S. Drinker of Lehigh University. E. E. inquired the Secretary of the College and University Council on April 25, 1918 about "whether 'Irving College' . . . has the power to continue to grant academic degrees in view of the fact that it seems not to comply with the provisions of the Act creating the College and University Council."[61] This council, established in 1895, protected potential students from institutions not granting the degrees allowed by the state or laid out in their charter. According to the Attorney General, Irving was an approved women's college for instruction leading to state public school teaching (as evidenced by the 1912 action mentioned previously), and E. E. could breathe more easily as Drinker wrote Campbell: ". . . It seems to me that the Attorney General has most advantageously and admirably decided the matter and it ought to put at rest the questions with which you have been troubled."[62]

Building upon the awards initially offered by Marlatt and Ege, students that excelled in various areas achieved medals and honors commemorating their accomplishments. The Board of Trustees Medal recognized the student with the highest average in the college course, the

---

60. Drinker, Henry Sturgis. Letter to the Hon. Francis Shunk Brown, Attorney General of Pennsylvania, July 17, 1918.

61. Schaeffer, Dr. Nathan C., Superintendent of Public Instruction, Office of the Attorney General of Pennsylvania. Letter to E. E. Campbell, July 2, 1918.

62. Drinker, Henry Sturgis. Letter to E. E. Campbell, July 19, 1918.

President's Medal saluted the winner of the annual elocution contest, and the Faculty Medal awarded the greatest progress in art.[63] In 1894, the Alumnae Association suggested the Alumnae Medal award for the student showing the most progress in instrumental or vocal music, and the following year the alumnae decided upon a $10 prize for a member of the senior class who wrote the best essay on a literary subject of their choice. At other times, alumnae prizes consisted of various gifts, most notably when the alumnae gave a complete set of Washington Irving's works to a student in 1905, and a set of the works of the great composers for the best grade in music in 1916. Beginning with the 1901–1902 school year, the A. W. Lilly Jr. Latin Medal congratulated the student who achieved the highest grade on a Latin exam throughout the year, while a sophomore excelling in mathematics began receiving recognition with a medal in 1904–1905.[64] All students could achieve recognition with honors: "HONOR STUDENTS are those who receive 100 percent deportment for the quarter."[65] Irving students occasionally won national or regional awards as Bessie Winder '03, won the $50 Julia K. Hogg Testimonial Prize offered to all seniors in women's colleges across Pennsylvania by the Daughters of the American Revolution.

The Board of Trustees bestowed an additional honor in 1910 with the addition of the Mistress of Arts (M.A.) as an honorary degree conferred by presidential recommendation. Any Irving graduate could receive the honor as well as any other graduate who has "pursued literary or professional studies for a period of five (5) years following graduation."[66]

As Irving continued through the 1920s, the classical course suffered, drawing fewer and fewer students each year, losing them to the home economics and secretarial tracts. Because of the popularity of the latter courses, E. E. realized the need for the assignment of departmental assistants since the department heads found it difficult to handle all the students and classes themselves. "Our Home Economics department [*sic*] is growing in numbers and interest. Miss Agnes Hunsicker, at the head

---

63. The Board of Trustees Medal was first offered in 1895 and renamed the Jacob Hurst General Excellence Medal in 1904. The President's Medal began in 1892 and was renamed the President's Medal in Oratory by 1905.
64. A. W. Lilly Jr. was Irving's Board President from 1890 until his death in 1902.
65. Irving College Term Report, January 31, 1924.
66. Irving College Board of Trustees Minutes, May 31, 1910.

of this department, is an excellent, faithful and most competent teacher. Her students are very enthusiastic over her and over their work[,]"⁶⁷ but with new classes added each year, more faculty were needed. In 1921, another year was added to the home economics' two-year course, and another teacher added to meet the growing demands.⁶⁸ The Secretarial Department under Miss Esther Lau in 1921: "compares very favorably with the course as given in other institutions. Its graduates are quickly employed and are commanding salaries in advance of those given to the teacher of high school subjects."⁶⁹ Taking dictation and transcribing it neatly, the twenty-four students in the course in 1921 took classes ranging from typewriting, stenography, and bookkeeping to office training, commercial law, and business writing.

The reasons for the declining classical curriculum and the popular home economics and secretary paths were evident to President Campbell. At the 1921 board meeting, he discussed the shift in student interest:

> During the war [WW I] the Government was over-stressing the vocational courses, and indeed it is still doing so, and also the fact that the Classical Course requires four years to complete it by a student who graduated from a first-class, four-year high school. Then, too there is a very noticeable unwillingness to study Latin, and our state seems to be encouraging this unwillingness in its policy. It seems to me that it is more than a pity for I know of no substitute for Latin in the Classical Course.⁷⁰

Campbell wanted women to receive the same education and opportunities as men, and the fact that many young women longed for the appealing vocational curriculums now available to them only saddened

---

67. Irving College Board of Trustees Minutes, May 31, 1921.
68. It is uncertain whether Irving ever established a four-year course in Home Economics, but college catalogs never promote its length, if it indeed did become a four year program. However, Domestic Science classes were added almost annually in the 1920s. After the course increased to three years in 1921, there were two classes added in the fall of 1922, one added in 1923, six new offerings in 1924, six in 1925, two in 1926, three in 1927, and five in 1928. However, some of these classes may have been restructured from previous classes with a new name, and several may have been eliminated (or were not offered in particular years) without mention.
69. Irving College Board of Trustees Minutes, May 31, 1921.
70. Irving College Board of Trustees Minutes, May 31, 1921.

him. However, with the practicability of the vocational classes toward job placement, incoming students flocked to those classes. In Campbell's mind, real education consisted of learning the classics that he had studied as a college student, and not the vocational work of the present, though it offered women more possibilities in the working world other than teaching. In 1921, two students graduated from the classical course, while nine completed the home economics requirements, two the secretarial, seven the different music courses offered, and three the expression (or elocution) course.

The growth and reputation of the music conservatory at Irving also lured students away from the classical curriculum. Knowing how to play the piano well was the mark of a polished young lady and it appears that many women's colleges developed fine music departments for which to draw students. Through the efforts of Harry C. Harper, Irving's musical director from 1895–1918, music at Irving rose to new levels of popularity as Harper and his work in the Music Department established a statewide and regional reputation for music. The first music students graduated in 1896, the same year in which sixty-four piano forte, twenty-five vocal, and two violin students enrolled in classes. The course consisted of six grades beginning with a preparatory year and the sixth year being an advanced post-graduate study. Harper required students to memorize preludes by Bach; sonatas of Clementi, Haydn, Beethoven, and Mozart; etudes of Chopin and in the final year, pianoforte concertos of Mozart, Moschelles, Mendelssohn, Haydn, and Beethoven. Most students tried to take both the music and classical concentrations, often graduating with two degrees earned over five years; even most non-majors took several music classes. Campbell upgraded the curriculum of the Music Department in 1910, making it more difficult for students to carry both concentrations at the same time, with the reduction in the number of students in the college course. "A strong tendency among the students is to take the music course and the English, History, and Reading included in this course. We find it more and more difficult to persuade students to take the Regular College Course."[71] Unfortunately for Irving's classical

---

71. Campbell, E. E. Presidential Report to the Irving College Board of Trustees. Contained in Board of Trustees Minutes, June 6, 1911.

course, Irving College garnered much fame as a music conservatory and little else.

At Irving, a student could specialize in a variety of instruments while learning the basics about music: harmony, theory, and sight reading, among others. Piano was the staple instrument and most students learned on the more than 20 pianos at the school, before moving into different areas. Similarly, the Music Department offered a pipe organ instruction curriculum, enabling students to become church organists, which, after music teachers, tended to be the future occupations of Irving's music graduates. Violin, banjo, guitar, and mandolin instruction was available for music students, but other students could also study voice. The department incorporated voice culture with piano accompaniment in order to teach fundamental music knowledge and create a well-rounded music student. A Glee Club existed on campus under the direction of music faculty, with voice students performing operettas and cantatas to student and local audiences.

Growing in popularity throughout the early twentieth century, the music course at Irving became quite difficult. Students were not allowed sheet music for lessons, performance, or examination, so the students memorized every piece of music. Generally, students played in graduation recitals during commencement week, sang in Sunday church services, performed scattered concerts at Columbian Hall, and provided accompaniment for students plays, soirees, and commencement services.

Because of the widespread reputation of the Music Conservatory, music students were involved in a variety of activities within the community and on campus. Though its popularity (along with the secretarial and home economics tracks that gained popularity in the 1910s) undermined the classical course, the Music Department thrived during the Campbell years and helped to draw new students to the college.

Campbell tried his best to develop Irving into a first-class small college for women, upgrading the curriculum at every chance presented to him. Through an application process that involved somewhat stringent college admission standards which were also continually raised, students were still admitted at any educational level, entering the college level upon required achievement, with the ability to enroll in preparatory classes. Despite this move toward accentuating the classical curriculum of the school, the popularity of home economics and secretarial courses undermined the Latin and Greek classes Campbell saw as the backbone to a collegiate education. The possibilities for work directly out of college lured many students away from the difficult classics and into the more applicable courses that began appearing for degrees about 1910.

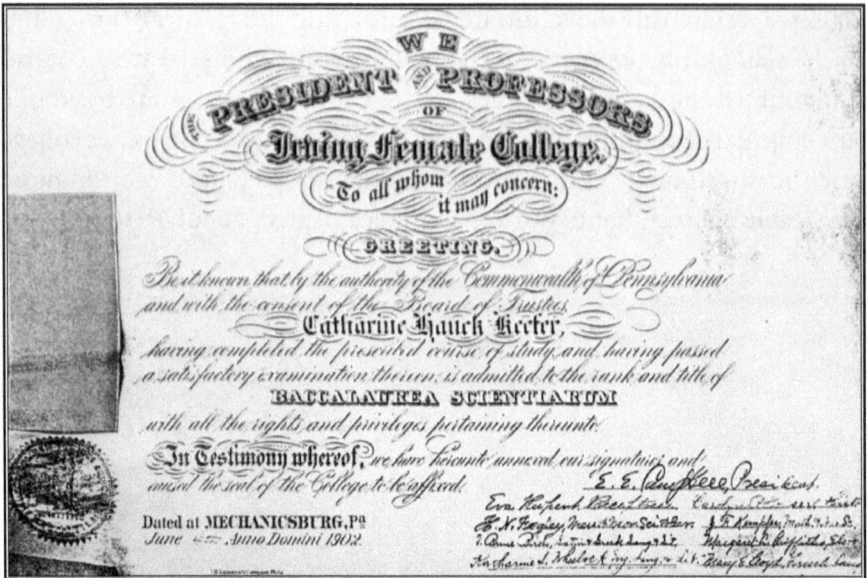

An Irving College diploma from 1912. Although most known for degrees in music, Irving handed out degrees in home economics, art, science classical studies and other bachelor's degrees.

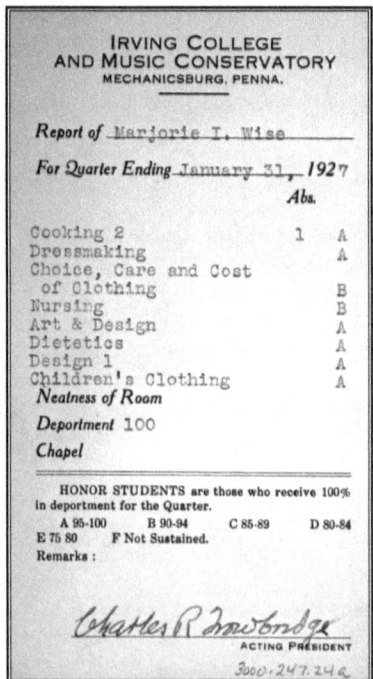

A report card of a student at Irving College in 1927. Student grades largely centered on results from final exams, though educators also graded student deportment, chapel attendance, and at times in the school's history, church attendance, punctuality, table etiquette and neatness.

CHAPTER FOUR

FACULTY LIFE, 1856–1929

In what year did the war of 1812 begin?
—Professor Howard Pennington Stemple, A.M. 1904[1]

Little evidence survives concerning the faculty of Irving College, making a reconstruction of their lives there challenging. Few copies of the Minutes of the Faculty Committee survive, thus giving a researcher only a taste of the business affairs of the teachers, and little college correspondence from Campbell or the school exists regarding hiring procedures, salary, or benefits. Background on the faculty's education and training appears occasionally through faculty sketches in yearbooks and college catalogues, though no primary source survives suggesting the reason for a large faculty turnover in the school's history.

From the start of the school in 1856, faculty resided in Irving Hall with the students, presiding over them as monitors, one per student residence hall floor. Campbell maintained this system throughout his tenure, allowing male faculty to live in Mechanicsburg and requiring female faculty to live at the school. Though no evidence suggests where male faculty lived while at Irving, most women's colleges maintained the standard of women faculty on the campus and men off, which was probably

---

1. "Jokes," *The Sketch Book,* Vol. VI, No. 4, February 1904, 10.

the case at Irving.² One professor who applied for a position at Irving in 1867 was informed by President Ege that he would receive a "warm and Comfortably furnished room, with everything as convenient as in a private family. Light and fuel included."³ Faculty members probably had rooms only slightly bigger than students, and ate in the school dining room, washed clothes through the school laundry, and received letters through the school's mail. For the school faculty, they lived at Irving as if they were student boarders: "The constant aim of every member of the College Family is to contribute to the pleasant social life of mutual confidence and cheerful acquiescence in College rules and to do the right *because it is right*."⁴

The women faculty performed a wider range of responsibilities than the professors at today's colleges. Acting as monitors at night to ensure students were asleep, the faculty monitored their students at the dinner table, on field trips, on afternoon walks, at church, and in the classroom. When interviewing teaching applicants, Ege described the teaching at Irving as not too laborious, giving recitation 5–6 hours per day in addition to required weekly attendance at church with students, and assistance with morning and evening school prayers. The teachers appeared to have no social lives while at Irving and the majority of the faculty who came to Irving tended not to be married (especially women), presenting problems for meeting companions. If married teachers arrived at Irving, it is doubtful that their entire family would reside at Irving, since town accommodations needed to be arranged for families. During lulls in school schedules, boyfriends visited teachers in the college parlor the same as student visitors. Adele Eichler was "an elocution teacher that the girls all loved . . . and she had a boyfriend who came to see her, and the girls were all thrilled about that."⁵ It must have been difficult to live at Irving nine or ten months out of the year and many faculty members may have resigned because of this, causing the high turnover of teachers.

---

2. There were not large numbers of faculty while Ege was president, so could it have been possible that he had male faculty living at Irving Hall with students and his family? Though most colleges kept male faculty off campus, and since Ege established student monitresses during his tenure, it appears likely that the men lived in town rather than at Irving.

3. Ege, T. P. Letter to Professor C. R. Gearhart, July 27, 1867.

4. *Greater America*, 4.

5. Oral History with Mary Lu Shaffer Heinz, (1925–1927), May 12, 1993.

Faculty Life, 1856-1929

According to Horowitz's *Alma Mater*, the constant interaction with students and lack of a private life caused many women teachers to quit at a college though deep down they enjoyed teaching,[6] but in order to remain in teaching and receive an independent salary, women had few other choices but to give up their social lives for nine months of school. Faculty also had to remain on their best behavior, acting as examples for the students, though by Campbell's tenure they could not mask everything as one student witnessed: "I know [Miss Naomi K. Hade] smoked because I saw her."[7] For the seemingly endless responsibilities, Ege offered $400 in salary for a professor, which could be considerably less if the educator lacked an advanced degree.

Though no concrete evidence survives of faculty salaries, some account books suggest what the Irving teachers may have been paid. In October of 1894, E. E. Campbell paid out $40 to Mary Kessler, $30 to M. Anna Griffiths, $40 to W. G. Campbell, $50 to Mrs. H. S. Kirkland, $50 to Mr. Harry Harper, $30 to Miss Elizabeth Kincheloe, and $30 to a Mr., Mrs., or Miss Pick. All of these individuals were faculty members, so it appears that this may have been their monthly paycheck, though long-time faculty member Rev. H. N. Fegley is absent from the books, and no one named Pick is listed in the college catalogues.[8] Another question with these numbers representing faculty salaries is that nine days after E. E. made these payments on October 12, Mr. Harry Harper is paid an additional $25, with no special mention made of it. These teachers could be paid different amounts relating to their experience and level of education as Harry Harper (the Music Director with a degree from the Boston Conservatory of Music) and Mr. H. S. Kirkland (who taught voice and piano) were paid $50, Mary L. Kessler (the former Irving Principal) and Rev. W. G. Campbell, A.M. were paid $40, while the remaining teachers listed, Griffiths (elocution and physical culture), Kincheloe (math), and Pick received $30. From this breakdown of payments, it appears that E. E. paid his experienced music faculty ($50/month, $450/school year) more than his college course faculty, who received more money

---

6. Horowitz, 182–184.
7. Oral History with Betty Boffemmyer Stram, '29, April 22, 1993.
8. No college catalogue still exists for this 1894–1895 school year, therefore a teacher named Pick could have been present. Fegley appears in both the 1893–94 and 1895–96 catalogues suggesting he taught at Irving over this year though he could have been away from the school for a term. Fegley also may not have accepted payment for his services, being a local minister in addition to teaching at Irving.

according to their experience: $40/month ($360/school year) for an advanced degree, and/or high-experience and $30/month ($270/school year) for a lesser degree and less experience. Since the trustees offered E. E. $1,800 as a salary in 1902 (as a beginning to transferring the college property over to the board), a sum that was about the standard wage for a small-college president, it is safe to assume that the faculty under him could not be earning salaries close to this amount.

The wages among the faculty differed according to their educational level and Irving faculty varied in their amount of education. The school usually had only one or two teachers at a time holding a Ph.D. and about one-third to one-half holding a master's degree. In the earliest days of the institution, few faculty members had advanced degrees; no Ph.D.'s are reported in college catalogues [Ph.D.'s were offered at U.S. universities starting in the 1880s], though several ministers, A.M.'s, and A.B.'s appear. The highest education level of the 257 educators known to have taught at Irving break down as follows: five had Ph.D.'s, four had D.D.'s, three had M.A.'s, one had just a B.A., forty-two had A.M.'s, forty-three had A.B.'s and eleven had B.S.'s [see Table 4.1]. In addition, nineteen of the faculty were ministers, twenty-four were listed as professors in the college catalogues, and there was a great deal of overlap, with many faculty members earning multiple degrees. The majority of the women faculty attended women's colleges—the only available education at the time—representing Metzger College in Carlisle; Smith College; Frederick and Hagerstown Female Seminaries in Maryland; Wellesley; Mt. Holyoke; Radcliffe; Simmons College in Boston; Goucher College in Baltimore; Wells College in Aurora, New York; Bryn Mawr, and Irving itself. A few of the women faculty achieved success at male-dominated schools such as Johns Hopkins, Columbia, the University of Pennsylvania, Northwestern, the University of London, Drexel, Cornell, and the University of Chicago, though nearly all of these women attended these colleges in the 1910s and 1920s after they opened more programs to women. The male faculty came from area colleges representing Dickinson, Roanoke College in Virginia, The Pennsylvania College at Gettysburg (Gettysburg College), University of Pennsylvania, Pennsylvania State College (Penn State), Millersville, Princeton, and even as far away as the University of Colorado. The art and music faculty studied at highly regarded schools, such as the Academy of Fine Arts in Philadelphia, the New England Conservatory of Music in Boston, Peabody Conservatory in Baltimore, the Maryland Institute of Art in Columbia, the New York School of Music and Arts, the Emerson School of Oratory in Boston, the Harrisburg Conservatory of Music, the Royal Academy of Music in London, and the London College of Music.

TABLE 4.1. VARIANCE OF DEGREES OF FACULTY AT IRVING COLLEGE, 1856-1929. The following table lists the number of faculty who earned the degrees listed. This material was derived from the faculty listed in the college catalogues and their degrees listed therein. Since some catalogues are missing not every faculty member is accounted for in this table, and there is some skepticism as to their listing of degrees. There is some overlap in this table as some of the faculty earned multiple degrees, therefore the number of degrees is listed in this table and not the number of faculty.

DEGREE	# AT IRVING	DEGREE	# AT IRVING	DEGREE	# AT IRVING
A.B. (atrium baccalaureus)	43	A.M. (Masters of arts)	42	B.S. (bachelor of science)	11
Mus.B. (bachelor of music)	5	Ph.D. (Doctor of Philosophy)	4	Ph.B. (bachelor of Philosophy)	4
D.D. (doctor of divinity)	4	M.A. (master of arts)	3	M.E. (master of English)	2
B.Ped. (bachelor of physical education)	1	M.E.L. (mistress of English literature?)	1	B.A. (bachelor of arts)	1
M.D. (doctor of medicine)	1	Sc.D. (doctor of science)	1	B.E. (bachelor of English)	1
B.O. (bachelor of oratory)	1	Esq.(Law)	1	–	–

Many of the individual educators developed quite a resume by the time they reached Irving. Mildred L. Smith, who taught Latin and Spanish in the late 1920s, received her A.B. from Grinnell College and did graduate study at the University of Minnesota, the University of Hawaii, and *La Sorbonne* in France. Myrtle Pider, on staff teaching English in Irving's last year, received an A.B. and A.M. from Northwestern, a Diploma in English at Columbia, and also studied at the University of London. Mary Alice Port, who never taught classes while at Irving holding the preceptress position, obtained a wide variety of schooling, receiving an A.B. from Smith in 1890, and did graduate work in education at Clark University in Worcester, Massachusetts, graduate work in Greek, Latin, and education at Columbia, and additional graduate work in Greek and Latin literature and archaeology at Oxford University in Great Britain.[9] Miss Winefred Sterrett Woods of Carlisle came to Irving as a new art teacher in 1907, after graduating from Metzger College, studying at the Academy of Fine Arts in Philadelphia, teaching at Albright College in Reading, and directing the Art Department at Conceptión College in Chile, South America for five years. Maud Thompson taught at Irving for only two years (1902–1904) but achieved a remarkable record with an A.B. from Wellesley, an M.A. from Yale in 1902, and a Ph.D. from Yale in 1906. Described by Lenore Embick Flower, '04 as a "true feminist," she had a strong personality that either made students believe in suffrage for women or become starkly against it: "[t]o defend the proposition that women have the right to vote is like defending justice[–]the abstract idea of Justice. In fact the defence [*sic*] of women's political rights is defence [*sic*] of Justice. If people do not believe in equal suffrage[,] they do not believe in Justice."[10] Surely frustrated with the conservative students, faculty and atmosphere at Irving, Thompson left Irving, taking her strong educational background elsewhere.

---

9. Port had a busy schedule and remarkable life. After graduating Smith in 1890, she was the principal of a high school in Maltoon, Illinois for two years, from where she moved on to become a teacher and associate principal of the All Saints School in Sioux Falls, South Dakota from 1892–1896. In the summer of 1897 she did her graduate work at Clark, and she became the head mistress at the Tacomic School in Lakeville, Connecticut, where she stayed until 1899. For the next year and a half, she did her graduate work at Columbia, until she moved to Tacoma, Washington to accept the principal position at Annie Wright Seminary from 1900–1903. From 1903 until she took the preceptress position at Irving in 1905, she underwent graduate work at Oxford and traveling in Europe.

10. Flower, 24.

Before these remarkable women however, the most educated faculty members tended to be the ministers usually hired to teach biblical history, mental and moral science, or lead chapel services. In Irving's early days, the most educated men were Rev. Henry I. Comfort, A.B., who taught math (1857–1859?), Rev. R. D. Chambers A.M. from the East Baltimore Conference, who taught ancient and modern language (1859–1863), Rev. J. Jewett Parks A.M. (1865–1867), and Rev. J. R. Bailey (1867–1869?), who taught mental and moral science. In the Campbell years, Rev. George Fulton (1916–1929) achieved his A.B. from Centre College (in Danville, KY), his A.M. from Princeton, and his D.D. at Centre College, while Rev. J. K. Robb (1918–1921), A.M., Ph.D. taught Physics, Chemistry, and Math in addition to his chaplain duties. Rev. Henry N. Fegley was a mainstay in the Irving faculty for 20 years (1892–1912) teaching German along with his ministerial classes. Graduating from the University of Pennsylvania in 1869, Fegley graduated from the Mt. Airy Lutheran Theological Seminary three years later and went on to pastor St. Mark's Lutheran Church in Mechanicsburg. Rev. T. B. Birch A.M., taught Latin language and literature in addition to religion (1896–1902), though spending only a short time at Irving.

A few non-clergy faculty achieved excellent educational backgrounds and taught at Irving, though for only a short time, since tiny Irving and its smaller paychecks could not afford to keep the top scholars for long.[11] Howard P. Stemple (1902–1914) became a noted member of the Irving faculty teaching history, sociology, and economics only one year after teaching high school, two years after achieving his A.M. in history and economics at Princeton, and four years after receiving his A.B. from Roanoke College in Virginia. Stemple left Irving to study at Oxford and then to teach at Allegheny and Ohio Wesleyan Colleges. William H. Ames Ph.B., taught sociology and economics for only one year at Irving (1901–1902), Professor E. D. Weigle, D.D. of Greek and Latin literature lasted four years (1896–1900), while Professor F. P. Matz, Ph.D., Sc.D. taught math, astronomy, and natural science and lasted only four years (1895–1899).

11. According to Flower, 23, the salaries that Campbell could offer the faculty at Irving were not enough to keep the more learned scholars from obtaining better positions elsewhere. Thus, many tended to stay for only a short time.

The variation of faculty education levels and the wages they earned probably resulted in the high turnover of teachers at Irving from the outset. The faculty, aside from the president, changed completely in 1867 and 1869, while Ege listed in college catalogues that empty positions would be filled during each summer from 1869 to 1873, and probably several years afterwards. Marlatt had better stability with his faculty, though he did hire three teachers of instrumental music and four in vocal music in five years. But Ege was much more severe, going through four art teachers (including several vacancies) in four years, five vocal music teachers in nine years, four English teachers (including one vacancy of three years), and no permanent math or moral science teachers after 1869. Campbell had a revolving door of teachers too, though more teachers stayed for longer periods under him. Harry Harper, Rev. H. N. Fegley, Katherine Steck Wheelock, and Rev. George Fulton were among those who remained the longest, though Campbell did have his own turnover problems. Under Campbell, Irving had three different math teachers in three years from 1892–1895, three different people teaching economics and sociology from 1900–1903, and had nine new faculty in 1892, nine new faculty in 1895, seven new people in 1904, six in 1915, seven in 1916, seven in 1917, nine in 1918, six in 1924, and six in 1926. Despite this changing of the guards, Campbell paid ten veteran faculty (including himself) out of twelve in 1907, with six members teaching at Irving longer than five years and two for a period of ten years. In 1923, Campbell employed thirteen veterans out of nineteen, with eight of them in place for three years and three of them in place longer than five years. Regardless of Campbell's success as an administrator and drawing students to Mechanicsburg, he failed to completely prevent Irving's history of high faculty turnover.

Of the faculty positions, the one with the most responsibility at Irving was the preceptress, who was the disciplinarian and administrator of the pupils for Dr. Campbell. Any student questions or problems went through the preceptress, who also examined dresses before dances and gave permission to walk downtown or visit Harrisburg. According to Irving students, the preceptress was "[o]ur nurse when we are ill; our giver of punishment and reward, when we deserve it; our teacher of etiquette at all times; our college mother, who gives her time to our wants, desires, and troubles, when our own mothers are far away."[12] The fire alarm bell and the master light control switch were situated in the preceptress' room to allow for student control and the constant knowledge of campus occurrences. In fact, every night at 10:00 P.M., just to be sure the students would do nothing but sleep, the preceptress pulled the fuse located in her room which cut all the lights in the dormitories, preventing last-minute, nighttime studying. The preceptress instilled an air of respect and fear in the students, and many of the women who held the position tended not be as liked as much as other members of the faculty. The preceptress even scared the kitchen help. Mae Noss, a dining room server in 1929, broke the preceptress' quiet bell in the dining hall when horsing around one day. Scared of what would happen despite the student laughter with the preceptress absent, Noss quickly brought the bell to a jewelry store in town to have it fixed before the preceptress returned later that day. Luckily for Noss, the preceptress never found out.

Marlatt and Ege employed competent faculty members, though little is known about many who taught at Irving before 1890. Rev. Henry I. Comfort, A.B. (1856–1858) received commendation from the *Weekly Gazette:* "[Comfort is] a young man of good attainments, and experience in the art of teaching, and his affibility [sic] and gentlemanly deportment amply qualify him for the responsible position to which he has just been chosen [to teach at Irving].[13] Miss Katherine A. Bradley (1868?–1873) "was a most thorough, efficient, and conscientious teacher, infusing into her subjects a personality and enthusiasm that made them an ever recurring delight" while teaching under President Ege.[14] Standing as second in authority to Ege (according to the boarding students), Bradley acted as the Ege-era version of a preceptress, while also teaching *belles lettres* and history.

Campbell had exceptional faculty commended by the board or by the students. Harry Clyde Harper developed the music conservatory at Irving from its small beginnings into a thriving and popular program.

---

12. *The Sketch Book*, 1923, 22.
13. *Weekly Gazette*, Vol. II, No. 49, October 22, 1857. Henry I. Comfort taught mathematics.
14. Kramer, Mary W. "Miss Katherine A. Bradley," *The Sketch Book*, Vol. II, Nos. 4–5, February/March 1896, 110.

Graduating from the Boston Conservatory of Music, Harper established a strong Music Department which grew beyond his twenty-three years at the college (1895–1918). "[Harper] deserves special commendation for the very superior work done in his department. He has developed it year by year until now Irving's Music Department is second to none in the state. The strong tendency of our student-body is to run toward the Music Department . . ."[15] A dashing and handsome young man, whom all the students especially liked, Harper went on to head the Music Department at the University of South Dakota, and also became a member of the Hood College (Frederick, Maryland) faculty. While teaching at Irving, he resided nearby at 410 East Main Street, and remained close to his students, giving each of them a studio photograph of himself before resigning his position at Irving. The board of trustees recognized his fruitful efforts upon his resignation in 1918:

> Mr. Harper identified himself with the musical life of Mechanicsburg and always showed a very willing and generous spirit in promoting and aiding things musical in town. His friends in town are many. His connection with Irving College covered a period of 23 years. During this time he had entire charge of the music at the College and established a reputation for thoroness [sic] in his department that has made the College known thruout [sic] Pennsylvania and in other states of the Union.[16]

As he did with Harper, Campbell thought very highly of Miss Elizabeth Jane Rae, who taught expression, English classics, and physical culture from 1913 to 1917. E. E. thought Rae owned an uncanny personality: "always bright and happy and cheery, with a smile and good word for everybody on all occasions, which is wholesome and sincere, has done much to place her department on a very high plane. She is one of the best teachers in this department we have ever had."[17]

---

15. Campbell, E. E. Presidential Report, Irving College Board of Trustees Minutes, June 2, 1908.
16. Irving College Board of Trustees Minutes, June 4, 1918.
17. Irving College Board of Trustees Minutes, June 1, 1915.

Adele Eichler "was the most interesting teacher I ever had[,]" said Betty Boffemmyer Stram, '29. Eichler, a charming and well-read person who knew how to teach, taught dramatics at Irving from 1925–1927, teaching many of the students how to act, speak, walk, and stand. Intent on memorization in her classes, Eichler drew from a strong background from which to teach, learning the finer points of dramatics with the Shakespeare Players in England. After Irving, Eichler started the Harrisburg Community Theater, which is still in operation today.

Though students liked handsome teachers like Harper or professors with a lot of personality like E. E. Campbell, students also liked teachers they could manipulate:

> if we didn't know what [Rev. Dr. George Fulton] was talking about, or what he had assigned to us, we'd get him started on one of his pet projects, or one of his pet sermons, and he'd forget the time, and he'd talk. Then we'd keep asking him questions and he would take a whole period and discuss this one thing. We didn't have to answer anything. No wonder I got A's![18]

With the wide variety of classes taught at Irving, students learned from a diverse crew of teachers, some of whom faced other difficulties at Irving: "I remember taking French from a French woman who could barely speak a word of English which was a trial and tribulation. She was very peculiar as far as her manners and her clothing were concerned, and of course it was a subject for the girls to talk about."[19] Though Campbell hired the best faculty he could, and some situations caused difficulties for students, he was usually on top of such issues.

Women enjoyed occupational opportunities while at Irving, since women constituted a majority of the faculty. Many of the women's colleges hired few women, if any at first, and it appears that smaller women's colleges installed women teachers out of necessity, whether they wanted them or not. With the low salaries that Irving and other smaller colleges offered, it is quite possible that male faculty could not always be hired,

---

18. Oral History with Ruth Hoy Diffenderfer, '26, June 9, 1993.
19. Oral History, Mary Lu Shaffer Heinz, (1925–1927), May 12, 1993.

therefore women teachers filled many of the small college positions. Out of the nine faculty Marlatt paid in 1857, three were women, teaching *belles lettres* and physiology; piano, guitar, and singing; and painting in oil and colored crayons. For his staff, he hired six more women in the next five years. Women held three out of five faculty positions with Ege in 1867, and four out of five in 1869, as he added six more women (and one man) to the faculty in the next six years. When Irving reopened in 1889 under Kessler, she employed eight women out of the nine faculty under her, featuring graduates from Smith, Wittenberg, and Wilson Colleges. When Campbell assumed the presidency, five of his eleven faculty were women, in 1892, seven out of thirteen were women, in 1900, eight out of sixteen were women, in 1907, seven out of twelve were women, and in 1922, twelve out of sixteen were women. Women taught nearly all of the home economics classes, the physical education, dramatics, elocution, English and foreign language, and most of the secretarial classes, while men faculty members usually taught the math courses, religion, psychology, and science. The classics, music, history, and art courses employed the efforts of both men and women. There were exceptions to these rules; Miss Catherine Hemperly teaching chemistry, physics, and math in 1913 and Mr. H. W. Stratton teaching French language and literature in 1907. In most classes, faculty generally fell into traditional roles at Irving with the courses they taught.

A Faculty Committee held monthly meetings to discuss topics and resolve issues relating to the school's rules and curriculum. They voted on student expulsions, decided upon changes in the students' caps and gowns, and scrutinized questions affecting the education of the school. This committee acted more like an administrative governing body for student punishment, possibly working closely with the student government, though the faculty and President Campbell had the final word on severe issues such as expulsion. The committee may have had further reaching responsibilities, but due to the few committee minutes that survive, it is difficult to determine what those may have been.

Aspects of faculty life outside of teaching are also scarce in the records that survive. Apparently, the teachers had their own social time, which often consisted of receptions held by E. E. in his home or in Columbian

Hall after the students were asleep. Evidence suggests that Miss Sarah Elizabeth Trump (preceptress, 1920–1929) had at least one party, living in the most space in Irving Hall, taking up school room thirty with her living room and room thirty-one with her bedroom. Since Trump was relatively young when at Irving and many other female teachers accepted teaching positions immediately after obtaining their college degrees, they naturally desired socializing too, so it is likely that these parties may have occurred somewhat frequently. Students remembered Trump meeting frequently with different men in the parlor, and since most of the younger teachers hired were not married, this was probably a common practice. However, the faculty worked a tight schedule keeping an eye on students when they weren't preparing for classes or grading coursework, so the free time teachers actually received was surely minimal.

Though the faculty had the most contact with and the most influence over the students, other individuals worked at Irving to maintain the everyday running of the college. Different staff, some of whom came from the surrounding area, worked in the kitchen cooking the food, serving the students, and washing the girls' laundry. Mae Noss, who worked as an Irving dining hall server in 1929, brought meat and vegetables out from the dumb waiter connected outside to the kitchen, but did not directly serve the students herself. Servers, always wearing simple black dresses with aprons, only worked during the mealtime periods, going home at about 10:30 after the breakfast shift and coming back to the dining hall just before each subsequent meal. Unlike today, the administration forbade students from working on the campus, so most of the kitchen and dining help lived nearby. In the 1920s, for example, the dishwasher lived on Locust Street and the vegetable prep person on Simpson Street, two streets within a short walk of campus. For those workers who lived further away, Campbell owned a row of houses on Chestnut Street near the school, where there were several apartments with a bedroom and kitchen for out-of-town help to stay overnight (Campbell may also have used these living spaces for male faculty). Noss obtained her job at Irving through word of mouth when someone recommended her to the head waitress in the dining hall for an open position. Helping for only everyday meals, servers received holidays off in addition to every third Sunday. Most Sundays involved a lighter workload for servers, since only one server had to come in for the morning shift to feed the Campbell family (nearly all the students slept in, missing Sunday breakfast) and at nighttime, as the cooks often prepared picnic lunches, which the students picked up from the servers downstairs in the Irving Hall lobby. The servers were paid $7 per week, with the cooks and maintenance help probably being paid a little more, and the chambermaids probably about the same. In addition to the servers, Irving College hired cooks who received additional kitchen help from the chambermaids, dishwashers, laundry help, a handy man, and both a head server and head maid who governed the work done by the appropriate workers under their responsibility. Though only evidence late in the Campbell tenure describes the kitchen and office staff at Irving, workers under Ege and Marlatt most likely had similar job duties and characteristics.

The dining staff fed the student's appetites for food, and the office staff handled the students' money and updated their files, records, and other business. In the 1920s, E. E.'s son Paul worked in the college office taking care of transcripts, grades, and selling the books and supplies to the students. "The office maintained things that the students would want, like stamps and we'd order books from them, and when the books would come in they would come get them. There was a pencil sharpener [and] students would sharpen pencils [there]."[20] Paul maintained this office: "[y]ou could always depend on Paul. He was always there [at the college office]. He was always willing to help you."[21] "Paul would mostly have been [in the office], and he knew everybody . . . I imagine . . . he knew more of the students than anybody else."[22]

Another campus worker, Daniel Jackson, was a full-chested African American man, who had a very friendly demeanor and acted as the caretaker for the college. He would release a huge security dog named Max on the college campus to roam around at night and scare off prowlers and young men trying to sneak by. Max had quite a reputation for ferocity and a rumor states that the dog even scared the students into staying

---

20. Oral History with Jane Campbell Beard, '29, April 12, 1994.
21. Oral History with Ruth Hoy Diffenderfer, '26, June 9, 1993.
22. Oral History with Jane Campbell Beard, '29, April 12, 1994.

in their dormitory rooms. But Max's reign of terror ended one evening when Mrs. Campbell tried to come onto campus and was "assaulted by Max, who, I just suppose jumped up on her, or snarled at her . . . and managed to tear her dress."[23] Max was not seen on campus after that incident, but during his stay, Daniel cared for the dog and fed him, bringing him inside or chaining him during the day.

The students appreciated the job Jackson did, commemorating him in *Irvingiana '03* explaining him as "Daniel Jackson R. H. M., O. M. H., Professor of Boiler Engineering, . . . instructor in Domestic Arts at Irving 1893–1901," referring to the fact that he kept care of the furnace boiler and general upkeep of the school (making him an instructor in domestic arts).[24] "His works on 'The Best and Quickest Way of Handling Trunks,' and 'The Baneful Effects of Electric Lights,' are now in press," displays the variety of responsibilities that Jackson had despite the joke made here by the *Irvingiana* staff.[25]

In addition to general maintenance and kitchen staff, the board of trustees played a significant part in the school. Solomon Gorgas, the school's founder, was a trustee, as was Dr. Ira Day (1799–1868), who was Irving's first board president and remained so until his death [see table 4.2].[26] Rev. A. R. Steck, D.D., a close friend of E. E. Campbell from their days working together at Tressler's Orphans Home in Loysville (Campbell was director, Steck one of its trustees), became board president in 1899. Born in Lancaster on August 8th, 1861, he graduated from Gettysburg College in 1882, graduated from Gettysburg Theological Seminary in 1886, and received his ordination the same year. He served as a Lutheran minister in Stewartsville, New Jersey, the First Lutheran Church of Indianapolis, the St. James Church in Gettysburg, and Union Lutheran Church in York. A well-liked man and a fabulous speaker, Steck served as the Irving Board President through its closing and the board's

---

23. Oral History with Jane Campbell Beard, '29, April 12, 1994.

24. *Irvingiana '03*, 109. This citation of Daniel Jackson was done as a humorous aside for the student's yearbook. The letters beside his name appear as "degrees earned" though I believe that R. H. M. stands for Residence Hall Maintenance, and O. M. H. could stand for Overall Maintenance Help (or something similar).

25. *Irvingiana '03*, 109.

26. Ira and his wife Elizabeth Day (1807–1865) gave birth to 10 children: Alfred (1830–1884), Annette (1832–1909), Caroline E. (1834–1835), John Emory (1836–1857), Mary (1838–1884), Susan A. (1840–1873), Jacob F. (1842–1865), Ira, Jr. (1845–1845), Francis B. (1847–1875), and Lizzie (1852–1877).

dissolving in 1940, watching his daughter Catherine attend Irving as a high school student from 1915–1918. Rev. S. W. Herman, D.D., joined the trustees in 1917 and served as the Board Vice President from 1920 until after the school's closing in 1940. Herman helped out with college affairs, signing college applications, and probably helping Campbell in deciding upon students for admission. Unusual for a non-profit organization, Presidents Ege and Campbell, both proprietors of the college, sat on the school's board of trustees, making their approach to the school multi-dimensional as well as illegal, according to Irving's charter.

TABLE 4.2. IRVING COLLEGE BOARD OF TRUSTEES PRESIDENTS, 1856-1940. The following is a list of Irving's Board Presidents as listed in the trustee minutes.

IRVING PRESIDENT OF THE BOARD	YEARS AS PRESIDENT (AS A TRUSTEE)
Dr. Ira Day	1855-1868 (1855-1868)
Dr. P. H. Long	1869-1877 (1855-1877)
David Coover	1877-1883 (1855-1883)[1]
A. W. Lilly	1890-1902 (1890-1902)
Rev. A. R. Steck	1902-1940 (1902-1940)

---

1. No record of Coover's death is listed in the board minutes, but the David Coover who is buried at Chestnut Hill Cemetery, dies on March 31, 1883 and is reported to be a trustee of the College along with his brother John. Since no board minutes survive from 1879–1889 it is difficult to determine whether the board stopped meeting during Irving's hiatus from 1883–1888, or that those minutes just did not survive.

Rev. A.R. Steck was Irving College's longest serving President and a close confidante of E.E. Campbell, serving with him also as a trustee of Tressler's Orphans Home. A Lutheran minister, Steck graduated from Gettysburg Theological Seminary.

CONCLUSION

IRVING'S LEGACY

ALTHOUGH this work appears to be a complete history of Irving, from Gorgas and *The Sketch Book* through Harry Harper and domestic science, many questions remain unanswered about the school itself. Future archival donations to the Joseph T. Simpson Library or other successful searches may eventually provide more information. Due to unfortunate bad timing, at the initial time of this research, many microfilmed newspapers were largely unavailable from before 1965, which encompasses every year that Irving was open. While some editions of Mechanicsburg's *Weekly Gazette*, *Cumberland Valley Journal*, and *The Daily Journal* resided at other repositories, the majority of the rest of the newspapers remained unavailable for reference. Much information concerning the school might be found in these newspapers, including further information regarding life at Irving during the 1870s and 1880s, of which almost nothing remains in sources investigated herein. Clarification on Matthew H. Reaser's purchase of the college and Campbell's "retirement" in 1917, Kessler's reopening of the school, local reaction to Kessler in charge, and the school's final closing in 1929 all could be accentuated further with possible newspaper articles.

With the Simpson Library publicizing their Irving College Collection of yearbooks, student records, college catalogues, and trustee minutes at the time of this initial research, more primary sources are coming into the library's hands at every turn. Though most of the recent donations have been additions to sources already in the collection, it is quite possible that

Conclusion: Irving's Legacy

new accessions will come to the library that could shed more information concerning student organizations, private lives, and the Campbell family. Additional oral histories were supposed to be conducted with other living Irving students and employees (some of which are not necessarily the positive view that permeates the currently available ones) in the later 1990s, so additional information about student life in the dormitories, classroom structure, and course load might be obtained. Very little material survives concerning the faculty at Irving, and while it seems doubtful at this point that much new light could be shed on this subject, there are always other ways to approach the question for new insights.

Irving could also be examined in more detail concerning several administrative and student issues that are only generally mentioned in this work. Campbell's fight with William Gies over the ownership issue of the school appears not only in the board minutes but also in letters that were salvaged in the luggage of Paul and Lilly Grace Campbell. Extensive student records, including transcripts and letters of reference, are present for nearly all of Campbell's tenure and the last three years of the school, making a small study of class registration and student grades viable options for future research. Though Irving is compared to several schools in each of the chapters in different subject areas, there is certainly more room for comparative histories between Irving and other women's colleges, co-educational colleges, and even men's schools. Curriculum between many schools and Irving is scrutinized in considerable detail in this work, but comparisons of student and faculty life with other colleges could make for an interesting study. Horowitz's *Alma Mater* outlines the entire Seven Sister women's colleges and comparing Irving with these is certainly worthy of consideration to discover the similarities and differences between large, successful colleges and smaller, lesser-known schools. Comparisons between Irving and other colleges of its size (about 100–130 students each school year) could shed additional light on unanswerable questions concerning Irving which may be available in other school's archives.

Irving College does not stand out as the first women's college, nor does it stand out as the first women's college in Pennsylvania. However, it does provide a history of a school with characteristics similar to other women's colleges of the time (strict rules, originally one building for student and faculty residence), and yet different (it lasted seventy-three years with no endowment; it is an example of the liberal idea of educating women in a conservative Pennsylvania town). It is through the examination of these smaller and more widespread "Division B" schools, that a sense for the experience of a majority of women and their college educations can be understood. Not every woman could go to Smith, Vassar, or Bryn Mawr, and just as the histories of Harvard, Yale, and Penn do not describe the story of the majority of young men's experiences at college, nor should Smith, Vassar, or Bryn Mawr. With their excellent courses and strong admissions standards, many women attended smaller and lesser-known schools like Irving instead of the well-known and largely written-about Wellesleys, Mount Holyokes, and Radcliffes.

Irving and these other lesser-known schools tell the story of these women. These smaller colleges often started without an endowment or state support, struggling with their proprietors through economic depressions and financial hardships. Irving grew as its educational leaders took command; Kessler reopened the school after it was closed by the Commissioner of Education, and Campbell constructed additional buildings and increased the number of students, raising the college to heights never before reached. Schools suffered from competition and many of the women's colleges closed in the twentieth century since more and more young women preferred to attend colleges where men enrolled, rather than in segregated schools. Often affiliated with religious denominations, many schools could be supported through local synods or church establishments; Irving was not so lucky, being only loosely tied with the Methodists and later with the Lutherans.

Students established their own organizations on campus, and these grew in the twentieth century, providing musical, literary, and social pursuits. A student's life at college, with its required hours of study and widespread participation in plays, recitals, college annuals, and student publications, resembled that of a person in business with no time in his or her schedule. Students established sororities and pushed for more privileges while at school, but sororities and their selectivity were abolished at Irving. Men, smoking (though in secret), and dancing appeared more widespread by the 1920s, as they did on other campuses. Students generally studied and obeyed the many regulations placed upon them, forcing them to bed by 10 P.M., requiring walks to the movies to be chaperoned, and mandating chapel services and study hours.

As colleges such as Irving strove for strength within their classical courses by providing additional Latin classes and advanced levels of Greek, most women initially were excluded, needing preparatory classes in order to enter the collegiate level. As the colleges upgraded their courses to equal men's colleges by 1900, women, somewhat ironically, raced to take the new classes offered in secretarial training and home economics, leaving the regular college courses with fewer and fewer students. The immediate employment opportunities of secretarial and home economics courses drew large numbers of students away from the standard curriculum in women's colleges which usually only offered teaching—and perhaps diminished chances for marriage—as a viable occupational option.

For women faculty, life at Irving at times mirrored student life, since women teachers had to give up outside social lives to live with the students—teaching their minds, watching their table manners, and monitoring their every behavior. Male faculty lived off-campus and enjoyed more freedom, but both men and women teachers at these smaller schools frequently left for more money and better positions elsewhere; even the most devoted of teachers could not stay for their entire careers. Many other teachers left not because they grew to dislike teaching, but because the constant demands placed upon them to teach and monitor students were too much to take. Wanting social lives of their own, since many of the arriving faculty had just graduated from colleges themselves, women faculty left for marriage or for sanity, while highly experienced male faculty took their Ph.D.'s to larger schools that could offer them higher salaries.

With an effervescent personality and a strong teaching background, Rev. A. G. Marlatt brought Solomon Gorgas's dream of a women's college to life. Thompson P. Ege brought that dream to a close, facing economic depressions, declining enrollments, financial incapability, and a direct order from the Commissioner of Education. Mary Kessler rolled up her sleeves and reestablished Irving, working hard, and facing hardships from conservatives who disagreed with the idea and the fact of a woman in charge. Dr. E. E. Campbell brought Irving to a new level. With a sense of humor and zest for life, Campbell adopted Irving as his own to plant, cultivate, and care for. Giving up his college only once to M. H. Reaser, who chose afterwards not to continue its educational path, Campbell *was* Irving College until his death when, despite many hard-fought attempts, Irving ceased to exist.

For nearly seventy-five years, Irving brought educational opportunities to Cumberland Valley women (and beyond) who just began to realize their potential and possibilities with higher education. By admitting students at any age and educational level, Irving provided services to many diverse young women. Some used Irving to achieve a college degree as a steppingstone to a teaching career, others attended one class or a few as a curiosity. Today its legacy largely unknown, its educational fruits forgotten, its structures all but disappearing, Irving College is a far outcry from when it once stood as an educational earmark in Mechanicsburg, admitting Northeastern, Southern, and Midwestern students, providing town residents with social functions, receptions, and an educational atmosphere, and allowing a liberal idea to expand within a conservative shell. Even facing criticism and especially financial hardship throughout its history and certainly at its end, Irving College stood as an influential and important place that was well-liked by residents, adored by many of its alumnae, and was one of the pillars standing to aid women in their progression throughout the nineteenth and twentieth centuries.

APPENDIX A

IRVING COLLEGE ADMINISTRATION

TABLE 1. DR. CAMPBELL'S REAL ESTATE ESTIMATE, 1901. Taken from the Board of Trustees Minutes on November 29, 1901, Dr. Campbell submitted the following as the value of Irving College, which he then owned. The Board was seeking to obtain the college property from him since the original charter vested the property in the hands of the trustees, though in 1901 that was not the reality.

Irving College Holdings Estimated Cost	
Property including campus, Irving and Columbian Halls	$28,000
Subsequent additions to college real estate	2,000
Four-acre addition and improvements thereon	1,000
First cost of pipe organ	1,350
Present valuation of all other musical instruments consisting of 2 concert grand "Knabe" pianos, 3 small practice claviers, and 16 other pianos	6,650
Valuation of all furnishings at present not including musical instruments	12,000
Total Valuation	51,000
Amount asked for all the property	60,000
Apparent profit demanded	9,000

TABLE 2. CAMPBELL'S FINANCIAL SUMMARIES, 1898-1901. At the board's request, Campbell submitted estimated amounts of his earnings through his ownership of Irving College. The committee of the board that reviewed these numbers said that the "'earnings' in exact figures are slightly greater," meaning that E. E. had rounded the numbers.

	1898-1899	1899-1900	1900-1901
Receipts	$24,000	$23,000	$32,000
Expenditures	13,000	15,000	22,000
Earnings	11,000	8,000	10,000

TABLE 3. IRVING COLLEGE'S NET WORTH 1873-1929. The following is a list of the monetary worth of Irving College's buildings, grounds, apparatus, etc. taken from trustee minutes and Reports of the Commissioner to the U.S. Board of Education for selected years.

Year	College Worth	Year	College Worth
1873	$30,000	1899	$65,000
1875	33,000	1900	70,000
1876	30,000	1901	60,000
1877	35,000	1902	50,000
1880	40,000	1903	75,000
1888	20,000	1906	100,000
1894	40,000	1907	75,000
1898	80,000	1910	100,000

TABLE 4. IRVING COLLEGE INCOME 1888-1915. The following lists further financial information for selected years of the school during Kessler's and Campbell's terms relating to how successful the college was financially. Net income, money collected from tuition and outside sources are all included from *Reports of the Commissioner of Education of the U.S.*, 1888-1915.

YEAR	INCOME FROM STUDENT FEES	INCOME FROM OUTSIDE SOURCES	TOTAL INCOME
1888	$1,200	$0	$1,200
1894	30,000	0	30,000
1895	25,000	15,000	40,000
1896	5,000	0	5,000
1897	NA	NA	25,000
1898	9,175	0	9,175
1899	9,100	14,600	23,700
1900	12,000	18,000	30,000
1905	15,800	0	15,800
1906	32,000	0	32,000
1907	29,000	0	29,000
1910	32,000	0	32,000
1912	31,100	0	31,100
1913	33,590	0	33,590
1915	35,541	0	35,541

APPENDIX B

IRVING COLLEGE STUDENT STATISTICS

TABLE 1. **IRVING'S STUDENT ORIGINS.** The following table outlines from which states Irving students had come as listed in the college catalogues for the particular years. Some years are not included since the catalogues or information are not available. Other years contain scant information on the total number of students enrolled and were estimated according to student records and board minutes. Additional abbreviations used include CN for Canada, PR for Puerto Rico, CU for Cuba, and NR for Norway.

[see facing page]

Irving College Student Statistics

States of Student Origin and Number of Students from Each State
plus: New England (NE), South[1] (SO), Midwest (MW), Great Plains (GP)

Year	PA	MD	DE	VA	OH	NY	DC	WV	NJ	NE	SO	MW	GP	Other
1857-1858	72	2	9	3	2	1	0	0	0	0	0	2	0	0
1859-1860	40	18	9	1	1	0	0	0	0	0	0	1	0	0
1861-1862	37	17	0	0	1	0	0	0	0	0	0	0	0	0
1864-1865	48	19	2	2	0	1	4	0	0	0	0	0	0	0
1865-1866	54	23	3	1	0	0	2	0	0	1	2	0	1	0
1866-1867	46	8	0	0	0	0	1	2	0	0	0	1	0	0
1867-1868	47	4	0	0	2	0	1	1	0	0	0	2	0	0
1869-1870	36	11	0	0	0	1	1	0	0	0	0	0	0	0
1870-1871	27	17	0	1	0	0	0	0	1	0	0	1	0	0
1871-1872	20	18	1	1	0	1	1	0	0	0	0	1	0	0
1872-1873	22	10	1	1	0	1	4	0	0	0	0	0	0	0
1873-1874	26	8	0	2	0	1	1	0	0	0	0	0	0	0
1875-1876	33	4	0	3	0	0	1	0	0	0	0	1	0	0
1889-1890	37	0	0	0	0	0	2	0	0	0	0	0	0	0
1890-1891	54	0	0	0	1	1	0	0	0	1	0	1	0	0
1891-1892	69	1	0	0	0	0	0	0	0	0	0	0	0	0

1. This category of southern states does not include the previously mentioned Virginia, Maryland, or Delaware.

	PA	MD	DE	VA	OH	NY	DC	WV	NJ	NE	SO	MW	GP	OTHER
1893–1894	58	7	2	1	1	0	3	1	0	0	2	3	0	0
1895–1896	93	1	0	4	0	1	0	1	2	0	3	4	1	0
1896–1897	86	3	0	1	0	1	0	1	2	0	3	3	0	0
1897–1898	103	7	0	6	0	2	0	0	0	0	1	0	1	0
1898–1899	105	4	0	5	3	2	0	0	0	0	0	0	0	0
1899–1900	112	5	0	1	0	1	1	1	0	1	1	0	0	0
1900–1901	120	1	0	3	1	4	0	1	0	2	0	0	0	0
1901–1902	130	5	0	4	0	2	0	1	0	0	0	0	0	0
1902–1903	106	3	0	2	0	0	0	1	2	0	0	0	0	1 (ID)
1903–1904	121	5	0	4	0	0	1	0	1	0	1	0	0	2 (ID, AZ)
1904–1905	128	6	0	4	1	0	0	1	1	0	0	0	0	2 (ID, AZ)
1905–1906	114	3	2	3	0	0	1	5	3	0	0	0	0	0
1906–1907	123	7	1	3	0	0	1	3	0	0	1	0	0	0
1907–1908	128	4	0	0	0	0	0	0	0	0	0	0	0	2 (ID, SD)
1908–1909	121	5	0	0	0	0	0	0	0	0	0	1	0	1 (SD)
1909–1910	125	4	0	1	0	0	0	1	0	0	0	1	0	1 (SD)
1910–1911	115	3	1	1	0	0	0	1	0	0	1	3	1	0
1911–1912	123	3	0	1	1	1	0	0	1	0	0	0	0	0

Irving College Student Statistics

	PA	MD	DE	VA	OH	NY	DC	WV	NJ	NE	SO	MW	GP	OTHER
1912-1913	124	3	0	1	1	1	0	2	0	0	0	2	0	0
1913-1914	98	2	0	0	0	1	0	1	1	0	0	1	0	1-CN
1914-1915	96	2	0	0	0	1	0	0	0	0	0	1	0	0
1915-1916	105	1	0	0	0	1	0	0	0	0	0	0	1	0
1916-1917	85	3	0	0	1	3	0	1	1	1	0	2	0	3-CN, PR, CU
1917-1918	93	3	0	0	0	3	1	0	1	1	0	0	0	1-CN
1918-1919	90	6	0	0	0	2	0	1	0	1	1	0	0	1-CN
1919-1920	114	5	1	2	0	3	1	3	1	1	0	1	0	3-CN, CU, NR
1920-1921	101	2	0	2	1	2	1	2	2	0	1	1	0	2-CO, NR
1921-1922	112	2	0	0	1	1	0	2	2	0	0	0	0	0
1922-1923	90	3	0	0	1	0	2	3	0	0	0	1	0	0
1923-1924	119	3	0	0	1	0	0	1	0	1	0	0	0	0
1924-1925	113	2	0	1	1	0	0	2	3	0	1	1	0	0
1925-1926	131	2	0	0	1	1	0	1	3	0	0	0	0	0
1926-1927	113	2	0	2	2	0	0	0	6	0	0	0	0	0
Totals	4,263	277	32	67	24	40	30	40	33	10	18	35	5	20

TABLE 2. STUDENT RESIDENCE POPULATION AT IRVING, 1889-1929.
The following table lists the number of boarding students versus the number of day students who commuted daily to school. The building of Columbian Hall in 1893 and possibly the completion of Campbell's Sunnyside residence by 1895 may be attributed for the increased number of boarding students. At several points Campbell used rooms in his home, Argyle (1907), for students when enrollment exceeded Irving and Columbian Halls. A single asterisk [*] refers to approximate figures. Years that are missing did not contain any approximation of boarding enrollment.

Year	Total Student Enrollment	Number of Student Boarders	Number of Boarders at Argyle[2]	Number of Day Students
1889-1890	39	15	-	24
1890-1891	58	11	-	47
1891-1892	70	26	-	44
1894-1895	102	78	-	24
1895-1896	110	78*	-	32*
1898-1899	119	80	-	39
1899-1900	123	80*	-	43*
1900-1901	132	106	-	26
1905-1906	131	100*	-	31*
1906-1907	138	105*	0	33*
1907-1908	135	105*	0	31*
1908-1909	128	105*	0	24*
1909-1910	133	107*	0	26*
1910-1911	128	107*	0	21*
1911-1912	130	107*	0	23*
1919-1920	135	109	8	26
1920-1921	117	106	10	11

2. According to the 1904-05 college catalogue, several overflow students stayed at Sunnyside in September 1901. This may have occurred at other times before the building of Argyle as E. E. seemed willing to place several "choice" students in his home. It also seems likely that there would not have been students in Argyle after E. E. Campbell's passing, though this could have occurred on a must need basis as before. Though zero appears frequently in this column, it is placed here since it is believed that in those years no students lived at Argyle, but these are also estimates since no information provides the correct number.

Irving College Student Statistics

1922-1923	100	95*	10	5*
1923-1924	125	95	0	30
1924-1925	124	92	0	32
1925-1926	139	107*	8	32*
1926-1927	125*	80	0	45*
1927-1928	125*	80*	0	45*
1928-1929	125*	80*	0	45*

TABLE 3. STUDENT SCHEDULE AT IRVING COLLEGE CIRCA 1910.
Henrietta Thomas's Memory Book describes her Irving years from 1909–1911. This schedule was taken from that scrapbook. The "practice" sessions refer to the one piano and one theory practice that a music student had daily. Note the classes on Saturday morning and the scarcity of classes on Monday.

Time	Mon	Tue	Wed	Thu	Fri	Sat
7:00		Practice, room 19	Practice, room 19	Practice, room 20	Practice, room 19	Practice, room 19
9:15		History	History	History	Bible History	
10:00	Practice, room 12	German		Practice, room 21	German	German
10:45		Bible History	Practice, room 21	Geometry	Rhetoric	Rhetoric
11:30		Piano Lesson (11:45)	Latin	Rhetoric	Elocution	Geometry
1:00		Geometry	Rhetoric	German		Practice, room 9
1:45		Latin		Elocution		
2:30		Theory		Theory	Practice, room 18	
3:15				Latin	Latin	
4:00						
4:45	Practice, room 14					
6:30 7:15 8:00						
8:45		Practice, room 3				

Irving College Student Statistics 231

TABLE 4. COLLEGE SCHEDULE OF CLASSES AT IRVING 1924–1925. Taken from the student records of the 1924–1925 school year, this table represents all the classes offered for Irving for a particular term and at what times. The number to the right signifies the room number with a [c] representing the chapel in Columbian Hall. It is important to note that the class "Livy" must not have been assigned a classroom when this schedule was printed since no class number exists for it. The key for the abbreviations is at the bottom of the table. Note that classes start at 9:00 and end by 3:00 (though no music classes are on this schedule) and that no Saturday classes exist.

Time	Mon	Tue	Wed	Thu	Fri	Sat
9:00	French III 4	Psych 4 Rhetoric 2	Psych 4 Rhetoric 2	Psych 4 Rhetoric 2	Spanish I 1 Jr Educ 5	
10:00	Soph Educ Livy 5	Ethics 4 Spanish I 1	Ethics 4 Spanish I Livy 1	Bible 4 German I 1 Com Arith 5	Sol Geom 5 Amer Lit 2	
11:00	German I 5 M+M His 4 Com Arith 1	French I 1 M+M His 2 Jr Educ 5	Bible 4 German I 1	Ethics 4 French II 1	M+M His 1 French IV 2	
12:00	L	U	N	C	H	
1:00	Spanish I 5 Amer Lit 4	French II 1 Voc Educ 4	French I 1 Eng Lit 2 Amer His 4	Sol Geom 5 Amer Lit 2	French I 1 Eng Lit 2	
2:00	French I 4 Eng Lit 6 Amer His 4	Amer His 4 Sol Geom 5	Soph Educ 5	Ancient His 4 French IV 1 Drama 2	Voc Educ 5 Anc His 4 French III 1	
3:00	Ancient His 4 Voc Edu 5 French IV 1 Drama 2	Soph Educ 5 French III 1 Livy	French II 5 Drama 1	Jr Educ 5 Pub Speak C	Pub Speak C	

Abbreviation Key: Psych = Psychology; Jr Educ = Junior Education class; Soph Educ = Sophomore Education class; Livy = Latin class studying works of Livy; Com Arith = Commercial (Business) Arithmetic; Sol Geom = Solid Geometry; Amer Lit = American Literature; M+M His = Medaeval and Modern History; Voc Educ = Vocational Education; Eng Lit = English Literature; Amer His = American History; Anc His = Ancient History; Pub Speak = Public Speaking.

TABLE 5. PREPARATORY STUDENT CLASSES AT IRVING COLLEGE, 1924–1925. This table lists the schedule of all the classes for the college preparatory students at Irving College from the student records of the 1924–1925 school year. Abbreviations used are at the end of the table.

Time	Monday	Tuesday	Wednesday	Thursday	Friday	Saturday
9:00	Gram II	Gram I	Gram I	Gram I	Gram I	Cicero
10:00	Classics II	Eng His	Eng His	Caesar	Gram II	Virgil
11:00	Latin I		Caesar	Latin I	Pl Geom Cicero	Caesar
12:00	L	U	N	C	H	
1:00	Eng His	Latin I	Algebra	Gram II	Eng His	
2:00	Algebra	Classics II	Cicero Classics II	Algebra		
3:00		Gram II Classics I	Latin I	Classics I	Classics I	
	Caesar	Cicero Pl Geom	Virgil Pl Geom	Virgil Pl Geom	Virgil Algebra	

Abbreviations Key: Gram = Grammar; Cicero = Latin study of Cicero's writings; Eng His = English History; Caesar = Latin study of Caesar's writings; Virgil = Latin study of Virgil's writings; Pl Geom = Plane Geometry.

TABLE 6. "SCHEDULE OF A SPECIAL" OF IRVING COLLEGE. "Schedule of a Special" originally appeared in *Irvingiana '03*, 93. Notice the variability of the schedule of classes as opposed to the regular course schedules. Actual Irving classes are in bold.

Time	Monday	Tuesday	Wednesday	Thursday	Friday	Saturday
6:30	Rise	Rise	Rise	Rise	Rise	Rise
8:00	Make Bed	Make Bed	Make Bed	Make Bed	Make Bed	Make Bed
9:15	Shopping	**Chemistry**	**Chemistry**	Read	**Chemistry**	Sweep
10:00	Practise	Practise	Practise	Practise	Practise	Practise
10:45	Sweep	Read	**Geometry**	Study	**Literature**	Gossip
11:30	Visit	Practise	Study	Write	Read	**Piano Lesson**
12:15	At Home	Read	**Elocution**	Practise	Write	**Elocution**
1:45	Make Fudge	Make Fudge	Make Fudge	Make Fudge	Make Fudge	Make Fudge
2:30	Read	**French**	**French**	**French**	Sleep	Read
3:15	Practise	Practise	Dress for Gymnasium	**Piano Lesson**	Dress for Gymnasium	Sleep
4:00	Walk	Walk	Gymnasium	Walk	Gymnasium	At Home
4:45	Write	Visit	Visit	Visit	Visit	Practise
5:30	Dress for Dinner	Dress for Dinner	Dress for Dinner	Dress for Dinner	Dress for Dinner	Dress for Dinner
7:15	Practise	Practise	Study	Practise	Study	Dance
8:00	Study	Study	Practise	Study	Practise	Dance
8:45	Doze	Doze	Sleep	Doze	Sleep	Feast

TABLE 7. STUDENT TRANSCRIPT FROM IRVING COLLEGE 1904-1908. The following offers a fine example of the courses a student at Irving would take in a four year period.

Year	Class	Terms/Year	Periods/Week
1904-1905	Rhetoric	4	4
	Essays	4	2
	Class Elocution	4	2
	English History	4	3
	German I	4	4
	Piano	4	2
	Hand Culture	2	1
	Painting	4	1
	Physical Culture	2	2
1905-1906	Essays	4	2
	Class Elocution	4	2
	English Literature	4	3
	Ancient History	4	3
	Biblical History	4	2
	Geometry	4	3
	German II	4	3
	Latin	2	3
	Piano	4	2
	Ear Training	3	2
	Physical Culture	2	2
	Botany	1	1
1906-1907	Essays	4	2
	Class Elocution	4	2
	American Literature	4	3
	Modern History	4	3
	Chemistry	2	3

Year	Class	Terms/Year	Periods/Week
	Ethics	2	2
	German III	4	3
	Piano	4	2
	Physical Culture	2	2
	Evidences of Christianity	2	1
1907–1908	Essays	4	2
	American Advanced History	4	3
	Geology	2	1
	Logic	2	2
	Economics	4	2
	Sociology	2	1
	German IV	4	3
	Piano	4	2
	Chorus	4	1
	History of Art	2	1
	Astronomy	2	1
	Psychology	2	2
	Natural Theology	2	1

TABLE 8. STUDENT TYPES AND ENROLLMENT INTERESTS 1899-1927. The following table lists the types of studies at Irving and how many students were enrolled in each for the years 1899-1927. The number of preparatory students, specials, and boarding students are also included for reference. The total enrollment of students is located in the last column. Home Economics as a program did not exist until 1914 and thus no students were enrolled until then. Students could be in more than one of these categories at one time, so there is overlap between columns which prevents all the columns adding up to the total column at right. The data was obtained from the college catalogues of the appropriate years.

Year	Prep Students	Specials[3]	Piano	Organ	Voice	Violin	Art	Home Econ.	Total
1899-00	5	12	75	3	25	5	26	–	123
1900-01	11	16	86	7	32	5	19	–	132
1901-02	14	0	95	7	29	3	13	–	142
1902-03	33	0	66	8	19	2	13	–	115
1903-04	58	18[4]	85	11	15	5	13	–	135
1904-05	39	0	94	18	23	3	17	–	143
1905-06	18	10	78	8	24	4	6	–	131
1906-07	14	0	90	9	22	6	6	–	138
1907-08	12	0	91	14	31	5	7	–	135
1908-09	4	0	86	16	35	4	8	–	128
1909-10	37	2	87	12	39	4	11	–	133

3. Specials are listed as "irregular students" in the 1905–06, 1909–10 and 1911–12 catalogues. They were listed as "unclassified students" in 1913–14.
4. 18 students were listed as being in a partial course which were assumed to be the special students.

Year	Prep Students	Specials[5]	Piano	Organ	Voice	Violin	Art	Home Econ.	Total
1910-11	23	0	94	14	42	4	10	–	128
1911-12	4	3	84	16	37	6	6	–	130
1912-13	5	0	75	14	31	5	10	–	132
1913-14	16	4	65	8	38	4	7	–	136
1914-15	12	0	59	10	34	5	9	–	100
1915-16	6	0	45	3	28	2	5	17	125
1916-17	17	0	43	11	22	0	4	22	100
1917-18	12	NA	47	4	25	0	6	19	103
1918-19	14	NA	51	6	24	0	5	17	102
1919-20	28	NA	55	5	38	3	10	22	135
1920-21	0	NA	52	2	36	3	0	29	117
1921-22	7	NA	38	11	28	0	0	48	120
1922-23	9	NA	29	11	24	0	0	26	100
1923-24	6	NA	36	10	30	2	0	27	125
1924-25	11	NA	31	10	20	0	0	30	124
1925-26	7	NA	39	13	15	0	0	25	139
1926-27	8	3	35	11	13	2	0	23	125[6]

5. Specials are listed as "irregular students" in the 1905–06, 1909–10 and 1911–12 catalogues. They were listed as "unclassified students" in 1913–14.

6. 125 is an approximate number for enrollment in 1926–27.

APPENDIX C

WOMEN'S COLLEGES

TABLE 1. **FOUNDING DATES OF WOMEN'S COLLEGES.** The following table lists the founding of many women's colleges in chronological order as they are previously mentioned. Only women's colleges are listed, though many co-educational schools did admit women before some of these colleges opened; these co-ed schools are not listed. The schools listed in <normal> typeface are seminaries (or schools without four year degrees, pre 1870), the schools listed in <**bold**> typeface declared themselves colleges, though many were even below the requirements and curriculum of women's seminaries. The schools are listed by the oldest date of their founding (according to the school itself) since in many cases the Commissioner's Report to the Board of Education does not signify dates in which they received a state charter. Many schools were founded but not included during their founding date either because they never had a state charter or because they did not offer four-year degrees (see footnotes). Modern two-year colleges (defined as after 1870 for this purpose) are not included here. This information was obtained through the Commissioner's Report to the Board of Education for various years, or for colleges still in existence, through each college's web site.

College or Seminary	College Location	Founding Date
Troy Seminary	Troy, NY	1821
Hartford Seminary	Hartford, CT	1828
Ipswich Seminary	Ipswich, MA	1828
Georgia Female College[1]	**Macon, GA**	**1836**
Howard Female College	**Gallatin, TN**	**1836**

---

1. Georgia Female College went on to become Wesleyan Female College in Macon.

College or Seminary	College Location	Founding Date
Mount Holyoke[2]	South Hadley, MA	1837
Athens College	Athens, AL	1843
Hollins Institute	Botetourt Springs, VA	1843
Memphis Conference Female Institute	Jackson, TN	1843
Southern Female College	La Grange, GA	1843
Virginia Female Institute	Staunton, VA	1844
Limestone College	Gaffney, SC	1845
University Female Institute	Lewisburg, PA	1846
Illinois Woman's College	Jacksonville, IL	1847
Bessie Tift College	Forsyth, GA	1849
Rogersville Synodical College	Rogersville, TN	1849
Mary Sharp College[3]	Winchester, TN	1850
Millersburg Female College	Millersburg, KY	1850
Brownsville Female College	Brownsville, TN	1851
Christian College	Columbia, MO	1851
Cumberland Female College	McMinnville, TN	1851
Ohio Female College	College Hill, OH	1851
Auburn (Elmira) College[4]	Elmira, NY	1852
Chickasaw Female College	Pontotoc, MS	1852
Richmond Female Institute	Richmond, VA	1852
Stillman Collegiate Institute	Clinton, LA	1852
Beaver College[5]	Beaver, PA	1853
Chapel Hill Female College	Chapel Hill, TX	1853
Maryland College for Women	Lutherville, MD	1853

2. Mount Holyoke began as a seminary in 1837. Though a strong seminary from the start, extended its course to four years in 1861, and petitioned the state to become a college in name in 1887.

3. Mary Sharp College was originally called the Tennessee and Alabama Female Institute which was founded in 1851.

4. Auburn College became Elmira College in 1855.

5. Beaver College purchased Beechwood College for girls and moved to Jenkintown, Pennsylvania, from Beaver, Pennsylvania, in 1925. It is now known as Arcadia University.

College or Seminary	College Location	Founding Date
Ohio Wesleyan Female College	Delaware, OH	1853
Pennsylvania Female College	Harrisburg, PA	1853
Pennsylvania Female College	Collegeville, PA	1853
Alabama Brenau College	Eufaula, AL	1854
Bethel Female College	Hopkinsville, KY	1854
Caldwell College	Danville, KY	1854
Columbia Female College[6]	Columbia, SC	1854
Glendale Female College	Glendale, OH	1854
Greenville Baptist Female College	Greenville, SC	1854
Louisburg Female College	Louisburg, NC	1854
Pittsburgh Female College	Pittsburgh, PA	1854
Rockford Female Seminary	Rockford, IL	1854
St. Louis Female Institute	St. Louis, MO	1854
Woman's College	Oxford, MS	1854
Andrew Female College	Huntsville, TX	1855
Baptist Female College	Lexington, MO	1855
Hillsboro' Female College	Hillsboro', OH	1855
Martha Washington College	Abingdon, VA	1855
Oxford Female College[7]	Oxford, OH	1855
St. Mary's College and Academy	Notre Dame, IN	1855
Thomasville Female College	Thomasville, NC	1855
Irving College	Mechanicsburg, PA	1856
Kee Mar College[8]	Hagerstown, MD	1856

6. Although founded in 1854, Columbia College did not officially open until 1859, and was not an accredited college until 1938.
7. Though founded in 1854, Oxford did not have a four-year degree until 1855.
8. Kee Mar was originally called Hagerstown Female Seminary.

College or Seminary	College Location	Founding Date
Sunderland College[9]	Perkiomen Bridge, PA	1857
Judson College	Marion, AL	1858
Whitworth Female College	Brookhaven, MS	1859
Maine Wesleyan Seminary	Kents Hill, ME	1861
Lindenwood College[10]	St. Charles, MO	1863
Vassar College	Poughkeepsie, NY	1865
Wells College	Aurora, NY	1868
Chatham College	Pittsburgh, PA	1869
Wilson College	Chambersburg, PA	1869
Smith College	Northampton, MA	1875
Wellesley College	Wellesley, MA	1875
Wesleyan Female College[11]	Cincinnati, OH	1877
Georgia Baptist Female Seminary[12]	Gainsville, GA	1878
Spelman Seminary[13]	Atlanta, GA	1881
College of Bryn Mawr	Bryn Mawr, PA	1885
Sophie Newcomb	New Orleans, LA	1886
Alverno College	Milwaukee, WI	1887
Goucher College	Baltimore, MD	1888
Agnes Scott College	Decatur, GA	1889
Barnard College	New York, NY	1889
Converse College	Spartanburg, SC	1889
Radcliffe College	Cambridge, MA	1893
Randolph-Macon College	Lynchburg, VA	1893

9. Though originally Montgomery Female Seminary, and established as Sunderland College in 1853, it did not have a four-year course until 1857.
10. Though founded in 1827, Lindenwood did not offer a four year degree until 1863.
11. Wesleyan Female College offered a three-year course after it opened in 1843.
12. Brenau University was originally founded as Georgia Baptist Female Seminary.
13. Spelmen Seminary in Atlanta, Georgia was the first school for African-American women to offer college-level courses.

Women's Colleges

College or Seminary	College Location	Founding Date
College of Notre Dame of Maryland[14]	Baltimore, MD	1895
Hood College	Frederick, MD	1897
Trinity College	Washington, D.C.	1897
Simmons College	Boston, MA	1899
College of St. Catherine	St. Paul, MN	1905
New Jersey College for Women (Douglass College)	New Brunswick, NJ	1918
Emmanuel College	Boston, MA	1919
Bennett College[15]	Greensboro, NC	1926
Sarah Lawrence College	Bronxville, NY	1926
Scripps College	Claremont, CA	1927
Mount Mercy College[16]	Pittsburgh, PA	1929
Bennington College	Old Bennington, VT	1932
Cedar Crest College	Allentown, PA	1957

---

14. The College of Notre Dame in Maryland was the first Catholic women's college. Although founded in 1873, it did not offer a four-year degree of study until 1895.

15. Bennett College was founded in 1873 as a co-educational school but did not become a women's college until 1926.

16. Mount Mercy is today Carlow College.

BIBLIOGRAPHY

PRINTED SOURCES

Biographical Annals of Cumberland County Pennsylvania, Chicago: The Genealogical Publishing Co., 1905.

Bradley, Carol Jane. *Irving Female College*, Essay given at Hamilton Library, Carlisle, Pennsylvania, 1952.

Brunhouse, Robert. *Miniatures of Mechanicsburg*, Mechanicsburg, PA: Mechanicsburg Museum Association, 1928, reprinted, 1986.

Burstyn, Joan N. *Victorian Education and the Ideal of Womanhood*, Totawa, NJ: Barnes and Noble Books, 1980.

Clarke, Edward H. *Sex in Education; or, a Fair Chance for the Girls*, Boston: James R. Osgood and Co., 1873.

Donehoo, George P. *A History of the Cumberland Valley in Pennsylvania*, Harrisburg: The Susquehanna History Association, 1930.

Eschbach, Elizabeth Seymour. *The Higher Education of Women in England and America, 1865–1920*, New York: Garland Publishing, Inc., 1993.

Flower, Lenore Embick. *Irving College*, Mechanicsburg: Irving Alumnae Club, 1966.

Gordon, Lynn D. *Gender and Higher Education in the Progressive Era*, New Haven, CT: Yale University Press, 1990.

History of Cumberland and Adams Counties, Pennsylvania, Chicago: Warner, Beers, and Co., 1886.

Horowitz, Helen Leftkowitz. *Alma Mater: Design and Experience in the Women's Colleges from Their Nineteenth-Century Beginnings to the 1930s*, Boston: Beacon Press, 1984.

"Irving College, Mechanicsburg, PA.: Its Marked Prestige and Growing Importance in its Chosen Field. The Higher Education of Women," *Greater America*, Vol. II, Nos. 10 11, July-August 1899, 1–5.

Klein, Philip S. and Hoogenboom, Ari. *A History of Pennsylvania*, University Park, PA,: Penn State University Press, second edition, 1980.

Lloyd, Nettie Hesson. *Wilson College, 1870–1910: Forty Years of Wilson as told by her Presidents, Faculty and Students*. Chambersburg: Repository Press, 1910.

Pennsylvania School Journal, Educational Review, Vol. LXXVII, No. 3A.

Rossiter, Margaret. *Women Scientists in America: Struggle and Strategies to 1940*, Baltimore: Johns Hopkins University Press, 1982.

Solomon, Barbara Miller. *In the Company of Educated Women: A History of Women and Higher Education in America*, New Haven, CT: Yale University Press, 1985.

Wing, Rev. Conway P. *History of Cumberland County, Pennsylvania*, Philadelphia: James D. Scott, 1879.

Woody, Thomas. *A History of Women's Education in the United States*, two volumes. Lancaster, Pennsylvania: The Science Press, 1929.

PRIMARY SOURCES

Bruton, Ella. Letter to E. E. Campbell, March 2, 1896.
Campbell, E. E. President of Irving College, 1891–1926, Personal Letters, 1906–1914.
Drinker, Henry Sturgis. Letter to the Hon. Francis Shunk Brown, Attorney General of Pennsylvania, July 17 and 19, 1918.
Ege, T. P. Letter to Professor C. R. Gearhart, July 27, 1867.
Fegley, H. N. *Lectures on Biblical History, Given to The Sophomore Class In Irving College, Mechanicsburg, Pa.,* 1893, revised, 1910.
Geis, William J. Board of Trustees Member of Irving College, 1900–1918?, Personal Letters,1906–1918.
Hymns of Worship & Service, Chapel Edition, Personal notes written in by Marion Claire Fisher, 1922–1927.
Interview with Marion Strouse Scharf, Irving Student 1914–18, March 11, 1996.
Irving College Account Books, 1891, 1894–1896.
Irving College Alumnae Association Bankbook, 1925–46.
Irving College Alumnae Association Dues Book, 1890–1900.
Irving College Alumnae Association Dues Book, 1900–1922.
Irving College Alumnae Association Minutes, 1893–1931.
Irving College Alumnae Association Scholarship Fund Bankbook, 1927–46.
Irving College Alumnae Association Scholarship Fund Book, 1924–44.
Irving College Alumnae Association Treasurer's Book, 1918.
Irving College Alumnae Association Treasurer's Book, 1927.
Irving College Alumnae Balance Book, 1901–1933.
Irving College Calendars, 1906.
Irving College Faculty Minutes, 1901–1912.
Irving College Photo Collection, 1857–1957.
Irving College Student Composition Papers, circa 1915.
Irving College Student Diary Entries, 1925–26.
Irving College Student Newspaper. *The Blue and Yellow Streak,* Vol. I Ed. 1, September 28, 1928 — Vol. I Ed. 4, October 19, 1928.
Irving College Student Records, 1897–1929.
Irving College, Baccalaureate Programs, 1858–1929 [incomplete].
Irving College, Class Day Programs, 1898–1929 [incomplete].
Irving College, College Production Playbills, 1865–1929 [incomplete].
Irving College, College Recital Programs, 1865–1929 [incomplete].
Irving College, Commencement Programs, 1858–1929 [incomplete].
Irving College, May Day Programs, 1914–1929 [incomplete].
Irving College, State Issued Charter, March 12, 1857.
Irving College, Student Transcripts, 1900–1929 [incomplete].
Irving College. *Announcement of Irving Female College Twenty=First Year,* Mechanicsburg: Thomas and Demming, 1876.
Irving College. *Catalogue of Irving College, Mechanicsburg, Pennsylvania, Collegiate Year 1889–90,* Mechanicsburg: Thomas Printing House, 1890.

Irving College. *Catalogue of the Officers and Students of Irving Female College, for the academic year 1857–8*, Carlisle, Pennsylvania: The Herald Office, 1858.
Irving College. *Catalogue of the Officers and Students of Irving Female College, for the academic year 1859–60*, Carlisle, Pennsylvania: The Herald Office, 1860.
Irving College. *Catalogue of the Officers and Students of Irving Female College, for the academic year 1861–2*, Carlisle, Pennsylvania: The Herald Office, 1862.
Irving College. *Catalogue of the Officers, Alumnae and Students of Irving Female College, Irvington, Mechanicsburg P. O., Cumberland Co., Pa., 1867–68*, Mechanicsburg: Cumberland Valley Journal, 1868.
Irving College. *Catalogue of the Officers, Alumnae and Students of Irving Female College, Irvington, Mechanicsburg P. O., Cumberland Co., Pa., 1867–68*, Mechanicsburg: Cumberland Valley Journal, 1870.
Irving College. *Catalogue of the Officers, Alumnae and Students of Irving Female College, Irvington, Mechanicsburg P. O., Cumberland Co., Pa., 1870–71*, Harrisburg: Sieg, Printer and Stationer, 1871.
Irving College. *Catalogue of the Officers, Alumnae and Students of Irving Female College, Irvington, Mechanicsburg P. O., Cumberland Co., Pa., 1871–72*, Harrisburg: Sieg, Printer and Stationer, 1872.
Irving College. *Catalogue of the Officers, Alumnae and Students of Irving Female College, Irvington, Mechanicsburg P. O., Cumberland Co., Pa., 1872–73*, Harrisburg: Sieg, Printer and Stationer, 1873.
Irving College. *Catalogue of the Officers, Alumnae and Students of Irving Female College, Irvington, Mechanicsburg P. O., Cumberland Co., Pa., 1873–74*, Harrisburg: Sieg, Printer and Stationer, 1874.
Irving College. College Brochure, 1865.
Irving College. *Constitution and By-Laws of the Phi Rho Mu Society of Irving College, Mechanicsburg, Pennsylvania*, Mechanicsburg: Thomas Printing House, 1894.
Irving College. *Fiftieth Annual Catalogue of Irving College for Young Ladies, Mechanicsburg, Pennsylvania, 1905–06*, Philadelphia: Chas. H. Elliot Co., 1906.
Irving College. *Fortieth Annual Catalogue of Irving College for Young Ladies, Mechanicsburg, Pennsylvania, 1895–96*, Philadelphia: Chas. H. Elliot Co., 1896.
Irving College. *Forty-First Annual Catalogue of Irving College for Young Ladies, Mechanicsburg, Pennsylvania, 1896–97*, Philadelphia: Chas. H. Elliot Co., 1897.
Irving College. *Forty-Second Annual Catalogue of Irving College for Young Ladies, Mechanicsburg, Pennsylvania, 1897–98*, Philadelphia: Chas. H. Elliot Co., 1898.
Irving College. *Forty-Third Annual Catalogue of Irving College for Young Ladies, Mechanicsburg, Pennsylvania, 1898–99*, Philadelphia: Chas. H. Elliot Co., 1899.
Irving College. *Forty-Fourth Annual Catalogue of Irving College for Young Ladies, Mechanicsburg, Pennsylvania, 1899–1900*, Philadelphia: Chas. H. Elliot Co., 1900.
Irving College. *Forty-Fifth Annual Catalogue of Irving College for Young Ladies, Mechanicsburg, Pennsylvania, 1900–01*, Philadelphia: Chas. H. Elliot Co., 1901.
Irving College. *Forty-Sixth Annual Catalogue of Irving College for Young Ladies, Mechanicsburg, Pennsylvania, 1901–02*, Philadelphia: Chas. H. Elliot Co., 1902.
Irving College. *Forty-Seventh Annual Catalogue of Irving College for Young Ladies, Mechanicsburg, Pennsylvania, 1902–03*, Philadelphia: Chas. H. Elliot Co., 1903.

Bibliography

Irving College. *Forty-Eighth Annual Catalogue of Irving College for Young Ladies, Mechanicsburg, Pennsylvania, 1903–04*, Philadelphia: Chas. H. Elliot Co., 1904.

Irving College. *Forty-Ninth Annual Catalogue of Irving College for Young Ladies, Mechanicsburg, Pennsylvania, 1904–05*, Philadelphia: Chas. H. Elliot Co., 1905.

Irving College. *Irving College and Music Conservatory, Fifty-Eighth Annual Catalogue, Record of 1913–14, Prospectus of 1914–15*, Baltimore: Munder-Thomsen Press, 1914.

Irving College. *Irving College and Music Conservatory, Fifty-Fifth Annual Catalogue, 1910 11*, Baltimore: Munder-Thomsen Press, 1911.

Irving College. *Irving College and Music Conservatory, Fifty-First Annual Catalogue, 1906 07*, Baltimore: Munder-Thomsen Press, 1907.

Irving College. *Irving College and Music Conservatory, Fifty-Fourth Annual Catalogue, 1909–10*, Baltimore: Munder-Thomsen Press, 1910.

Irving College. *Irving College and Music Conservatory, Fifty-Ninth Annual Catalogue, Record of 1914–15, Prospectus of 1915–16*, Baltimore: Munder-Thomsen Press, 1915.

Irving College. *Irving College and Music Conservatory, Fifty-Second Annual Catalogue, 1907–08*, Baltimore: Munder-Thomsen Press, 1908.

Irving College. *Irving College and Music Conservatory, Fifty-Seventh Annual Catalogue, 1912–13*, Baltimore: Munder-Thomsen Press, 1913.

Irving College. *Irving College and Music Conservatory, Fifty-Sixth Annual Catalogue, 1911–1912*, Baltimore: Munder-Thomsen Press, 1912.

Irving College. *Irving College and Music Conservatory, Fifty-Third Annual Catalogue, 1908–09*, Baltimore: Munder-Thomsen Press, 1909.

Irving College. *Irving College and Music Conservatory, Seventieth Annual Catalogue, Record of 1925–26, Prospectus of 1926–27*, Baltimore: The Belvedere Press Inc., 1926.

Irving College. *Irving College and Music Conservatory, Seventy-First Annual Catalogue, Record of 1926–27, Prospectus of 1927–28*, Baltimore: The Belvedere Press Inc., 1927.

Irving College. *Irving College and Music Conservatory, Seventy-Third Annual Catalogue, Record of 1927–28, Prospectus of 1928–29*, Baltimore: The Belvedere Press Inc., 1928.

Irving College. *Irving College and Music Conservatory, Seventy-Third Annual Catalogue, Record of 1928–29, Prospectus of 1929–30*, Baltimore: The Belvedere Press Inc., 1929.

Irving College. *Irving College and Music Conservatory, Sixtieth Annual Catalogue, Record of 1915–16, Prospectus of 1916–17*, Baltimore: Peters Publishing and Printing Co., 1916.

Irving College. *Irving College and Music Conservatory, Sixty-Eighth Annual Catalogue, Record of 1923–24, Prospectus of 1924–25*, Baltimore: The Belvedere Press Inc., 1924.

Irving College. *Irving College and Music Conservatory, Sixty-Fifth Annual Catalogue, Record of 1920–21, Prospectus of 1921–22*, Baltimore: Peters Publishing and Printing Co., 1921.

Irving College. *Irving College and Music Conservatory, Sixty-First Annual Catalogue, Record of 1916–17, Prospectus of 1917–18,* Baltimore: Peters Publishing and Printing Co., 1917.

Irving College. *Irving College and Music Conservatory, Sixty-Fourth Annual Catalogue, Record of 1919–20, Prospectus of 1920–21,* Baltimore: Peters Publishing and Printing Co., 1920.

Irving College. *Irving College and Music Conservatory, Sixty-Ninth Annual Catalogue, Record of 1924–25, Prospectus of 1925–26,* Baltimore: The Belvedere Press Inc., 1925.

Irving College. *Irving College and Music Conservatory, Sixty-Second Annual Catalogue, Record of 1917–18, Prospectus of 1918–19,* Baltimore: Peters Publishing and Printing Co., 1918.

Irving College. *Irving College and Music Conservatory, Sixty-Seventh Annual Catalogue, Record of 1922–23, Prospectus of 1923–24,* Baltimore: Peters Publishing and Printing Co., 1923.

Irving College. *Irving College and Music Conservatory, Sixty-Sixth Annual Catalogue, Record of 1921–22, Prospectus of 1922–23,* Baltimore: Peters Publishing and Printing Co., 1922.

Irving College. *Irving College and Music Conservatory, Sixty-Third Annual Catalogue, Record of 1918–19, Prospectus of 1919–20,* Baltimore: Peters Publishing and Printing Co., 1919.

Irving College. *Thirty-Sixth Annual Catalogue of Irving College for Young Ladies, Mechanicsburg, Pennsylvania, 1892–93,* Philadelphia: Chas. H. Elliot Co., 1893.

Irving College. *Thirty-Sixth Annual Catalogue of Irving College for Young Ladies, Mechanicsburg, Pennsylvania, 1893–94,* Philadelphia: Chas. H. Elliot Co., 1894.

Irving College. *Thirty-Sixth Annual Catalogue of Irving College for Young Ladies, Mechanicsburg, Pennsylvania, 1891–92,* Philadelphia: Chas. H. Elliot Co., 1892.

Irving College. *Thirty-Sixth Annual Catalogue of Irving College for Young Ladies, Mechanicsburg, Pennsylvania, 1890–91,* Mechanicsburg: Thomas Printing House, 1891.

Irving Female College Board of Trustees Minutes, 1859–1940.

Irving Female College. *Irvingiana '01.*

Irving Female College. *Irvingiana '02.*

Irving Female College. *Irvingiana '03.*

Irving Female College. *Irvingiana '07.*

Irving Female College. *The Irvington Annual,* Vol. I No. 1, Carlisle, Pennsylvania: The Herald Printing Office, 1858.

Irving Female College. *The Irvington Annual,* Vol. I No. 2, Carlisle, Pennsylvania: The Herald Printing Office, 1859.

Irving Female College. *The Sketch Book,* published by the Senior Class of Irving College, Vol. II, 1923.

Irving Female College. *The Sketch Book,* published by the Senior Class of Irving College, 1922.

Irving Female College. *The Sketch Book,* published by the Senior Class of Irving College, 1929.

Irving Female College. *The Sketch Book,* April 1927.

Bibliography

Irving Female College. *The Sketch Book,* E. E. Campbell Dedication edition, December 1926.
Irving Female College. *The Sketch Book,* February\March 1927.
Irving Female College. *The Sketch Book,* June 1928.
Irving Female College. *The Sketch Book,* March 1928.
Irving Female College. *The Sketch Book,* May 1927.
Irving Female College. *The Sketch Book,* May 1928.
Irving Female College. *The Sketch Book,* November 1927.
Irving Female College. *The Sketch Book,* Vol. 1 No. 1, February 1895.
Irving Female College. *The Sketch Book,* Vol. 1 No. 2, March 1895.
Irving Female College. *The Sketch Book,* Vol. 1 No. 4, May 1895.
Irving Female College. *The Sketch Book,* Vol. 1 No. 5, June 1895.
Irving Female College. *The Sketch Book,* Vol. 2 Nos. 4–5, Feb\Mar 1896.
Irving Female College. *The Sketch Book,* Vol. 2 Nos. 6–7, Apr\May 1896.
Irving Female College. *The Sketch Book,* Vol. 3 No. 5, April 1897.
Irving Female College. *The Sketch Book,* Vol. 3 No. 6, June 1897.
Irving Female College. *The Sketch Book,* Vol. 4 No. 1, October 1897.
Irving Female College. *The Sketch Book,* Vol. 4 No. 2, November 1897.
Irving Female College. *The Sketch Book,* Vol. 4 No. 3, December 1897.
Irving Female College. *The Sketch Book,* Vol. 4 No. 4, February 1898.
Irving Female College. *The Sketch Book,* Vol. 4 No. 5, April 1898.
Irving Female College. *The Sketch Book,* Vol. 6 No. 1, November 1903.
Irving Female College. *The Sketch Book,* Vol. 6 No. 2, December 1903.
Irving Female College. *The Sketch Book,* Vol. 6 No. 3, January 1904.
Irving Female College. *The Sketch Book,* Vol. 6 No. 4, February 1904.
Irving Female College. *The Sketch Book,* Vol. 6 No. 5, March 1904.
Irving Female College. *The Sketch Book,* Vol. 6 No. 7, May 1904.
Irving Female College. *The Sketch Book,* Vol. 6 No. 8, June 1904.
Irving Female College. *The Sketch Book,* Vol. 6 No. 9, October 1904.[1]
Irving Female College. *The Sketch Book,* Vol. 7 No. 2, November 1904.
Irving Female College. *The Sketch Book,* Vol. 7 No. 3, December 1904.
Irving Female College. *The Sketch Book,* Vol. 7 No. 4, January 1905.
Irving Female College. *The Sketch Book,* Vol. 7 No. 5, February 1905.
Irving Female College. *The Sketch Book,* Vol. 7 No. 6, March 1905.
Irving Female College. *The Sketch Book,* Vol. 7 No. 8, May 1905.
Irving Female College. *The Sketch Book,* Vol. 8 No. 1, November 1905.
Irving Female College. *The Sketch Book,* Vol. 8 No. 1, October 1905.
Irving Female College. *The Sketch Book,* Vol. 8 No. 10, November 1906.
Irving Female College. *The Sketch Book,* Vol. 8 No. 11, December 1906.
Irving Female College. *The Sketch Book,* Vol. 8 No. 14, May 1907.
Irving Female College. *The Sketch Book,* Vol. 8 No. 15, June 1907.
Irving Female College. *The Sketch Book,* Vol. 8 No. 2, December 1905.
Irving Female College. *The Sketch Book,* Vol. 8 No. 4, January 1906.

---

1. This edition of *The Sketch Book* is actually misprinted and should be Vol. 7 No. 1. The November edition is printed correctly at Vol. 7 No. 2.

Irving Female College. *The Sketch Book,* Vol. 8 No. 5, February 1906.
Irving Female College. *The Sketch Book,* Vol. 8 No. 6, March 1906.
Irving Female College. *The Sketch Book,* Vol. 8 No. 8, May 1906.
Irving Female College. *The Sketch Book,* Vol. 8 No. 9, June 1906.
Irving Female College. *The Sketch Book,* Vol. 9 No. 1, October 1907.
Irving Female College. *The Sketch Book,* Vol. 9 No. 2, November 1907.
Irving Female College. *The Sketch Book,* Vol. 9 No. 4, February 1908.
Irving Female College. *The Sketch Book,* Vol. 9 No. 5, April 1908.[2]
Irving Female College. *The Sketch Book,* Vol. 9 No. 5, March 1908.
Irving Female College. *The Sketch Book,* Vol. 9 No. 7, June 1908.
Irving Female College. *The Sketch Book,* Vol. 10 No. 2, December 1908.
Irving Female College. *The Sketch Book,* Vol. 10 No. 3, February 1909.
Irving Female College. *The Sketch Book,* Vol. 11 No. 1, November 1911.
Irving Female College. *The Sketch Book,* Vol. 11 No. 2, January 1912.
Irving Reunion Club membership lists.
McCracken, Nelle, '18. Irving Student Scrap Book, 1917–1918.
Monitress' Journal, 1872–73.
Oral History with Betty Boffemmyer Stram, Class of '29, April 22, 1993.
Oral History with Catharine Steck, Irving Student 1915–1918, October 16, 1993.
Oral History with Jane Campbell Beard, Irving Class of '29, April 12, 1994.
Oral History with Mae Noss, Irving Employee 1929, February 1, 1995.
Oral History with Majorie Wise, Irving Class of '27, February 1, 1995.
Oral History with Marion Strouse Scharf, Irving Student 1914–18, May 18, 1993.
Oral History with Mary Belle (Jane) Baylor Havely, Irving Class of '29, May 9, 1995.
Oral History with Mary E. Shope, Class of '26, June 6, 1993.
Oral History with Mary Lu Shaffer Heinze, Irving Student 1925–27, May 12, 1993.
Oral History with Pauline Hege, Irving Class of '25, October 15, 1993.
Oral History with Ruth Hoy Diffenderfer, Class of '26, June 9, 1993.
Phi Rho Mu Constitution and By-Laws, 1894.
Pittsburgh Irving College Club Minutes, 1929–1940.
Pittsburgh Irving College Club Minutes, 1941–1960.
Schaeffer, Dr. Nathan C., Superintendent of Public Instruction, Office of the Attorney General of Pennsylvania. Letter to E. E. Campbell, July 2, 1918.
Schaeffer, Nathan C. Letter to E. E. Campbell, July 22, 1918.
Scharf, Marion Strouse. Typed reminiscences of Irving, 1982.
Sheet Music, "Silver Spring," (Hyers\Haas), 1860.
Shipman, W. A. Letter to E. E. Campbell, December 2, 1907.
Shope, Mary, '26. Irving Student Stunt Book, 1922–29.
Stansfield, Bernard. Letter to Paul Campbell, February 17, 1940.
Steck, A. R. Letter to E. E. Campbell, March 13, 1906.
Student's Hand Book, Mechanicsburg, Pennsylvania: Irving College, Presented by the YWCA, 1923.
The Pharetra, Vol. XVI (actually Vol. XVII), No. 1, October 1903.

---

2. This edition is also misprinted as it should read "Vol. 9 No. 6."

Thomas, Henrietta, (1909–1911). Irving Student Memory Book, 1909–11.
Trump, Charles S. Letter to E. E. Campbell, December 23, 1907.
United States Board of Education. *Commissioner's Report to the Board of Education*, Washington, D.C.: Government Printing Office, 1870–1920.

NEWSPAPERS

Carlisle Herald, Carlisle, Vol. 56 No. 23, February 6, 1856 — Vol. 57 No. 32, April 15, 1857; Vol. 61 No. 30, June 21, 1861 — Vol. 63 No. 29 July 24, 1863.

Cumberland Valley Journal, Mechanicsburg, Vol. 6 No. 1, December 20, 1861 [No. 261] — Vol. 10 No. 42, December 28, 1865 [No. 500] (incomplete).

Daily Journal, Mechanicsburg, Vol. 2. No. 1, November 20, 1901 — Vol. 2 No. 296, October 31, 1902.

Harrisburg Telegraph, Harrisburg, June 2, 1916, Vol. 96 No. 183, August 4, 1926.

Mechanicsburg Free Press, Mechanicsburg, Vol. 1 No. 9, July 7, 1894 — December 30, 1899.

Weekly Gazette, Mechanicsburg, Vol. 2 No. 1, November 13, 1856 — Vol. 3 No. 1, November 12, 1857.

ABOUT THE AUTHOR

CHAD E. LEINAWEAVER is the Director of the Morristown & Morris Township Library, and previously, served as the Head of the Special Collections Division of the Newark Public Library, the Director for the Library and Museum Collections for The New Jersey Historical Society and the Director of Library User Access Services of the New England Historic Genealogical Society. Chad has authored portions of the *Dictionary of New Jersey History* (New Library Press, 2006) and provided a chapter to *Preserving Local Writers, Genealogy, Photographs, Newspapers and Related Materials* (Scarecrow Press, 2012). He has authored many articles including a regular "Pocket Librarian" column for *New England Ancestors* magazine, and articles for *Archival Anecdotes* and other periodicals. Chad is a Mechanicsburg native, did research on Irving College while in graduate school at Northeastern University and met some of the former Irving College students in the 1990s.

www.ingramcontent.com/pod-product-compliance
Lightning Source LLC
Chambersburg PA
CBHW030137170426
43199CB00008B/102